Finding the Exit

Finding the Exit:

It's Not Where You Start, It's Where You Finish

by Lea A. Ellermeier

Mill Camp Press, Dallas, Texas

2018 Mill Camp Press

Published in the United States by Mill Camp Press, Dallas, Texas

ISBN 978-1-7323118-0-0

Library of Congress Control Number: 2018905728

Printed in the United States of America

Cover design by Gary Kaplow

Cover photo by Maksym Kaharlytskyi

Author photo by Mallory Kee

For Wayne.

For Ruedger.

For Will.

Contents

The Exit

Dallas, Texas – October 31, 2007

It's 11:38 in the morning and I'm sitting in my office, staring at the phone, tapping my lucky three-legged pig on the desk.

I purchased the egg-sized chancito five years ago, at a trinket shop in Santa Fe, New Mexico. The Peruvian shop owner spoke in a reverent tone when he plucked the little pig from a basket next to the cash register, handed it to me and explained its lucky nature. Having just left my job to start a new company, I forked over his two-dollar asking price. This small conduit of good fortune has occupied an honored place on my desk ever since.

The pig came through for me.

An hour ago, someone from 3M Treasury called to say they'd initiated a wire transfer.

The contracts have been signed, a press release went out on Business Wire at 9:00 and my employees have opened the 3M gift boxes shipped overnight from St. Paul – packages filled with sponges, sticky notes, sandpaper and bandages. But despite all of this, I will not believe the sale of my company is real until someone from Deutsche Bank calls to say the money has landed.

My co-founder and our resident technology guru, Ruedger Rubbert, stands outside my window, surrounded by our employees. Behind them, engulfed in a cloud of smoke, Sam the Hamburger Man sweats over his portable grill as he makes lunch for everyone.

It's a celebration.

Ruedger chats up two sales reps, talking more with hand gestures than words. His whole body radiates happiness. If he feels only a small measure of the relief that I do, he's floating.

Everyone gives me credit for the sale of our little healthcare technology company, Lingualcare. I'm the CEO, the public face, the one quoted in press releases and invited to speak at conferences. But without Ruedger, I would not have survived it.

Five years ago, I did not know the difference between "being in" a start-up company and "being" the start-up company. I was no CEO.

I reported to several over the course of a career littered with early stage technology companies from Berkeley to Berlin, and freely bitched about their decisions. But I had no clue about life in that little tiny rectangle at the top of the organizational chart, the one beholden to a cynical, inquisitorial board of directors and responsible for employees with families, mortgages and dreams of their own.

Ruedger's mantra, "Don't freak out today, freak out tomorrow," kept me from eating my weight in butter cookies on more than one occasion.

A knock on my partially open door pulls my attention from the party outside. One of my new 3M colleagues comes in. He's wearing a 3M polo shirt and a 3M employee badge attached to a bright red lanyard, decorated with even more 3M logos. There is no doubt to whom he belongs.

I received a similar lanyard and badge this morning, but I'm not wearing it, not yet. I want to belong to Lingualcare, the company I never wanted to start, just a little bit longer.

"Hey Lea, can I bring you a plate?" he says. "The burgers are terrific."

I shake my head. "I'll get something in a few minutes."

Maybe I will. Maybe I won't. I'm not hungry, even though I haven't consumed anything except the latte I drank this morning with my lawyer, sitting on a wood bench in the Dallas County Courthouse, waiting for a judge to finalize my divorce. My now ex-husband John didn't appear for the 8:00 a.m. proceeding. It was only me at the end, me to finish what we had both started.

Signed decree in hand, I expected to feel the crush of sadness, the flipside of our wedding day bliss. Despite the passing of eleven years, I remembered the intimate ceremony in sharp detail: my face tingling with nervousness, wet sand oozing between my toes as John kissed me beneath a Hawaiian rainbow, and the scraggly surfers who whooped and hollered when he scooped me off my feet and carried me across an imaginary threshold in the sand.

But this morning I felt nothing.

The demands of the last six months have hollowed me out. I've been running on anxiety, caffeine and Costco animal crackers since we hired an investment bank to chase the Holy Grail of every start-up company – an exit – while fighting with the man I used to love over the remnants of a shared life.

I'm not sure how the official end of my marriage and the sale of my company converged on the same sunny Halloween morning. Months of meetings with lawyers, negotiations, contracts and verbal sparring got me to this place. I have yet to absorb all the implications of crossing the finish line. What will life be like tomorrow when I walk into the office wearing my 3M badge, a single mother with a nine-year-old son and money in the bank?

No more lawyers, redlined documents and conference calls?

No more fighting with John?

No more stress?

Wishful thinking.

The phone rings. It's the executive director of Entrepreneurs for North Texas, a non-profit that helps small companies like mine give back to the community. She is a close friend, so I take her call.

"Your dad would be so proud of you," she says.

Her words catch me off guard, and tears threaten to ambush me. I take a deep breath and look up at the ceiling until my emotions settle. We agree to have lunch after things calm down.

Last year she heard me speak to a high school class in south Dallas. I told the students how my company had been turned down for financing multiple times and how dental industry experts said American patients would hate our product, orthodontic braces that go on the backside of the teeth.

A sophomore girl raised her hand and asked, "Why didn't you quit?"

Rather than throw out an inspirational poster answer like, "Winners never quit, and quitters never win," I told the story of how my father, a real estate entrepreneur, died suddenly, six weeks before my seventeenth birthday, and left me without a home. I told them how I dropped out of high school in the middle of my junior year, worked a series of menial jobs, landed in rehab for alcoholism at the age of twenty and afterward vowed to do something meaningful with my second chance, something that would make my father proud.

My father.

What would he say if he were here today, sitting on the other side of my desk?

When I was an eleven-year-old Girl Scout, I overheard him bragging about my cookie selling acumen. He told his business partner that I could sell ice to Eskimos. I vividly recall his crooked smile, his gravely, baritone voice and the joy I felt as each word spilled into my heart.

Tears escape from the corners of my eyes as rekindled grief and the uncertainty that accompanies a dream realized mingle in my empty stomach. I swivel away from the window so my employees can't see me dabbing my cheeks with a Kleenex.

At 11:51 Deutsche Bank calls.

When I hang up, I realize, for the first time since I can remember, I am not afraid.

Oh, Another Girl

Hastings, Nebraska – 1965-1973

I doubt if anyone knows the story of their birth as well as I do. My mother recounted mine every year on my birthday, starting with the back pains she felt during her Monday night bowling league and culminating near midnight with hysterical crying when she saw my face and realized that I'd inherited my grandfather Carl's large, beaky nose. Despite the doctor's reassurance that my face would fill out and Grandpa Carl's nose would become relatively smaller, she feared I would be ugly, a terrible fate for a girl.

My father had a more subdued reaction to my birth, one that my mother faithfully noted in my baby book. "Oh," he'd said, "another girl."

My parents had decided that my older sister Beth deserved a baby brother, a boy they would name Eric. When I arrived with the wrong equipment, they were caught off guard. No girls' names had been discussed.

Friends and family descended on Mary Lanning Memorial Hospital to see my mother and me, and they offered suggestions for naming the baby with the ugly nose. After much debate, my parents settled on Lea, pronounced like Lee not Leah, and Ann, the names of two spinster aunts on my father's side who no one liked.

My mother inevitably ended my birthday story on a positive note, proclaiming, "Dr. Dean was right, your little face fattened right up, and after a few weeks you weren't nearly so ugly."

And so I was welcomed into the world.

Lea Ann Ellermeier.

A name too long to fit on the small line provided at the top of my grade school worksheets, a name that invited mispronunciation and misspelling, a name unlike the one's given to my contemporaries – Tami, Vicki, Heidi, Lori, Jodi, Staci, Patti – a name that could not be made cuter by substituting a smiley face for the dot on top of the "i," a name that, like its owner, required explanation.

Our family lived in Hastings, Nebraska, population 15,000, an unremarkable community eighty miles southeast of Lincoln where most people made a living from farming or supporting those who did. In the 1990s, Hastings would be celebrated as the birthplace of Kool-Aid, the drink that kept many dentists in business, but in the 1960s and 70s no one paid homage to Kool-Aid or Hastings.

My father grew up on a farm ten miles outside of town. My mother, raised in Wyoming and Oregon, moved to Nebraska to attend Union College in Lincoln. She met my father in the early 1960s, while working at the Ingleside Hospital for the Insane.

I should clarify – my father was not an Ingleside patient. Having recently been discharged from the Navy, he was managing a Jack & Jill grocery store in Hastings when a mutual friend introduced them.

I don't know if my sister Beth's birth story included details of their shotgun wedding, but my parents, Sharon Lynn Koch and Marlyn Gene Ellermeier, married in March 1963 and Beth was born in September. I followed in March 1965. My brother Robb arrived in August 1968 and my sister Lara in November 1970.

My father had ambition.

He saved his Jack & Jill salary and bought a small fixer-upper house. After many nights and weekends remodeling and spiffing up the yard, he sold the house for a profit and bought two more. Dedicating his spare time to working on houses and studying for his real estate exam, my dad became a house flipper before anyone coined the term.

Not long after my birth, he left Jack & Jill to focus on real estate, obtaining his broker's license and buying apartment buildings and rental houses all over Hastings.

My mother opted to stay home and leave the moneymaking to my father.

She never spoke of the dreams that drove her to abandon Oregon for a life in Nebraska. If her actions reflected what lurked in her heart, she aspired to be the wife of an adoring, affluent man, the kind of man who showered his wife with praise, mink stoles and diamond drop earrings. I think she imagined herself a Midwestern version of Elizabeth Taylor, fiery and dramatic, a woman everyone would love unconditionally no matter how many plates she threw.

My mother's version of an ideal life also included perfect, obedient children who didn't speak unless spoken to and who did exactly as they were told.

The latter, she would embrace with fury.

And rage.

My first memory is hiding from my mother.

Curled up behind my father's galoshes in the downstairs coat closet, I squeezed my eyes shut while she screamed and spanked my three-year-old sister Beth for leaving toys in the living room. Beth's shrieks of "Please Mommy, stop, Mommy stoooooop," terrified me.

My mother stalked through the house, bellowing my name and demanding that I come into the living room this instant. I didn't budge, not until my father returned home for lunch and rescued me.

I was 18 months old.

Throughout my childhood, my mother's bouts of rage came and went with an unpredictability that kept everyone in our household on edge. Waiting for the eruption, anticipating it, wondering what shape it would take, made it impossible to ever feel safe.

I became acutely attuned to the warning signs, the way she gripped a water glass, the set of her mouth and tightening of the muscles in her throat. Seeing her mood shift spiked an electrical storm inside me. My heart pounded in my face, my skin prickled and I found it hard to form words. With each passing moment, my anxiety accelerated and amplified until my body pulsed with adrenaline.

In my mind, I felt the blows a thousand times before she landed the first one.

During the actual violence, I mentally shrank into a protective cocoon and focused on not crying out loud. I couldn't stop the tears from falling down my cheeks, or prevent my small body from shaking, but I refused to give voice to the pain. Even at a young age, this resolve lived inside me. My determination to confront chaos with stillness was the only power I possessed.

To my father, she justified her actions as "discipline," keeping her unruly children in line. He believed her, or pretended to. Sure, there were bruises and welts, but if no one required a trip to the emergency room, how bad could it be?

I never fit into my mother's idealized world. A tomboy from early on, I was prone to grass stains and required too many tetanus shots. My legs were covered in scrapes and scars from playing recess football, scrounging around junkyards and riding my bicycle too fast on uneven surfaces. I preferred G.I. Joe to Barbie, and only wore dresses when coerced.

My mother encouraged more feminine pursuits. She forced me into piano lessons, and hours of practice that kept me inside. She signed me up for tap and ballet and applauded when I twirled on the stage in my sequin-covered leotard and orange tutu. Unlike my sister Beth, who slept in her costume and cried when our mother would not allow her to wear it to school, I traded my sequins for cut off shorts and Converse sneakers as soon as I could.

"Talks too much" appeared frequently on my report cards, and my mother agreed. All too often I felt compelled to point out the inconsistencies in her parenting, believing that logic would triumph over fury if I could just make the right argument.

It never worked.

It took me years to figure out that there was no magic formula for averting my mother's attacks, because there was no correlation between my behavior and her response. The rage festered inside her, sparked by something that marred the perfect picture she had spun in her mind. As it ballooned, filling her to bursting, she had to find an outlet. Who better than a small child, someone incapable of fighting back, someone who would beg for her love tomorrow?

My mother ran a tight ship. In the name of "good health," she banned refined sugar, white flour, soda, processed food and pork products from our household. She insisted on early bedtimes so we'd get at least eight hours of sleep. And she limited our access to television, convinced that spending time with H.R. Pufnstuf and Captain Kirk would soften our brains.

Everyone had daily chores – cleaning our rooms, washing, drying and putting away dishes, setting the table, taking out the trash and helping in the yard. She expected us to perform these duties at a level of perfection that constantly shifted, making it impossible to trust our abilities and judge the quality of our own work.

I grew up afraid, doubting I could do anything well and longing for Oreo cookies.

The summer of 1972, at the age of seven, I took my first drink. My parents threw a 4th of July bash that year. Our house bulged with grown-ups, neighbors and people my dad knew from work. My siblings and I had been banished to the second floor, where our babysitter entertained us by playing Candyland and Chutes and Ladders.

When the babysitter put Lara to bed, I stole downstairs and grabbed a full glass from a side table near the living room door. It looked like Coca-Cola, a forbidden beverage in our no-sugar household. I chugged down its contents before anyone could stop me.

Warmth flooded my body, radiating from my stomach to my fingertips as the Seagram's Seven infiltrated my bloodstream. The taste had a bitter edge, but the sensation made up for it.

It was magical.

I searched for another glass, to see if drinking more would heighten the effect, but before I could find one, my mother spotted me and shooed me back upstairs.

It would be a few more years before I got my hands on alcohol again, but I remembered the warm flush of calm it delivered, and the desire to experience it again stayed with me.

* * *

That Christmas of 1972, one of my friends got a record player, the kind housed in a plastic clamshell case with a handle. She used the Christmas money her grandmother sent her to buy forty-five records at Musicland, and by Valentine's Day we could both manage a decent Cher impression, belting out "Gypsies, Tramps and Thieves" without fully understanding the meaning of the words.

With my eighth birthday looming, I started a campaign to get my own record player.

My father said, "It's up to your mother."

My mother insisted that I wouldn't take care of it.

I pressed her hard one morning while she made orange juice, an exercise that involved running warm water over a can of frozen concentrate until it became unstuck and then stirring in three cans of water. She used a wooden spoon to squish the unyielding frozen blobs against the glass until they softened and liquefied.

"Please, I'll take care of it, I promise," I said as I ate my Cheerios.

She turned on me. "You don't appreciate what you already have. I don't want to hear anything more about a record player." She swung the wooden spoon in my direction, ending our conversation in a spray of orange juice.

Her refusal only fed my yearning.

That summer, while perusing an Archie comic book, I saw an ad on a page next to a drawing of Sea Monkeys lounging outside a Tudor castle. The ad read, "Win $1,000 College Scholarship or other GRAND PRIZE AWARDS!" Underneath the headline were crude drawings of the grand prizes: tent, camping stove, bicycle, transistor radio and a record player. For a third grader, the college scholarship held no interest, but the record player was exactly like the one I'd coveted for months.

I couldn't believe my luck.

All I had to do was cut out and mail in the postcard with my name and address. They would send me a prize catalog, ordering kit and instructions for selling personalized Christmas cards. I'd also receive an I.D. badge verifying my membership in the Junior Sales Club of America.

I told no one, fearing that my mother would thwart my plan before I got started. I kept watch on the mailbox, and when the kit arrived, I hid it under my bed, only taking it out to memorize the selling script while everyone watched TV downstairs. After a week of practicing in front of the mirror, I hit the street.

Walking door to door, lugging the kit and sample cards up and down our block, I quickly figured out that selling Christmas cards in July would be a bigger challenge than I'd anticipated. No one wanted to buy cards with sparkly fir trees and snowy pastoral scenes when the temperature hovered above ninety degrees and the humidity made it hard to breathe. Even the neighbors who knew me well wouldn't open their screen doors for fear of letting in mosquitoes.

A day of lackluster sales made it clear that knocking on every door wouldn't work.

The next day, I started assessing the houses from the sidewalk, eliminating the ones that did not look promising. Old women without children, the ones who smelled funny and wore slippers in the middle of the day, never bought, so I avoided them. Houses with too many toys in the yard meant a mom with no time to talk, so I skipped those too.

Some people were nice when they opened the door and saw me standing there in the red bandana print shirt that my grandmother had sewn for me, kit in hand, a hopeful smile on my face. Others were just plain mean.

One old man who lived across the street from my elementary school scowled at me as soon as he saw me on his porch. Standing behind a scuffed aluminum screen door, he barked, "Where's your mother?" interrupting me before I could finish my pitch.

"At home," I answered.

"Well, she must be a lousy mother if she's letting you run around all by yourself," he said and slammed the door in my face.

I ran and hid behind a large oak tree. Sinking down into the grass, I hugged my knees and fought back tears. The aftershocks of his anger left me feeling small, too small to accomplish such a big goal.

What did I know about selling?

Nothing.

It was so much harder than the Junior Sales Club brochure said it would be.

I wanted to go home, to play badminton with my sister, but I wanted the record player more. Wiping the tears from my cheeks with the back of my hand, I decided to try again. I picked up the kit and walked over to the next block.

Near the end of the afternoon, the wife of our local fire chief invited me into her large, sunny kitchen and offered me lemonade and a bowl of strawberry shortcake. She added a blob of homemade whipped cream, the kind my mother only made at Thanksgiving and Christmas; it tasted like heaven.

Instead of pitching the merits of personalized Christmas cards, I told her about the record player and how I had been knocking on doors for two days to get it.

"How many more boxes do you need to sell?" she asked.

Instead of giving her an exact number, I said, "Only a few more."

"Maybe I can help you," she said as she filled out the order form.

She bought five boxes!

"I'm selling these cards to get a record player, and I only need to sell a few more to reach my goal," quickly became my sales pitch.

After three days of canvassing northeast Hastings, I hit my number.

While no one wanted to buy Christmas cards in July, it turned out that many people wanted to help a kid fulfill her dream of owning a record player. I didn't realize it at the time, but that summer I'd learned my first lesson about selling – people don't buy products, they buy emotional satisfaction.

My father praised me for my initiative. My mother grudgingly congratulated me, and then muttered to my father, "She'll break that in a week."

The record player arrived at the end of August. Every night after dinner I listened to "Half Breed" by Cher, playing it over and over again, singing and dancing in front of my bedroom mirror, until my mother came upstairs and demanded I turn it off.

I savored my small triumph. She could tell me to turn it off, but she could not take it from me. I had earned it, and in the process, discovered something important: I had the power to make things happen.

Prelude to a Start-up

New York, New York – March 2002

I didn't love New York.

Maybe because I only went there to beg: for press coverage, for analysts to say good things about my products and, of course, for investment money. During 2000 and 2001 I spent many weeks in Manhattan, tin cup in hand, raising twenty-five million dollars for Mordix, my employer.

Ours was not a sexy business.

Whenever I told someone I worked for a dental technology company, they served up a horror story. People I barely knew shared intimate details of ill-fitting crowns – usually accompanied by an open mouth and a view of the offending tooth – botched root canals and post-Novocain misadventures.

Fortunately, our product didn't require Novocain.

Mordix made robots that bent the wires orthodontists used to straighten teeth. We didn't plan to sell the robots, just the wires, the imaging device and treatment planning software needed to design them.

We had a cool product called SmilePerfect and a revenue graph that resembled a hockey stick, showing the kind of enormous growth that made investors salivate. But after spending thirty million venture capital dollars on two continents, Mordix hadn't come close to shipping a commercial product, and our story was losing its sheen.

On that day in March 2002, I hated New York because I was stuck in traffic. I needed to get to La Guardia, to Dallas, to my four-year-old son Will. My husband John took good care of him while I was on the road, but I missed my little guy. He was my only child, born with his hands wrapped around my heart.

I felt guilty being away for more than a few nights.

Guilt.

It erupted like hives when I forgot to buy juice boxes for a school party or when Will called me before bed and asked me to sing him a song. I pictured him in his blue Bob the Builder pajamas, blond hair damp from the shower, sitting on my lap while I sang "Country Roads" and "Sunshine on my Shoulders," invoking my best John Denver voice.

I wanted to be a great mother and a great vice president of sales and marketing. Unfortunately, the latter was easier to quantify; Will didn't send me spreadsheets every month measuring my performance against plan or grill me at board meetings.

The taxi driver rolled down his window to let in some air. He asked the crucial question, "You wanna take the tunnel or the bridge?"

"Bridge."

I hated tunnels, especially ones that passed under a body of water. I'd seen too many disaster movies where a small trickle on the side of a tunnel erupted into a crushing torrent that no one could outrun, except for one hero and a trusty sidekick who would manage to escape through a maintenance hatch with a water-tight door.

I was no hero. Panic would prevent me from locating the hatch, and I'd never had a trusty sidekick.

My phone rang halfway over the Triborough. It was an executive recruiter from Dallas, a friend who specialized in placing high-level talent at start-up companies backed by venture capital.

"Roscoe is shopping your job," he said.

Roscoe was Mordix's new CEO. The board of directors had hired him in February, after I raised the money to pay his salary. Venture firms loved guys like Roscoe, a well-pressed man with a Fortune 50 pedigree, start-up experience (at a failed dotcom in Florida), expensive shoes and puckered lips.

My friend continued, "I got the spec this morning. It doesn't say Mordix but let me read it to you."

My hands grew cold as he read the job description: vice president of product marketing for an orthodontic technology start-up company in North Dallas.

There was only one of those.

"How can the board let him fire me? I closed a financing six weeks after the World Trade Center attacks, when they were ready to turn off the lights," I said, raising my voice too high for the small interior of the cab.

The cabbie looked at me in the rearview mirror with scrunched eyebrows.

"New CEOs want their own teams, people who are loyal to them. The board has to let Roscoe run the company his way."

I flashed back to Roscoe announcing at the last board meeting that he intended to "upgrade positions where talent gaps exist."

Mind the gap.

Did my talent resemble a grubby subway platform?

On the flight back to Dallas, I mentally scrolled through recent interactions with my colleagues, searching for clues in shifting glances or stilted conversations. I couldn't recall anything suspicious.

As I picked cashews and pistachios from my small bowl of warm roasted nuts and sipped a Diet Coke, I considered my friend's words. CEOs wanted people around them who were loyal. I got that. Maybe I hadn't done anything to indicate feelings of loyalty toward Roscoe, but I didn't think I'd done anything to indicate disloyalty either.

When would Roscoe drop the bomb? After he hired someone new? After it was too late for me to fight back?

Instead of heading home from the Dallas-Fort Worth airport, I drove to Mordix. It was a Friday, but traffic going into the city was light, so I arrived before 6:30. I hoped to find Roscoe in his office catching up, his routine since starting the job.

I parked my black Mercedes C230 in the deserted parking lot. I'd bought the car at the height of the dotcom bubble, splurging when I should have been saving. Two years earlier, when I drove it out of the showroom, the technology industry felt bulletproof. My husband John and I were in-demand tech executives with impressive resumes and the ability to command big salaries. Now he was unemployed, and it looked like I was about to be.

John's company, the one we thought would go public in the summer of 2001 and make us millionaires, had just been sold for pennies on the dollar. The acquirer offered John a job at their headquarters in Colorado, but we could not move. John had two children from his previous marriage who lived in Dallas. So, he'd taken the severance package and started a job search.

The office was quiet. I passed a warren of empty cubicles as I made my way down the hallway to Roscoe's executive lair.

Like many companies started in the late nineties, Mordix hadn't skimped on furnishings. Herman Miller Aeron chairs and modern desks filled the space, creating an impression of prosperity that didn't align with the company's financial performance.

As I neared Roscoe's open door, I felt my heart beating behind my eyeballs. The adrenaline rush that preceded imminent doom made me lightheaded.

A wiser person would go home and think it over, confer with their spouse before engaging in this sort of confrontation. But what good would that do? If Roscoe intended to fire me, he would fire me. Talking to him on Friday afternoon instead of Monday morning wouldn't alter the outcome, and I preferred to spend the weekend mourning my job rather than agonizing over the possibility of losing it.

Breathe, I told myself, breathe.

As they say in Texas, he can't eat you and he can't take your birthday.

Roscoe sat with his back to the door, typing furiously on his computer, his pumpkin-shaped head, covered in tight gray-blond curls, bent in concentration. I drew a deep breath, knocked on the doorframe and leaned in.

"I hear I'm on the upgrade list."

He swiveled my direction and gave me a wide-eyed glare. "Uh…"

"Dallas is a small town," I said. "It's hard to keep a secret here."

Pointing to the chair across from his desk, Roscoe got up, peered down the hallway and then closed the door. He sat across from me and smiled.

I smiled back. I'd learned early in my career that silence made people uncomfortable. Most would start talking and give away their position to avoid that discomfort.

Roscoe cracked first.

"After consulting with the board, I decided to split your job in half, put you in charge of sales and service only, and have someone else manage marketing."

"You want me to be the vice president of sales?"

"Everyone speaks highly of your sales skills," he said with a grin that reminded me of a certain plastic clown who hawked hamburgers on television.

"I have a four-year-old. I can't be a road warrior."

I hated to play the mom card, but running sales meant at least sixty percent travel. Although technically I already owned sales, the job was limited to recruiting early customers and managing the beta test program. I'd always assumed the company would hire a dedicated sales leader when we launched SmilePerfect nationally, and I could go back to product marketing, the job I liked best.

I stopped short of telling Roscoe that I wouldn't hire myself as vice president of sales. I could sell Christmas cards in July, but I didn't have the Genghis Khan personality that great sales leaders possess. I hated managing salespeople. The best ones were too smart and creative for the company's good. They uncovered loopholes in every comp plan and never turned expense reports in on time. The bad ones were like old pack mules; they required non-stop flogging to make the numbers.

As much as I despised sales management, I loved product marketing. The process of interviewing customers, sweating through the product development cycle and building things that people didn't realize they wanted put me into a focused place that bordered on obsession. Successful product launches, big sales numbers and strong reviews from editors and analysts gave me a huge rush.

That's what I did best.

That's where I shined.

Roscoe broke the silence. "Well, that's what I have for you. I hope you decide to take it."

I wanted to argue, but I remained silent. Better half a job than no job.

I mentally replayed the conversation on the drive home. Did he want me to resign? Was this the first step in a master plan to drive me out the door?

Roscoe was a product of the Deep South. I knew his type – they graciously dispensed poison, smiling as they spooned it into your tea cup and offered it to you with a warm-from-the-oven peanut butter cookie. I couldn't trust that his words matched his intentions.

I did have a few things working in my favor: solid job performance, good relationships with the board of directors, and my status as the only female on the executive team. Firing me without cause would be a bad optic.

As I considered all the facts, one question kept popping up in my head – even if Roscoe didn't fire me, did I still belong at Mordix? With him at the helm, would it ever again feel like the company I'd fallen in love with?

* * *

I dreaded going home to tell John what had happened. The weight of his own unemployment kept him on the edge of despair. Every day I put on a happy face and tried to be cheerful and optimistic enough for us both, keeping conversations light and centered around Will, the bright spot in our shared life. But I couldn't hide this from him.

After putting Will to bed, I unpacked my suitcase, cleaned the kitchen and arranged all the spices in the pantry in alphabetical order. Creating order calmed me. Even the smallest mundane tasks, shining a pair of shoes or lining up books according to height and thickness, dampened my internal chaos.

After aligning the bottles of tarragon and thyme so the labels were centered, I went into John's study and blurted out, "I think Roscoe is going to fire me."

He turned away from his laptop screen and rubbed his face with both hands. Fourteen years older than me, John had ridden the ups and downs of the tech industry since the mid-1970s when he took his first job at IBM. He'd worked at big companies as well as start-ups and knew how rapidly the landscape changed when a new CEO arrived. If anyone could empathize, surely John could.

"What did you do to piss him off?"

"I didn't do anything," I said.

"Well, you must have done something or he wouldn't want to fire you. Didn't he give you a reason?" John gripped the arms of his office chair with both hands. He leaned back, as if he wanted to put as much space between us as possible.

I searched his brown eyes for understanding. Why didn't he get up and hug me, reassure me that everything would be okay? Why was his first response to throw blame at me? I swallowed, pushing down the emotion that threatened to turn this into a full-blown fight.

"Roscoe plans to give marketing to someone else," I said. "He wants me to run sales and implementation."

"So, you're okay for right now," John said, exhaling loudly. "Jesus, Lea, why didn't you say that right up front?"

"Because I don't trust the guy."

"You need to get on his good side, kiss his ass if you have to."

After six years of marriage, I thought John knew me better, knew I lacked the ability to convincingly suck up to anyone. After being far too vocal in my twenties, I'd rekindled my friendship with silence and stopped telling co-workers and bosses exactly what I thought.

Silence I could manage. Fawning was out of the question.

"I'll do what I can," I said, and left him to his Internet surfing.

When I met Roscoe for the first time, back in February, I sensed he didn't like me. He shook my hand and peered over my shoulder, not meeting my eyes. He moved on to the next person before I could finish saying, "Welcome to Mordix."

Maybe he expected me to kiss his ring and swear fealty the first day, which I would never do, not to someone unproven. Or maybe he just didn't like anyone hired by the old CEO.

Naively, I believed my past accomplishments, like raising tens of millions of dollars, finding the first beta customers and driving the specifications for our first commercial product, had earned me goodwill, or at the least an opportunity to prove my value.

But now it seemed past performance and loyalty to the enterprise didn't matter. Taking marketing away from me was the first step to pushing me out the door. I was sure of it.

The next day I called Ruedger Rubbert, our Chief Technology Officer (CTO) who worked in the Berlin office, to see if he had any insights.

A mechanical engineer and serial entrepreneur, Ruedger founded Mordix in the mid-nineties and served as the company's first CEO. Now he managed research and development and ran German operations. The U.S. venture capital investors (VCs) insisted that he step down as CEO when they funded the company, but allowed him to keep his board seat.

Ruedger was my best inside source. He'd tell me the truth and wouldn't care if I called him at home on a Saturday afternoon.

"Roscoe never talked about hiring a new VP of marketing during the closed session of the board meeting," said Ruedger. "He probably called the board members individually. But he didn't call me. He knows you and I are friends."

"What do you think?" I said. "Is this the first step to firing me?"

"I agree with your headhunter friend," he said. "Roscoe wants his own people on the executive team. We all need to watch our backs."

Aaron, a buddy of Roscoe's from the failed dotcom in Florida, showed up in Dallas a few weeks later. Apparently, the job spec sent to recruiters was a ruse to create the illusion of an extensive search. Roscoe planned to hire his pal all along.

Although Aaron seemed amiable and more competent than I wanted him to be, he had a weird habit that made me seriously question Roscoe's judgment. In meetings, Aaron chewed and sucked on the collars of his shirts until they were stained and dripping wet.

Our CFO christened him "suck-shirt."

* * *

When I received the April financial statements in early May, I stared at the numbers, not believing what stared back.

I did the calculations twice; each time they came out the same. Aaron, the usurper with less education and experience than me, the guy who sucked on his shirt collars, had been given a larger salary and received a bigger stock option grant than I had.

Maybe I could have accepted it if Aaron brought a Rolodex full of dental industry contacts, or a big bag of pixie dust to transform SmilePerfect into an overnight sensation, but he hadn't spent one day in dentistry. In fact, Roscoe had tasked me with "helping Aaron get up to speed on what we do."

Printout in hand, I marched down the hall to Roscoe's office.

"Is this correct?" I said, pointing to the bottom of the page where I'd handwritten Aaron's salary and stock option numbers.

Roscoe seemed surprised that I possessed the basic math skills to calculate the pre-Aaron, post-Aaron payroll and capitalization table deltas.

"I'm not going to discuss this with you," he said, pushing the offensive spreadsheets across the desk and turning back to his computer.

As I walked back to my office, choking on the words that I wanted to scream, all of which would yield an R rating, I heard a voice in my head. It belonged to an old boyfriend who liked to say, in his thick West Texas drawl, "I'm so damn mad I could spit."

Thinking about it stopped the tears.

I hated that I wanted to cry, that my physiology would betray me at a time like this. I'd rather spit than be seen weeping in the hallway.

I closed my office door, slid into the inviting embrace of my Aeron chair and turned away from the glass wall that exposed my soul to the inhabitants of the cubicles on the other side. A screen saver morphed across my monitor, a multicolored cube turning inside out, twisting, expanding, contorting and contracting like my insides.

I thought about the nights I'd spent at the dining room table hunched over my laptop, finishing one more task before the work day began in Germany, about all the street hot dogs and gyros I had consumed while fundraising in Manhattan the year before, bits of which were probably still lodged somewhere in my intestinal tract, and about the weekends promoting SmilePerfect at orthodontic society meetings in garden spots like Cleveland and Kansas City. I gave big chunks of myself to Mordix and in return, Roscoe and the board were giving me the finger.

As I forced myself to take deep breaths, I realized that I wasn't angry.

I was heartbroken.

* * *

I couldn't accept it. There had to be some recourse, some path to justice.

The next morning, I called a Dallas board member and requested a meeting, offline. Breaking the chain of command and talking to me without Roscoe's knowledge was taboo. But we shared a common bond; we were both scrappy kids from the Midwest who had overcome difficult circumstances to find our way to Dallas. I considered him a friend.

He offered to buy me lunch.

"It's a mulligan," he said over cashew chicken at a Chinese place near his office at the Galleria Mall in North Dallas.

We dined in the atrium area, overlooking the Galleria's famous indoor ice rink. Three stories below us, a pack of little girls in pink and purple leotards skated around the oval with two instructors. I envied their grace and balance. The closest I'd ever come to gliding across the ice was getting a Dorothy Hamill haircut in 1977.

"I don't get it," I said.

I pushed a cashew across my plate, wishing I'd asked for silverware, something I never did when my dining companion requested chopsticks. The slippery cashews threatened to fly out of the smooth plastic chopsticks if I applied too much pressure. I imagined the stain it would leave on my board member's buttery yellow polo shirt, so I speared soft, greasy chunks of brownish chicken with the end of a chopstick instead.

"In most of my companies the CEO has one weird hire, a guy who doesn't fit, who you end up paying too much money. But you can't veto the guy because the CEO wants him on the team. Aaron is Roscoe's mulligan." He shrugged and turned his palms skyward.

"Does this not seem completely unfair to you?" I said.

"Roscoe doesn't think you're loyal." He held my gaze, as if trying to detect a hint of loyalty in my green eyes, judging if I deserved Roscoe's consideration.

"Should I have sliced open my palm and sworn a blood oath?"

"Tell Roscoe you are excited to be on his team." He offered me a big smile and added, "Come on, you can do it."

Despite his good instincts, my board member was wrong.

Since his arrival, Roscoe had treated me with indifference. He avoided making eye contact when he passed me in the hallway and never stopped in my office to chat, something he did every day with my male colleagues. Since I'd confronted him about hiring Aaron, it had gotten worse. He no longer asked for my opinions in meetings. I had to inject them into the discussion and endure his icy glares.

Roscoe definitely wanted me out of Mordix. He just hadn't figured out how to make it happen.

As the summer closed in, I spent my days avoiding the occupants of Dante's Ninth Circle – the icebound realm reserved for the treacherous. I hid my heartbreak as best I could and made nice with Roscoe and Aaron.

The charade reminded me of the time I tried to stay friends with a boyfriend who cheated on me. One minute I wanted to scream, "You are such an asshole!" and the next, I yearned for him to tell me I was special.

I hated watching *my* marketing team file into the conference room for meetings with Aaron. I hated the sound of Roscoe's laughter in the breakroom and the smell of Aaron's burnt microwave popcorn wafting in the hallway. Most of all, I hated plastering a smile on my face when I walked into the office and cheerfully saying good morning to everyone in the disingenuous tone of a nurse about to administer an enema.

In late May, right after Roscoe's Monday morning staff meeting, where he gave me less than two minutes of airtime,

Ruedger called. I was at my desk, contemplating what to do about lunch. Lately, I'd been eating Subway sandwiches in my car instead of going out to lunch with friends. I didn't want to answer the question, "How are you?"

"Can you go outside and call me?" Ruedger said.

"It's ninety-five degrees out there."

"This is important," he said.

I left my suit jacket on the chair, grabbed my cell phone and went out the back door, to the side of the building that faced a grassy slope and a grove of trees. This secluded entrance was frequented by smokers and people who didn't want their phone calls overheard, mostly cheaters and clandestine job seekers.

The maintenance people had just mowed the lawn and the scent of cut grass mixed with gasoline filled the air. That sweet smell always reminded me of my childhood, when I mowed yards to make money during the summer. Back then I didn't know the smell was a chemical distress signal sent by the grass after being injured by the mower. Back then I believed working outside on a hot, humid day was the worst job anyone could have.

I dialed Ruedger's cell phone number and paced, trying to avoid the piles of discarded cigarette butts that rimmed the no man's land between the pavement and the grass.

"Roscoe is hiring a new CTO to replace me," he said. "He asked me to hand over all my projects before I go on vacation in July."

No, no, no, no, no. How could this be?

Mordix and Ruedger were one. He'd dreamed it, created it and shaped it from a tiny spark of an idea into a multinational company. Every patent, every product feature, every technological breakthrough began in his subconscious.

How could Mordix exist without Ruedger? How could I exist at Mordix without Ruedger? He was my ally, my friend. Without him, I would have to navigate Roscoe's duplicity alone.

"What are you going to do?" I whispered, afraid that my voice would crack.

"I have an idea."

The Only Way off the Hairy Edge Is to Jump

Dallas, Texas – June 2002

It wasn't a new idea, but it was a good one.

Last year Ruedger and Thomas Weise, Mordix's best systems engineer, partnered with a German orthodontist named Dr. Peter Hoffman to develop a new product: customized orthodontic braces placed on the lingual, or tongue side, of the teeth.

Back in March, Roscoe vetoed the project, despite my sound arguments to move forward. He didn't understand the product's potential or the full implications of his decision. By refusing to honor an earlier contract, Mordix would relinquish ownership of the intellectual property to Hoffman.

Roscoe didn't make his decision in a vacuum. Other, darker forces inside the company lobbied him to abandon it. Mordix's Chief Clinical Officer hated Dr. Hoffman, and good ideas not his own. He argued, rightly, that lingual orthodontics was a small market segment. But he didn't tell Roscoe that Hoffman's lingual braces solved all the problems associated with older systems and had the potential to put lingual treatment in the mainstream.

First invented in the late 1970s by an orthodontist in Beverly Hills named Dr. Craven Kurz and manufactured by OrthoCo, lingual braces never gained popularity in the United States. Big, bulky brackets cut up patients' tongues and mangled their speech. Orthodontists struggled to master the technique. Placing the brackets in the correct position on the backside of the teeth, and bending the much smaller wires, was difficult. Orthodontists had to take continuing education courses and invest in specialized instruments and staff training.

The U.S. dental market was a retail market. Patients paid orthodontic treatment costs out of pocket. U.S. orthodontists made plenty of money treating twelve-year-old patients with traditional "railroad track" braces. They had little motivation to seek out more aesthetically conscious adult patients to supplement their income.

Despite the steep learning curve, lingual braces became popular in Europe and Japan, markets where adults and older teens refused to wear traditional braces. For those orthodontists, providing a premium retail procedure not subject to price regulation by government insurance made the extra training worthwhile.

Fast forward to 2002: advances in computer-aided design (CAD), computer-aided manufacturing (CAM), robotics and rapid prototyping made it possible to customize almost anything.

Using CAD/CAM technologies, Ruedger, Thomas and Dr. Hoffman designed individualized lingual brackets that conformed to each patient's unique tooth anatomy and pre-bent wires customized with their prescription. The new brackets were 70% smaller than the old OrthoCo lingual brackets. And because they were contoured to follow the shape of the individual tooth, it was easy for orthodontists to place them correctly. Dr. Hoffman's early patients reported no problems speaking or eating.

The timing was right.

For two years I'd watched our biggest competitor Align Technology, makers of the Invisalign System, attack the orthodontic industry with shock and awe media campaigns that made Invisalign a standard of care faster than any orthodontic product that preceded it. By targeting adults who wanted straight teeth but would never wear regular metal braces, Align created a new market segment.

Despite the patient appeal of the Invisalign System, orthodontists complained about the treatment outcomes. Many patients who wanted the Invisalign System couldn't be treated to an acceptable standard. Orthodontists made them sign release forms agreeing to wear metal braces if the aligners didn't deliver a clinically acceptable result.

Align trained general dentists, the orthodontists' primary referral source, on how to use Invisalign. Their actions alienated many orthodontists, thus opening the door for an alternative like customized lingual braces.

"Stop selling Roscoe on the lingual idea," said Ruedger.

Despite my banishment from product development, I had continued to lobby for the lingual project. I still believed in the market potential and clung to the idea that with enough good data, I could change Roscoe's mind.

Ruedger continued, "I'm going to ask Hoffman for the license he planned to give Mordix. In exchange for selling rights in North and South America, we will help him with engineering and manufacturing."

"We?"

"Thomas, you and me," he said.

"You want to start another company?" I asked.

"Maybe you missed that target on your back."

There were times when I appreciated Ruedger's no-bullshit style. This wasn't one of them. What was he thinking? Where would we get money? I had pitched every investor I knew on Mordix. I couldn't turn around and pitch them on a new company less than a year later.

"What if I don't want to start a new company?" I said, pacing back and forth on the freshly cut grass. Little bits of it stuck to the sides of my patent leather shoes. I reached down to brush them off as I contemplated this possible new future.

Since Aaron's arrival I'd been calling people in my professional network, asking about opportunities in their companies, and putting out job feelers to friends. So far, I'd gotten only bad news. Still reeling from the dotcom crash, the job market for tech people in Dallas sucked.

As much as I mistrusted Roscoe, I wasn't ready to walk away from everything I'd built at Mordix. The most optimistic part of me still believed that if I continued to prove my value, my job would be safe. And starting a new company, well, that seemed even riskier than staying.

I was thirty-seven years old. I'd spent my career at modestly successful underdog companies where I'd made decent money, but not enough to stop living paycheck to paycheck. Like many of my peers, I'd ratcheted up my standard of living with each pay increase, expecting the next big stock option package to pay off my mortgage and cover retirement.

My career needed a big hit, not a failure.

"Let's see if we can get the license from Hoffman," said Ruedger. "Then we'll figure it out. If he won't give it to us, it's a moot point."

* * *

Dr. Hoffman planned to be in Berlin for a conference at the end of June. Ruedger set up a meeting.

Instead of spending money we didn't have on a lawyer, Ruedger and I dug up an old licensing agreement and reworked it. The agreement gave a new company, owned by Ruedger, Thomas and me, the rights to North and South America for Hoffman's lingual braces.

On a hot afternoon in late June, while Ruedger waited for Hoffman, I boiled spaghetti for Will's lunch and fretted.

Did I want Ruedger to succeed or fail?

I wasn't sure.

If Hoffman said no, the decision would be made for me, but I'd be stuck with an uncertain future at Mordix. If he said yes, I'd be forced into an even more uncertain future, albeit one that offered a potentially lucrative outcome.

My phone rang.

"Hoffman is coming over in an hour. We'll sit in the backyard and talk through the contract over a bottle of wine" said Ruedger.

"Do you think he'll sign?"

"He doesn't think the U.S. market is worth anything, he already told me that. Signing it away in exchange for our help with engineering and manufacturing is a good deal for him."

"Saying it and putting it in a contract are two different things," I said.

Hoffman might have been willing to sign away the North American rights to Mordix, a real company with a hundred employees and millions of dollars in the bank. But assigning those rights to Ruedger, Thomas and me, three individuals with minimal personal financial resources and no investors lined up was a different matter.

"I'll call you when he leaves."

I did laundry.

I removed suspicious items from the vegetable crisper.

I took out the trash.

I skimmed leaves from our swimming pool. The water appeared more green than blue. I dreaded calling the pool company, fearing they would tell me it needed a new pump. We couldn't afford one. Not knowing wouldn't make the pump any less broken, but I didn't want another big scary number keeping me up at night.

Will ran out the patio door in his swim trunks, ready to leap into the water. I caught him before he reached the edge and suggested a trip to the carwash instead.

He loved going to the carwash, standing on a platform built for people his size and watching through a window as cars were rinsed, soaped, rinsed again and dried with a gigantic blow-dryer.

When he saw my little black Mercedes, he pulled me away from my gossip magazine and insisted I watch each step of the process as he explained it to me. His eyes widened with delight when the giant blow-dryer drove rivets of water across the smooth surface of the car, leaving a mirror finish.

Three o'clock in Dallas, ten o'clock in Germany, and still no call from Ruedger.

What was he doing?

I decided to brave the heat and take Will to the park a few blocks from our house, cell phone tucked in my back pocket.

"Mom, watch me."

Will tackled the monkey bars, arms barely long enough to reach from one to the next. I stood close, ready to catch him if he slipped. His blond hair flopped into his eyes as he swung. He needed a haircut. I mentally added that to my to-do list for the following week and pushed away the twinge of guilt I felt for not doing it last week.

"I made it," he said as he reached the end, his face flushed with naked pride.

As he ran to the other side of the play area to join another boy on the merry-go-round, a smile broke across my face. He was a happy kid. Maybe I was doing something right.

My pocket vibrated.

"We have a contract." Ruedger sounded tipsy. "It took two bottles of wine, but not a lot of persuasion."

"What do we do now?"

Ruedger laughed. "I'm going to bed. Maybe you can figure that out and we'll talk in the morning."

We hung up.

Instead of sharing Ruedger's excitement, I felt tendrils of fear squeeze my stomach. The signed contract ended our theoretical discussion. Now, I had to decide.

I could pretend to be loyal and wait for Roscoe to fire me. I could look for a new job and hope I got one before Roscoe fired me, or I could start the company with Ruedger and Thomas and leave on my own terms.

Whenever I mentioned finding a new job, Ruedger reminded me that working for anyone but yourself came with a big, steamy pile of uncertainty.

"Do you want to be at the mercy of someone else or own your destiny? That's the question you need to ask yourself Lea."

I loved the lingual idea. That's why I'd fought so hard for the project at Mordix. It just made sense that if patients had a choice between braces on the front of their teeth or braces on the back, they would choose the more aesthetic option.

The answer seemed clear.

But as much as I loved the idea, I was afraid to start a new company. I did not know how to tell Ruedger that my reticence had nothing to do with my confidence in him and Thomas or the merits of our idea. It wasn't even about my wretched personal financial situation or my husband's unemployment.

It was about my father.

Being an entrepreneur had led him to a terrible place.

For Love of Money

Hastings, Nebraska 1974-1981

In the spring of 1974, my parents divorced and my mother quit drinking. Church basement AA meetings became her primary social outlet and she replaced her fun friends with a stream of somber coffee drinkers who left overflowing ashtrays on our kitchen table.

Getting sober and filing for divorce happened simultaneously, so I wasn't sure what made her crazier, the loss of alcohol as a crutch or the financial insecurity that accompanied leaving my father.

During the summer of 1974, my mother became more erratic than ever. She frequently woke in the middle of the night and went to the kitchen to count the silverware. If a fork or spoon was missing, she would scream, slicing into our dreams with the full force of her fury, and pull us from the warmth of our beds, regardless of the hour, to scour the house for the missing tableware.

"You don't care about *anything*. You're all *ungrateful!*" she would declare, swatting at anyone who entered her orbit during the search.

She accused us of throwing away packages of toilet paper she knew she'd bought and hiding her paperback novels before she could finish reading them.

"You want to make me look crazy to the judge," she'd yell. "All of you and your father, you're in it together!"

My three-year-old sister Lara used to hide under her bed to avoid the beatings that inevitably came when we didn't locate the misplaced butter knife or Harry Kemelman novel. One particularly bad night, my mother yanked Lara from under the bed by her ankles. Lara clawed at the orange and yellow shag carpet, her pink flowered nightgown bunching up around her chest as she fought. Her high-pitched wails pierced my heart.

When Beth and I told our father about these episodes, he threatened to sue for custody, but in the end, he wasn't ready to be the single parent of four little kids.

He abandoned us to her monstrous rage.

As part of her divorce settlement, my mother received the Redwood Motel, located at the end of Hastings' motel row on Highway 6, next to the KHAS radio tower.

The one-story wood structure, painted dark red with white trim, sat on the west side of a circular drive with a grassy lawn in the middle. It had seventeen air-conditioned rooms and a small house attached to the office.

The Redwood attracted a dubious clientele of traveling salesmen, third-rate lounge acts, and during the summertime, families traveling through town on their way to somewhere more interesting. Customers paid $9.27 per night for a room with one bed and $12.36 for a double.

Over our protestations, my mother insisted we live on-site. She would not consider buying a house in town and hiring someone else to run the motel, even though it meant changing schools and giving up our neighborhood friends.

For me it meant leaving my sunny, second-floor bedroom to live in the motel basement, next to the laundry room. It meant no longer being able to ride my bike to the library or walk to my dad's townhouse. That was the worst part. After the move I rarely saw my dad. He might as well have been living on Pluto.

I probably should have been thankful that the judge hadn't awarded her the other motel my dad owned, the DLD, also on Highway 6. It had a row of six rooms and four large white concrete teepees with red zigzags at the top. I hated my basement room, but at least it wasn't a concrete teepee.

On the plus side, the Redwood did have a Coke machine. Beth and I would frequently sneak the key to the machine out of the office drawer. One of us would keep watch while the other opened the metal door and grabbed a Coke or a Dr. Pepper, the nutritional equivalent of rat poison in my mother's eyes. We'd hide in the cornfield behind the motel and share our treasure. Fearful of getting busted with our sugary contraband, we'd drink it so fast we got brain freeze.

We'd only been living at the Redwood a few months when one of the customers, a traveling salesman named Jerry, began courting my mother.

A tall, white-haired man with big teeth and a mahogany tan, Jerry drove a lemon-yellow Cadillac and talked with a soft southern accent. Even though he had to be fifteen years older than my mother, she fell for his charms.

He acted nice.

Too nice.

Whenever Beth or I mentioned something we liked, he had it. When we said we liked horses, he told us he owned a horse farm in Kentucky. When we said we liked to swim, he said the horse farm had a big swimming pool with a diving board. When we said we liked roller skating, he bragged about the new skating rink with a disco ball in the town next to his farm.

After only a few months of dating, Jerry inserted himself into the motel operations, convincing my mother to buy a CB radio and entice truckers traveling on Highway 281 to detour over to Highway 6 to spend the night. He made plans to pave the large grassy area where my siblings and I liked to play and turn it into a parking lot for eighteen-wheelers.

Then he started talking about marriage.

Beth and I begged our mother not to marry Jerry, not to take us away from our father, but the promise of living the high life in Kentucky and not having to deal with four kids and a motel all by herself had left her starry-eyed with hope.

My mother had been searching for a silver bullet shaped like a man. And Jerry had just the right sheen.

Before finalizing the wedding plans, Jerry insisted on spiffing up the Redwood so my mother could sell it immediately for a big profit. He convinced her that the trucker's parking lot was the answer. If she were willing to invest a few thousand dollars for paving, she'd get her money back fivefold.

My mother gave Jerry the money.

We never saw him again.

When it became clear that Jerry hadn't been in an accident or misplaced her phone number, that her money was lost and so was her favorite Neil Diamond eight-track – a hard-to-find greatest hits volume that she'd accidently left in his car – my mother took it out on us, raging about unmade beds, scuffs on the linoleum floor and assorted acts of ingratitude.

She never talked about the financial loss or the humiliation of being conned by the slick Southerner in the yellow Cadillac, but she often complained about the stolen Neil Diamond eight-track. She vocally mourned the loss of "Sweet Caroline," and swallowed the betrayal.

In December 1976, my mother sold the Redwood and moved us to Ogallala, Nebraska, a town two hundred miles from Hastings, to pursue a man named Bill. A hot-tempered Irishman nineteen years her senior, Bill loved drama as much as she did. Their relationship included fire arms, broken door frames and visits from the country sheriff.

Ogallala, population five thousand, had little to offer beside gas for those traveling on Interstate 80 and a lake filled with rainbow trout. My siblings and I hated fishing and didn't want to move, but our family wasn't a democracy.

It was during those first few weeks in Ogallala that I realized my mother despised me. Her favorite insult was, "You're just like your father."

I had his blond hair, fair skin and quiet reserve. I'd even mastered the art of the impassive, empty-eyed stare, a tactic I'd seen him use to diffuse her angry outbursts.

Neither the new town nor the relationship with Bill improved my mother's disposition or impacted her pattern of violence. She fought with Bill constantly and took out her disappointment on everyone in the house.

I hated coming home from school, not knowing what would be waiting for me when I opened the front door. My stomach would clench as I neared our driveway. Sometimes I'd walk around the block, over and over again, until I could find the courage to go inside.

After we moved, I saw my father sporadically, when he could convince my mother to meet him at a rest stop on the Interstate halfway between Ogallala and Hastings or when he'd spring for Greyhound bus tickets.

I missed him and I longed for my friends and the familiar surroundings of Hastings. Being the new kid, and being afraid to invite anyone to my house, made for a solitary existence in Ogallala.

Loneliness and social isolation heightened the psychological impact of my mother's violence. Crying became part of my daily routine. I didn't have the word for it then, but I was depressed.

My twelfth birthday came and went with no card or phone call from my father. Despite my pleading, my mother refused to pay for a long-distance call. How could she afford it on the pittance he paid in child support?

I felt abandoned. Hopeless. Defeated.

Home alone, a few nights after my birthday, I took Bill's loaded .38 revolver from the hall closet and sat on the kitchen floor, feeling the weight and coolness of it in my hands.

I imagined my mother coming home and finding me dead in the kitchen, blood splattered on her flocked wallpaper. Would she cry? Would she be angry that I'd made a mess?

As I stared at the gun, one question ran in a loop through my mind. What kind of person must I be if my own parents couldn't love me?

I held the gun to my cheek, my finger resting on the trigger, and closed my eyes. All it would take was one small movement, one squeeze with one finger, and I would be free. I would never have to face my mother's hatred again.

Then it occurred to me that if I pulled that trigger, if I ended my twelve years of life with a bullet to the face, my mother would win and I would lose. I would lose. The thought made me put down the gun.

Unfiltered pain poured out of me in waves of tears that ran down my cheeks and neck. Sobs shook my shoulders. I hugged my knees to my chest and began rocking on the floor, back and forth, back and forth.

Was it too much to ask for a mother who did not leave welts on my legs, forcing me to skip gym class? Was it too much to ask for a father who cared enough to call me on my birthday? Had he forgotten about me because I was so far away?

He meant so much to me. How could I mean so little to him?

I was tired of being scared and tired of living in my head because I was too ashamed to tell anyone the truth about my family. I needed saving, but superheroes only existed in comic books and movies. If I wanted to be saved, I would have to do it myself. That night, I resolved to run away and live with my father.

A few weeks later, I landed a job working the drive-thru at Nelson's Dairy Crème. It paid $.95 an hour, plus tips.

I worked a few nights after school and during the day on the weekends, drawing smiley faces and writing cheery messages on cups and paper bags to get my tips up. Every night I volunteered to stay late, to mop the floors and wash dishes while the owner cleaned the fryer and scrubbed the hot griddle with a nasty-smelling charcoal briquette.

After three months at Nelson's, I'd saved enough to buy a bus ticket to Grand Island, the closest town to Hastings with a Greyhound bus depot. I kept the money in my jewelry box, waiting for the moment when my courage outweighed my fear. It came in September, after my mother whipped me with a belt until my back bled.

A few nights after the incident, I crept out the back door with the Samsonite suitcase I'd gotten for Christmas, heavy with my favorite Nancy Drew books: *The Mystery of the Tolling Bell, The Ghost of Blackwood Hall, The Clue in the Old Stagecoach* and *The Witch Tree Symbol.*

I lugged my suitcase through the dark streets of Ogallala, shifting it from one hand to the next, my arms burning with the weight of it. Slowly, I made my way to the bus stop a half mile from our house. Once there, I hid in the shadows by the trash cans so no one would see me before the bus arrived. Since I'd purchased my ticket the day before, when the bus rolled into the Sinclair station at 1:30 a.m., I slipped on without the gas station attendant noticing me.

Finding an empty row of seats near the restroom, I slept until the bus driver shook my shoulder in Grand Island at 6:30.

At the payphone outside I called my father collect.

He didn't answer.

Not knowing what else to do, I bought an Old Home Bakery fried cherry pie and a Coca-Cola and ate my sugary breakfast on an orange plastic bench. I was so focused on not getting cherry goo on my shirt, I didn't notice my dad walk in until he called my name.

His face was drawn. He hadn't shaved or put on socks.

At forty-four, his wispy blond hair barely covered the top of his head. The thin strands, usually combed meticulously into place, stuck out at odd angles. He'd obviously left the house without looking in the mirror.

"Your mother called me," he said, sitting down next to me. "Beth got scared and told her you were on the bus."

"Can we go home?' I set the pie down and hugged him.

"Why did you do this?"

I pulled away and raised my shirt so he could see the red slashes on my skin. "I can't live with her anymore," I said.

My father pressed his fingers into one of the welts, as if to test its truthfulness. He closed his eyes for a moment and dropped his head.

They announced the bus to Chicago.

Passengers threw away their Styrofoam coffee cups, snuffed out their cigarettes and filed out the door until only the old lady with cat-eye glasses behind the snack bar, my father and I remained.

"I'll talk to her," he said in a whispery voice. His blue eyes shone with tears.

He was going to send me back.

"No, no, no, please, please, please don't send me back. She'll kill me."

It had not occurred to me, in all my saving, planning and plotting, that my father would send me back to Ogallala. That he would reject me.

"Your mother loves you," he said.

"She hates me. She hates me because I remind her of you. I look like you. My smile is crooked, just like yours." I smiled to show him, to convince him that I belonged to him.

"I promised your mother I'd put you on the next bus," he said. "It leaves at 8:05."

He bought me a stick of beef jerky, another fried cherry pie and a Coke for the road. Consolation prizes, disguised as love, stuffed in a flimsy white paper bag.

"I promise you, everything will be okay," he said as he handed my suitcase to the bus driver and kissed me on the forehead.

It wasn't.

For a few months, my mother held back, limiting herself to verbal assaults. Bill living in the house helped. With him, we had one more victim in the rotation. On occasion, he would even defend one of us, convincing my mother that whatever punishment she'd decided to mete out wasn't warranted. But she could not be dissuaded for long. By Christmas her outbursts of rage were as destructive as they'd ever been.

* * *

Right before my thirteenth birthday, I met a Samoan girl named Maria, a recent transplant from Pago-Pago whose family had relocated to Nebraska in search of job opportunities.

A head taller than anyone in our sixth-grade class, Maria easily tipped the scales at two hundred and fifty pounds. Although only twelve, she could pass for thirty. Maybe it was the deep creases in her forehead, or maybe it was the housedress. I had never seen a twelve-year-old wear a housedress, the kind made of floral-print cotton with patch pockets on the front, a favorite of grandmothers throughout the Midwest. Sweat socks and sandals completed her ensemble.

I befriended Maria when I realized she could buy liquor.

Since my first drink five years earlier, I'd had a few bottles of Budweiser and a cup of sloe gin mixed with 7-UP, but it wasn't until Maria arrived that I had real access to alcohol.

Plied with a few dollars and a package of Twizzlers, Maria would shuffle down to the liquor store in her house dress to buy pints of peppermint schnapps for me. I hid the bottles and rationed out the contents over the course of several days. It took only a few gulps to calm the anxiety that accompanied daily life in my mother's house, and the warm fuzziness made it much easier to fall sleep.

In 1979, the year I turned fourteen and started eighth grade, Ogallala Junior High administered IQ tests and placement tests. The guidance counselor told me that I tested as a high school graduate on the placement tests.

"These scores surprised me," she said with a tight smile. "Given your grades, I thought we might have to hold you back a year."

I'd flunked Home Economics after I burned an iron-shaped hole in my sewing project and had gotten a C in Biology because I refused to dissect a frog, but my other grades weren't *that* bad. I left her office feeling a weird mixture of pride and shame.

I never saw the IQ test results.

Years later Beth told me the guidance counselor called our mother in for a meeting and told her I'd scored in the genius range. The school wanted to create a learning plan for me because my grades didn't reflect my potential. They suspected boredom as the culprit. My mother insisted the school not extend any special treatment or tell me about the test results. She didn't want me to get a big head.

In the fall of 1979, my relationship with my mother reached a new low. After one particularly bad fight, I ran away again – same bus depot, same suitcase, no Nancy Drew books.

When I arrived in Grand Island, I called my father and told him that if he did not take me in, I would board another bus, to New York or Los Angeles or some other place where runaways went to vanish. I refused to take my mother's abuse one more day.

By then he had married a grocery store heiress named Barbara, an alum of Stephens College, the same finishing school Joan Crawford attended. Since Barbara could pick me up from school and look after me when my father traveled, he agreed to take me. They had just finished building a large house on Lake Hastings with plenty of room for a teenager.

Barbara treated me with amiable indifference – hello, goodbye, pick up those shoes, what time will you be home for dinner and don't forget to put your dirty clothes in the laundry chute.

The indifference didn't bother me. Their house was deliciously quiet and that was enough.

I loved the quiet.

I loved that Barbara bought Oreo Cookies, Double Stuff even, and bags of Cheetos and pretzels. She didn't count the slices of

American cheese before going to bed, like my mother did, or berate me if she unearthed a Snickers wrapper at the bottom of the kitchen trash can.

I loved that I didn't have to work to pay for my school clothes and supplies. My father paid for everything and gave me an allowance of ten dollars a week.

I could come home after school and not be afraid of what was waiting on the other side of the front door. I fell asleep easily, without alcohol, not worried that I'd be roused in the middle of the night by high-pitched screaming and slamming doors.

My life quickly filled with new friends and activities. I was invited to sleepovers and went to football games and dances. I spent Saturdays at the mall perusing records at Musicland and eating popcorn balls at Karmelkorn. I invited friends over to listen to music and hang out in my room.

For the first time since my parents' divorce, I could concentrate on school. My first semester at Hastings Senior High I made the dean's list.

I felt like a normal person.

I felt proud.

Peaceful, even.

But my reprieve only lasted six months.

* * *

Barbara came into the marriage with three grown children, two girls and a boy. In March of 1980, two weeks before my fifteenth birthday, her twenty-two-year-old son raped me in our basement rec room.

It happened after a family celebration where I'd consumed several bottles of beer. Drunk and not wanting to be discovered, I went down to the basement to sleep it off on the pit sofa next to the ping pong table. A few hours later I woke up, struggling to breathe, my skirt gathered around my waist and my two-hundred-pound stepbrother on top of me, half naked with his knees between mine.

My eyes opened and met his. He covered my mouth with his hand and whispered. "Don't say anything."

I nodded. Anything to escape.

A few days later, so consumed with anxiety that I could barely get through the school day, I called my sister Beth and confessed what had happened. Even though she promised not to say anything, she told my mother. My mother called my father, and in an instant, my drama-free world exploded.

Barbara lost it.

"She's a lying little bitch!" Barbara yelled, her voice penetrating my bedroom door and the Billy Joel eight track blaring from my stereo. She insisted my father immediately drive me to the Adams County Sheriff's office to take a lie detector test.

He did.

Choking down sobs, I answered the examiner's questions and passed the polygraph while my father and the sheriff, a friend of his, watched through a large window. Afterward, burning with shame and puffy-eyed, I said nothing as my father escorted me to the car.

He didn't drive us home. Instead we stopped for bear claws and chocolate milk at Daylight Donuts, the place we always went to celebrate small things like an A on a test or me making the staff of the school paper. I didn't know why he took me to my favorite donut shop that day. Perhaps he thought a big dose of comfort food would erase the afternoon's trauma, or maybe he just didn't know what else to do.

Maybe he felt as lost as I did.

We sat at a table by a window that afforded a clear view of life as usual.

"I don't think you should press charges," he said as he tore a toe from his bear claw and licked bits of icing from his index finger. "It won't be good for anyone, especially you."

I pulled a thin napkin from the dispenser and dabbed at the tears leaking from the corners of my eyes. "You think this is my fault," I said.

"Maybe you didn't do anything wrong," he said, "but you didn't do many things right."

I had been drinking. I went to the basement instead of my room. It was my fault.

I swallowed the blame with a chocolate milk chaser.

Had I done something to make Barbara's son believe that I wanted him to do what he did? How could I know for sure? I'd passed out. Maybe I was the kind of girl who deserved to be raped, a drunken girl who couldn't protect herself.

My father reached across the table and squeezed my hand. "What if I promise he will never be allowed in our house again? You will never have to see him."

I nodded my agreement, unable to meet his eyes.

We left the donut shop, prisoners of a decision that would cost each of us much more than the integrity we'd left on the table with our crumpled napkins.

Everything was the same, but nothing was the same.

I made a half-hearted attempt to kill myself on my fifteenth birthday, the girly way, with a razor blade, slashing the wrong direction.

For a few months, I visited a counselor on Thursday afternoons. She probed around my outer defenses, but our sessions went nowhere. How could I talk about my feelings when I didn't have any? I was dead inside.

I didn't remember most of the rape, just the end, when I woke up and confronted him with my eyes. Were those few seconds enough to crush the determination that held me together during fourteen years of my mother's abuse? Could a man I barely knew wield that much power?

When the counselor asked me how I was coping, I mostly talked about school and my difficulties concentrating in class.

I didn't tell her that I'd started smoking Marlboro Lights and blowing the smoke out my bedroom window. I didn't tell her about drinking Barbara's scotch when I was alone in the house and watering it down to hide my theft. I didn't tell her about my secret relationship with a college-aged boy who lived in the neighborhood, that I would sneak out at night and meet him at the lake, drink beer and make out until the wee hours. I didn't tell her that the wonderfully quiet house I'd moved into a year ago was now enveloped in a new kind of silence, a silence sharper than razor wire.

On March 29, 1981, I turned sixteen and inherited Beth's starter car, a 1970 Ford Torino, white with a blue vinyl top and cloth seats that smelled faintly of bong water.

With the car came freedom, and for me that meant drinking.

Back then, every Nebraska driver's license was issued with 12 points. If someone lost all their points, they lost their license. Thanks to two speeding tickets and a DWI, in less than three months I was down to one point.

After my DWI arrest, my father hired a lawyer and tried to get the charges dismissed, but I'd blown a 0.18 on the breathalyzer and thrown a punch at a deputy sheriff.

There would be no leniency.

Grounded for the first six weeks of summer, I was only allowed out of the house to go to my new waitressing job at the Garden Café, a quasi-nice restaurant attached to our local Holiday Inn, and attend mandatory alcohol education classes at the mental health center.

I'd hoped the alcohol education classes might teach me how to drink and not black out, but they didn't. Our instructor started each class with the same preamble. "If you're under twenty-one, don't drink at all. If you're over twenty-one, drink in moderation, no more than one beer or glass of wine every ninety minutes."

Clearly, he'd never tried a beer bong.

Most of the time we watched films featuring mangled cars and bloody people, narrated by stern-faced law enforcement officers, with shots of crying relatives spliced in. But nothing I saw in the films, no matter how gruesome, could erase my need for alcohol. It was the only thing that made me feel okay, at least for a little while.

Figuring out how to drink just the right amount became my obsession. I wanted to drink enough to be funny, charming and sexy, without blacking out or wrecking my car.

Quitting early didn't seem like a good option; that wouldn't be fun. But blacking out wasn't fun either, especially when it led me to do something awful, like French kissing a stranger or puking on my favorite shoes.

I hated going to bed when I'd drunk enough to spin, but not enough to pass out. I incessantly searched for a line that kept shifting, a shimmery mirage of equilibrium that eluded me.

During the 1970s, my father's business empire had grown dramatically. He'd expanded beyond residential property management and a few motels in Nebraska to Sonic Drive-In franchises, storage facilities and motels in Kansas and Iowa. We'd gone from vacationing in Kansas City to touring Boston and Washington, D.C. While my friends pitched tents and grilled burgers in the Black Hills, I sipped lobster bisque at the Lenox Hotel.

From the outside, our lives seemed enviable.

Then disaster struck.

Its name was Jimmy Carter.

Ask anyone who worked in real estate back in the late 1970s and early 1980s what it was like, and watch their faces turn grim. Twenty-two percent interest rates killed the industry. Failed banks and savings and loans littered the landscape. It became impossible to liquidate anything.

Like many of his peers in the real estate business, my father relied on leverage and needed a constant supply of fresh cash to feed his empire.

In 1981, he made a series of unfortunate choices.

The first was floating money between banks in three states – Nebraska, Kansas and Iowa – where he owned properties or businesses. Back then, it could take up to a week for out-of-state checks to clear, so by the time one check written on an empty account cleared, my father had covered it with another check written on a different empty account. He had this practice down to a science.

The second mistake he made was using the U.S. Postal Service to send checks from state to state, compounding bank fraud with mail fraud, two crimes that fell under FBI jurisdiction.

The third mistake was asking his business partner Jack to deposit a check at the Hastings State Bank on a Friday afternoon in late August of 1981.

My father had given Jack specific instructions: go inside to deposit the check, get a receipt from the teller, make sure you do it between two-thirty and three o'clock.

Easy enough.

But Jack stopped for a late lunch and lost track of time. When he arrived at the bank at 2:50 and found the parking lot full, he pulled into the drive-thru.

Jack put the check and deposit slip in a plastic cylinder and hit the send button. After an initial WHOOSH, it made a strange sucking noise and then stopped. Leaning out the window of his car, he could see it in the pneumatic tube, hovering over a pickup truck in the lane next to his.

The bank manager tried to reset the system, but the tube wouldn't budge. They would have to call a technician from Omaha to fix it on Monday.

Three o'clock came and went.

My father only avoided being arrested the next week because my grandparents borrowed against their farm to cover his shortfall. He paid them back a few weeks later, after he closed the sale of the Tall Corn Motel in Davenport, Iowa, but things between them were never the same.

My grandparents feared they had raised a shyster.

If only the Tall Corn sale had closed a week earlier, if only Jack had gone inside the bank, if, if, if… If my father had been an honest person maybe none of the events that followed would have occurred.

But they did.

The first day of my junior year of high school I came home at four o'clock and was surprised to find him in the living room. He usually didn't arrive until just before dinner at six. As soon as I walked through the front door, he asked me to join him.

In his calm, even tone, he said, "I'm being investigated by the FBI. Be careful what you say on the phone. It's probably being recorded."

"Are you going to jail?" I said.

"Maybe."

It got worse after that.

From what I picked up while eavesdropping on his conversations with Barbara, he was desperately trying to sell properties and free up cash. He had several balloon payments coming due and no money to pay them. High interest rates deterred potential buyers who relied on mortgages. Cash buyers wanted to earn interest on their cash, not buy real estate.

By the end of October, my father had stopped smiling.

* * *

The Saturday after Thanksgiving, my father asked me to meet him at his office after I finished working the breakfast shift at the Garden Café. He'd sounded serious, so I didn't even go home to change out of my orange and tan polyester uniform.

Secretly I hoped he planned to divorce Barbara. Since the incident with her son, our relationship had gone from cordial to caustic. She rarely spoke to me except to bark instructions or complain about something I'd done. At meals, she talked to my father and ignored me.

When I arrived at his property management office, I found him sitting in the lobby, staring at the wall of windows that spanned one side of the room. He gestured for me to sit down across from him.

Without looking at me, he said, "I'm in a bad situation. I need to borrow money from Barbara's trust fund. She's agreed, with one condition. She wants her son home for Christmas."

It took a few seconds to absorb his words. I fought back tears but couldn't stop my hands from shaking. It hadn't even been two years and my father was already breaking his promise.

"How much?" I said, barely able to choke out the words.

"That's not important," he said.

"It's important to me," I said as I gripped the arms of my chair, trying to stop the shaking.

He shifted his gaze to the floor. "It's only for a few days. You can stay with your sister Beth. I'll come over to her place for Christmas dinner and we can all be together."

Beth had graduated from high school that spring and moved to Hastings for college. She lived in a five-bedroom house my dad owned, along with three roommates and two cats.

"How much?"

"I can't go to the bank. If I don't get this money from Barbara, I'll lose everything!"

"HOW MUCH?" I screamed. I would not leave without knowing how many pieces of silver I was worth.

He bit the fingernail on his thumb and mumbled, "Eighty thousand dollars."

After that, I became fluent in silence.

Make It Equal, Even When It's Not

Berlin, Germany – July 2002

The silence stretched between Ruedger and me as we stared out at the river Spree. The chipped wooden bench rocked slightly as I fidgeted, crossing and uncrossing my legs, thinking about how to start a conversation I knew would be unpleasant.

If we were going to start this new company, we had to decide who would do what, and then divide up the ownership.

I knew that Thomas would not contribute at the same level as Ruedger and me. We would create a legal structure, find investors and deal with the lawyers, accountants, landlords, investors, customers and employees.

We would own the scary parts, the parts most employees never saw or touched.

It would be up to Ruedger and me to manage the inevitable disappointment of investors when we didn't make our plan, because no start-up ever made their plan. We would sit in board meetings and defend bad decisions, under-performing employees and cost overruns. We would decide who to pay and who not to pay when money got tight. And we would put on a good face for the troops, shielding them from the threats our new business would inevitably face.

"This is not a third, a third, a third proposition and you know it," I began. "You and I will own ninety-five percent of the responsibility."

"If you want to tell him that he's not worth as much as we are, go ahead."

"How do I do that?" I asked.

"If you want to be a CEO," said Ruedger, "get used to being a bad guy."

Calling myself a CEO felt like playing dress-up. At any moment, I expected my mother to call me for dinner. I'd put my pirate costume and plastic sword back in the toy chest and resume my proper place in the world.

We walked to the restaurant, side by side. Despite the warmth of the evening, a cool breeze blowing across the water raised goose bumps on my arms. I untied the sweater around my waist and pulled it over my head.

"Can you live with an equal division?" I said.

"Yes," said Ruedger. "There are only three of us. Together you and I have a majority."

"Yes, and together you and Thomas have a majority," I reminded him.

He shrugged. "At some point we have to trust each other."

"What if one of us leaves?" I said. "What do we do then? Thomas walked out when he was at Mordix. He left for a year and a half because working with you made him crazy."

"He came back."

At the restaurant, a small Italian café with a large outdoor patio, Thomas greeted me with a hug. The waiter guided us to a table under a pergola shrouded in vines and small twinkling white lights. It seemed like a better setting for a first date than a business negotiation.

I studied Thomas' long, angular face and serious gray eyes, slightly distorted by the thick lenses of his glasses. How would I tell this nice man that I valued him less than Ruedger?

We ordered drinks, shared a basket of bread and a plate of olives, and talked about everything except the equity.

For almost three years we'd been colleagues with clear roles and responsibilities, working toward a known set of objectives. Through that process, we'd forged a strong friendship. Starting a

new company required us to redefine everything, to fight for
territory that was, to some extent, unknowable.

Ruedger told me that when he started Syrinx, the company that
would morph into Mordix, there were six co-founders who divided
the stock equally. Although they held equal ownership, the
founding team had not contributed equally. Everyone expected
Ruedger to run the day-to-day operations, get the company
financed, manage technology development, build a patent portfolio
and make all the strategic decisions while they worked in their
silos. His resentment grew as the gap between responsibility and
compensation widened. He swore he'd never do it again.

I drew closer to the subject, asking Thomas, "What do you see
yourself doing at the new company? What role do you want to
play?"

He took off his glasses and rubbed the bridge of his nose, then
put them back on. "I know what you're asking. You want to know
if I'm going to do as much as you and Ruedger."

"Yes."

The waiter appeared with our food. The quattro formaggi pizza
I'd ordered reeked of Gorgonzola, my favorite cheese. I welcomed
the distraction of a few bites before returning to the topic on the
table.

Ruedger saved me from having to spell it out. "How much of
the company do you expect to get?" he said to Thomas. "I think
that's the real question Lea is asking."

Thomas said, "I thought we would divide it equally, between
the three of us, like we did at Syrinx."

I waited for Ruedger to jump in, tell Thomas why it didn't work
at Syrinx and why it won't work now. But he said nothing.

I didn't have Ruedger's Syrinx experience and it seemed cheap
for me to feed it to Thomas. What would I propose instead? Forty,
forty, twenty? Tell him he's worth half as much as we were?
Thirty-five, thirty-five, thirty? That sounded petty.

Feeling trapped, and unwilling to kill our venture before it had a chance to find its legs, I blurted out, "I'm okay with an equal division of equity."

Ruedger turned to me, eyebrows scrunched. "Are you sure?"

Thomas jumped in. "I know you and Ruedger are going to contribute more on the business side, but I will work on the patents and build the manufacturing technology with Hoffman. So, I think this is fair."

Ruedger nodded.

We discussed titles and I agreed to be the CEO. Ruedger would serve as President and Thomas would take the CTO title. In a weird twist, Ruedger asked to be the Chairman of the Board of Directors, effectively making him my boss while I was his boss.

Smiling, Thomas wiped his hand on his napkin and extended it across the table to me. "Do we have a deal?"

We had a deal.

After dinner, instead of returning to my hotel, I walked in the direction of the Brandenburg Gate and called Will to see if he was home from camp.

He answered the phone breathless, like he'd run in from outside. "When are you coming home?"

"On Sunday."

"Can you come today?" he said in a soft voice that made me want to scoop him up and squeeze him.

"Tell me what you did at camp," I said.

He'd painted a pirate ship. A mean kid named Luke kicked him repeatedly during nap time, when the counselor wasn't looking. He and his dad were going to Home Depot on Saturday to build a birdhouse.

I smiled as he wove the stories of his day into a picture for me.

"I'm bringing you a surprise from Germany." I told him.

"Is it an airplane?" His voice rose with excitement.

Will loved airplanes as much as he loved building airports with Legos. The last few trips I'd brought back miniature airplanes that were hard to find in the U.S.: Iberia Airlines, Aeroflot and Sabena. A small metal Lufthansa 747 was no substitute for a mother's time, but Will didn't hold it against me.

It was past ten o'clock when we hung up. Grayish pink light clung to the horizon. The river glittered. Party boats streamed by, the sounds of music and bits of conversations drifting along in their wakes. Every café had a few tables on the sidewalk full of late night diners.

Unlike people who lived in Dallas, where outdoor dining in August could be life threatening, Berliners relished cool evenings on the river. They lingered, having one more drink, maybe a cappuccino or a dessert just to draw out the experience. It was one of the things I liked most about the city.

When I reached Unter den Linden, I sat on a bench and gazed up at the bronze sculpture that sat atop the Brandenburg Gate, a statue of the goddess of victory in a chariot pulled by four horses. Spotlights illuminated her triumphant face, casting a yellow light against the darkening sky. I thought about my dinner with Ruedger and Thomas, and the big steps I'd just taken. I'd negotiated the ownership structure and agreed to be the CEO of a company I didn't feel confident enough to start.

Sure, I'd like to be one of those successful entrepreneurs who graces the cover of Forbes and rings the NASDAQ bell. It would be great if I no longer had to agonize about my lack of retirement savings and paying for Will's college. But that outcome felt like a silly fantasy, like believing I could win the lotto.

Recently I'd been having dreams about falling from high places, being pulled underwater and running from dark, menacing shapes that I couldn't identify but knew would kill me if I stumbled. I woke up most mornings feeling unsettled.

I didn't want to be an entrepreneur.

I didn't want to be my father.

Plop, Plop, Fizz, Fizz

Hastings, Nebraska – 1982

Early in the morning on the 26th of January, my father had a heart attack. Barbara called an ambulance and they went to the hospital without waking me.

He spent two weeks in the hospital recovering.

I did not visit him, send a card or call.

Beth went daily and pleaded with me to go along. "Dad wants to see you," she said. "He feels terrible about Christmas."

"He should feel terrible," I said, my voice swimming in bitterness. Not only had he kicked me out of the house for Christmas, when I returned I discovered that Barbara's son had stayed in my room. She'd washed the sheets, but my bedspread reeked of his cologne.

The injustice of it burned like a fireball in my chest. I'd never experienced anger that intense, and I feared that if I spoke to my father, the fireball would explode and annihilate both of us.

He left the hospital on a Monday afternoon. I skipped his homecoming and went directly from school to work. I hung around the hotel after my shift ended, flirting with the night clerk and playing Pac Man in the game room until I burned through all my tips.

Quiet darkness greeted me when I unlocked the front door. Not wanting to wake my father and Barbara, I removed my shoes. As I tip-toed past their bedroom door, I heard snoring, confirmation of my father's presence in the house.

I fell asleep dreading the morning, imagining my father's accusatory stares across the breakfast table, unsure if I could maintain my silence if he pressed for a conversation.

Sirens woke me at two in the morning. I came out of my room and peered down into the foyer. My father was on a gurney, being wheeled out of the house. Barbara, wearing a bathrobe, held the door open, a burning cigarette between her fingers.

Barbara saw me and said, "He's having stomach pains. We're going to the hospital. Go back to bed."

She called a few minutes after my alarm went off at 7:00. "Go to school," she said. "He has indigestion. They're just going to keep him a few hours."

That afternoon, in my Home Furnishings class, I was looking through fabric samples and passing notes back and forth with my friend Heidi. The merits of silk curtains versus polyester didn't interest me. I'd only taken the class because it fulfilled my Home Economics requirement and gave me a chance to gossip with Heidi at the end of the school day.

When they called my name on the PA system, I didn't hear it.

Heidi shook my shoulder. "They're calling you to the office," she said.

The school secretary delivered the news in an even tone. "Your father has taken a turn for the worse; you need to go to the hospital right now. Your stepmom said to bring a friend with you." Then she added, "Don't take Heidi, she's missed too much school this semester."

I went alone.

The Torino's heater had just started blowing warm air when I pulled into the hospital parking lot. I wished that I'd worn my rabbit fur coat to school instead of the fashionable pink cotton trench coat I'd purchased two weeks earlier. An icy wind cut through the thin fabric and raised bumps on my arms. Spring had only arrived at the Imperial Mall, not the Mary Lanning Memorial Hospital parking lot.

I knew it was bad when I exited the elevator and saw my father's cousin sitting in the ICU lounge. He only showed up for funeral potlucks.

"Your dad's not going to make it," he said, looking up at me with red-rimmed eyes.

I slid into the molded plastic chair next to his, trying to make sense of his words. How could this be? How could my father go from indigestion to "not going to make it" in only a few hours?

This had to be a mistake.

My father couldn't die.

The realization of how much I still needed him hit me hard. Underneath my anger, deep below the sick feeling of betrayal that stoked my resentment, I loved my father and I desperately wanted to hear him say that he loved me too.

Beth came out of a room at the end of the corridor and hurried over to me. She hugged me tight. Her tears rolled down my neck.

"I think he bought some Alka Seltzer when we stopped at Walgreens on the way home from the hospital yesterday," she said. "He made me wait in the car."

My father believed that Alka Seltzer was a magic elixir, capable of curing everything from heartburn to the bubonic plague. The little blue packages lurked all around the house, in medicine cabinets, kitchen drawers, his briefcase, his desk drawer and always in the glove box of his car, just in case. As children, my siblings and I quickly learned to hide stomach-related ailments, anything to avoid the fizzy, gritty concoction that coated our tongues and induced enormous burps.

"They think something was wrong with his kidneys and taking the Alka Seltzer made it worse," Beth continued. "The doctor specifically told him not to take it with the nitroglycerine."

Plop, plop. Fizz, fizz. What had he done?

The man in the bed seemed smaller than my father. His cheeks, always pink from the sun, hung loose and pale. It had been only two weeks since I'd last seen him, and in that time, he had morphed into someone else.

I squeezed his fingers and said a silent prayer.

Please God, don't take my father. Maybe I acted like I didn't want him to be my father anymore, but I didn't mean it. I love him. I'm so sorry. Please, please, please, please, please don't take my father.

Someone placed a firm hand on my shoulder. I was surprised to see Dr. Dean, the man who brought me into the world, the man who had assured my mother I would not be ugly. He'd seen me though the measles, pulled a rusty nail out of my foot and administered numerous tetanus shots over the years. I wondered if he still kept lollipops in his jacket pocket, the kind attached to a loop of stiff string just the right size for a child's finger.

"If they can stabilize your dad, he'll go on a Care Flight to Omaha tonight." He patted my shoulder.

We listened to silence, punctuated by the beeping monitor.

When Beth knocked on the door, signaling my time was up, I squeezed my father's hand and slipped out of the room.

I wanted to click my heels three times and be magically transported to a safe place far, far from the plastic chairs, the flecked linoleum and the dark windows that offered nothing but unflattering reflections.

Suddenly, the light above the door to my father's room began to flash and a pulsing alarm filled the hallway with electronic urgency. Nurses and a doctor rushed into the room, rolling a cart in front of them.

When Dr. Dean emerged a few minutes later, grim-faced, I knew. There would be no reconciliation, no forgiveness.

My father would never smile at me again with his crooked grin and say, "Don't worry Lea Ann, everything will be okay."

* * *

The day after the funeral, I returned to the house at 2900 Lakeview Cove to find my belongings on the front porch, stuffed into green lawn bags. My key wouldn't open the locks on the front door or the side door. I rang the doorbell, knocked and pounded with both fists, but no one answered.

I loaded the bags in my car. As I squeezed the last two into the back seat, I noticed Barbara's son's car parked a few houses down. Had he packed my things? Was he living in my room? I wanted to drag my keys from the headlight to the tail light, digging into the paint until metal showed through, but I resisted the urge.

Unsure where to go, I drove to the public area of Lake Hastings and parked next to the boat ramp. I looked out at the partially-frozen lake, the scene of many afternoons waterskiing with friends and late nights of heavy petting in the back seats of cars. I'd always felt proud telling people, "I live at the lake." It implied a social status I could no longer claim.

Where did I live now?

In the Torino?

Was I homeless?

I drove to Beth's house, called my mother and told her that Barbara had kicked me out without warning. "I don't know what to do," I said, trying to hold it together. I hated showing my mother any kind of weakness. "Barbara changed the locks."

If I was looking for sympathy, I'd dialed the wrong number.

In a flat tone, my mother said, "My divorce from Bill was final last month and I've met someone new. His name is Wayne. I don't want you to ruin my relationship with him the way you ruined your dad's relationship with Barbara." She added, "You made your choice when you ran away, so now you need to live with it."

Even though I didn't want to move back to Ogallala or live with my mother again, the rejection hit me like a sucker punch. I wanted her to claim me. I wanted her to want me.

Beth found me that night on the floor of her spare bedroom, passed out in a fetal position, clutching a bottle of peppermint schnapps that I'd pilfered from one of her roommates, surrounded by the trash bags that contained my life.

She joined me on the floor and stroked my hair. "You can stay with me," she said. "You'll always have a place with me."

My father died without a will, so Barbara inherited his entire estate.

And just when I thought things couldn't get any worse, she repossessed my twelve-year-old Ford Torino. My father had registered it as a company car for tax purposes. As she now owned his company, the Torino belonged to her.

I'd officially lost everything.

How Will You Ever Get Another Job?

Dallas, Texas – August 2002

Ruedger resigned first, on the last Monday in August, right after he returned from a three-week vacation on Spiekeroog, a tiny barrier island in the North Sea where he and his family went every year to enjoy blinding rain showers occasionally interrupted by short bursts of sunshine.

Roscoe claimed to be shocked by Ruedger's decision to leave, even though he'd hired the new CTO to take on most of Ruedger's responsibilities.

He was waiting outside my office when I arrived that Monday morning.

"Did you know about Ruedger's plan?" He closed my door and paced from it to the window of my small office, hands shoved deep in his pockets. "What is he going to do next?"

"You should ask him."

"Well, he can't hurt us. His non-compete is rock solid."

This was not true, but I didn't enlighten Roscoe.

Ruedger had signed a restrictive non-compete with Mordix Inc. Unfortunately, Mordix Inc was not his employer. He'd never received a paycheck from the Inc. Ruedger worked for Mordix GmbH, the Germany entity. Somehow the expensive international labor lawyer that Mordix had hired didn't realize it when he structured the company's employment agreements back in 1998.

German law required companies to pay former employees a salary during a non-compete period, and it narrowly defined the restrictions of a non-compete. U.S. companies had no such obligation and, depending on the states where they operated, could make it almost impossible for former employees to find work in their area of expertise. The bottom line – Mordix had to either let Ruedger compete or ask him to sign a retroactive non-compete with the GmbH and pay him a salary for the next year.

When this came to light, Roscoe and the board of directors accused Ruedger of acting in bad faith, claiming he knew about the loophole from the beginning.

Ruedger refused to accept culpability. "It's my job to educate the expensive lawyer the VCs hired to box me in?" he told Roscoe. "How exactly should that work?"

Eventually, after much finger-pointing and bickering, the board decided to pay him for a year. Ruedger agreed to sign a retroactive non-compete with the GmbH as long as it clearly carved out lingual orthodontics as an area where he could work.

With Ruedger's departure, Roscoe's paranoia level rose to DEFCON one. I saw him through the window of the IT director's office, red faced, gesturing with his hands while the IT guy typed furiously. I suspected they were scouring Ruedger's emails, probably mine and Thomas' too, looking for evidence of a conspiracy. They wouldn't find anything. We had left nothing for them to find.

* * *

Although John and I had been talking about the possibility of me starting this new company with Ruedger and Thomas, Ruedger's resignation put pressure on me to declare my commitment.

The night Ruedger resigned, John and I talked about it after I put Will to bed. John was in our living room, sprawled on the sofa watching CNN. I sat down across from him and said, "I have to make a decision soon."

He put the TV on mute. "What kind of decision is there to make? It's not a company yet, you don't have funding. You can't leave your job and have no income."

"I can't raise money for a new company if I'm still working at Mordix. You know that."

"Then let Ruedger do it," he said as he unmuted CNN. "You can join him once he has money in the bank."

John's argument was logical, but unrealistic. Ruedger could not raise money for a U.S. company without a U.S. person on the management team. It would never happen, and John knew that. He was telling me "no" without saying the word "no."

* * *

Thomas resigned two weeks after Ruedger.

The morning Thomas announced his resignation I had a dental appointment, so I didn't get in until after ten o'clock. Roscoe must have asked the receptionist to report my arrival because once again he was waiting outside my office door.

"Are you next?"

All the employees knew that Ruedger, Thomas and I were tight, that we spoke on the phone frequently and huddled over lunches and dinners. Even though Ruedger wanted to keep our plans secret as long as possible, I could not look Roscoe in the eye and lie outright.

"Yes," I said.

"What's going on?"

"The only reason I'm still here is because you haven't built a strong enough case for firing me." I dropped my briefcase on the floor and leaned back against my credenza so I could meet his eyes.

Roscoe's ears turned from pink to crimson. "You want today to be your last day?"

"No, and you don't either."

He raised an eyebrow and cocked his head.

I continued. "It's September. At the rate this company burns cash you will be broke by next summer. You can't close a financing in less than six months, that means you'll have to start raising money in February. You won't find new investors if you don't have some paying customers."

Mordix had reached an important crossroads. The SmilePerfect System was finally ready for clinical use, and the company needed commercial validation. If I left, Roscoe would have no one to sell SmilePerfect. He couldn't hire someone and get them up to speed in time to have an impact. And without sales, there would be no financing.

Recognition clouded his face. "Go on," he said.

I'd been thinking about a way to resign and still get a severance package. Until that moment, it hadn't gelled for me, but suddenly I knew how to make it happen.

"I'll stay until the end of the year and close at least ten paying customers," I said. "In exchange, I want three months of severance and benefits." I added, "And we don't have to tell anyone that I'm leaving."

The last part provided more benefit to me than him. I didn't want to be a lame duck; no one helped those who no longer mattered.

"Are you going to work with Ruedger and Thomas?"

"We are starting a company to develop the custom lingual product with Dr. Hoffman."

"There's no market for that," he said.

As much as I wanted to defend our idea, I didn't. Why give Roscoe a reason to regret signing Hoffman's termination contract?

"Then you don't have anything to worry about," I said.

"I'll let the board know, but not the management team. We'll keep it between us."

We shook hands.

As soon as Roscoe rounded the corner, I went outside and called Ruedger. Despite my enthusiastic spin on the arrangement, he responded negatively.

"You're staying until the end of the year?" His tone reminded me of my fifth-grade home room teacher, a humorless woman with a fierce bouffant who constantly reprimanded me for talking in class.

"Thomas and I are counting on you," he said.

By staying at Mordix, I'd provoked the paranoia he and Thomas shared. I'd never discussed the real reason for my reluctance to start a company, but they both sensed my hesitation.

After assuring Ruedger that I was still on the team, I called John to break the news. "Roscoe would have fired me eventually," I said, explaining that this way I would get a salary and benefits for three months that I wouldn't have gotten otherwise. "This buys me time to raise money for the new company."

John said, "You think you can get it funded in ninety days?" It sounded more like an accusation than a question.

"I'm going to do everything in my power to make that happen," I said.

"We will be in a terrible position if you don't."

That night I decided to go to Germany for the weekend to reassure Ruedger and Thomas. It would mean a serious case of jetlag, but I needed to look my new partners in the eye. Maybe I needed to reassure myself as much as much as I needed to reassure them that we were doing the right thing.

Thomas and Ruedger collected me at the baggage claim in Hannover. We piled into Ruedger's minivan and headed toward Bad Erlangen, the town where Dr. Hoffman lived.

"What do we want from Hoffman?" I said as Ruedger entered the autobahn.

"Documentation," said Thomas.

Coming from the world of software development, I had no idea how much documentation was required to sell medical devices until I landed at Mordix.

Conformité Européene (CE) and U.S. FDA regulations stipulated that every medical device be manufactured to Good Manufacturing Practices (GMP) standards and be traceable, whether it was a tube of toothpaste, a pain killer or a hip implant. The specifications and lot numbers of every material used to make a product had to be recorded and saved until the end of time. This translated into mountains of paper and cost, an enormous barrier for small, bootstrapped companies like ours.

We also needed before, during and after photos of patients. Orthodontists expected clinical photos as proof the product worked.

"Hoffman probably already has documentation," I said.

Thomas laughed a hearty laugh. "You're kidding, right?"

"Doesn't he need it for the lab he's already running?" I said.

"No one audits dental labs in Germany, so most of them don't bother with the documentation."

This gave me a glimmer of hope. If Hoffman didn't need documentation and we were buying from him, then maybe we could skip it too.

"Do you want anything from Hoffman?" Thomas asked me.

"Sales leads," I said. Hoffman attended lingual conferences all over the world. He had to know a few U.S. orthodontists interested in lingual.

"Hoffman does not want us to sell the product yet," said Thomas.

"I thought it was ready to go?"

"He has been treating patients with it since last October, and several have already finished," said Thomas, "but he won't let anyone else in his clinical group use it yet."

"That's a problem," I said.

Ruedger added, "You need to convince him to let us sell."

We had reservations at the Wald Hotel, a wellness hotel and sauna garden about a kilometer from the city center. Almost a hundred years old, it was a typical German-style building: three stories, white stucco, brown wood trim, an abundance of large windows and an orange tile roof. The hotel had beautifully appointed, spacious rooms with high ceilings and fantastic views of the surrounding forest.

When it was time for dinner, we walked the kilometer into town, along the edge of the forest, taking in the damp smell of leaves and crisp autumn air.

We met Hoffman at an Italian restaurant near his office. One side of the restaurant had a glass wall with a view of the patio and a fence covered in vines and twinkling white lights. It seemed funny to be having another serious business meeting in a romantic setting.

"Hello, hello." Hoffman kissed both my cheeks and shook hands with Ruedger and Thomas.

I couldn't decide if Hoffman was good-looking. My age, a few inches taller than me, with thinning blond hair and the kind of skin that turned deep red when he drank too much wine, Hoffman had a pleasant face, but not a particularly handsome one. It was a little too square and his receding hairline made his forehead look enormous. He flashed crooked teeth when he smiled, an oddity given his line of work.

Even with this amalgamation of less-than-movie-star features, Hoffman had a magnetic effect on the female half of the species. At orthodontic society meetings, women of all ages flocked to him. He aggressively flirted with the thin blondes under thirty.

He'd cycled through six gorgeous girlfriends in the short time I'd known him, most of them Russian, all of them deferential and clingy. His current girlfriend, Dr. Lilli Thalman, a German-Israeli orthodontist, had worked her way through dental school as a runway model. Smart, independent and well-spoken, Lilli didn't fit the fawning girlfriend profile at all.

After we ordered, I went straight to the biggest issue. "When can we start selling it in the U.S.?"

Hoffman shifted his gaze to Ruedger and then back to me. "I only want competent people using the new system."

"How will you judge that?"

"They have to take a course from me."

Hoffman had a lucrative side business. He taught lingual orthodontic courses all over Europe on the weekends. The courses promoted OrthoCo's lingual bracket, the bracket he used at the EUROTOP Laboratory before developing the new one. OrthoCo, the largest manufacturer of orthodontic products in the world, marketed the courses to their customers. Hoffman charged attendees EUR 1,000 for the two-day course, netting EUR 30,000 to 40,000 every weekend.

"You're going to come to the U.S. and teach?" I asked, knowing Hoffman hated airplanes. He preferred to travel via red Ferrari with a girlfriend in the passenger seat.

"Everyone has to take a course, or they will fail," he insisted.

We couldn't allow Hoffman to be a limiting factor to our business, nor could we force U.S. doctors to fly to Europe for a course. But every product was made individually in his production facility, so there was no way to avoid his involvement. We needed to find a compromise.

The conversation turned to technical issues. Hoffman worried about Mordix. He bought a certain type of wire from them and feared they would terminate the supply once I left the company.

My three companions lapsed into German, a language I didn't speak, and left me to ponder how we could productively work with Hoffman if he held all the cards.

After dinner, Hoffman went to the restroom. Ruedger leaned my direction and said softly, "Don't worry, he's starting to turn. Lilli wants to come to the U.S., so he will teach her to give the course and she can train our doctors."

Before Hoffman returned to his seat, he pulled a folded piece of paper from the back pocket of his jeans and handed it to Ruedger. "I received this from OrthoCo today."

The letter, written in English, came from their European business development manager. It said that if Hoffman wished to continue receiving OrthoCo's marketing support for his courses, he needed to sign a letter of intent promising OrthoCo an exclusive license for his new lingual product.

Ruedger read it carefully and then handed it to me.

I read it and handed it to Thomas.

"They have been my partner for three years with the EUROTOP courses," said Hoffman. "I think I owe them."

"Did you tell them you have new partners?" Anger rose in Ruedger's voice.

Thomas refolded the letter, handed it back to Hoffman and said, "They aren't offering you any money. What is their intention exactly? Do you know?"

Hoffman shook his head. "They want to sell the system, and they want to take a closer look at the production."

"OrthoCo is suing Align Technology," I said, "for patent infringement. And they threatened Mordix with a similar lawsuit. Don't show them the manufacturing line, don't let them see what you're doing."

Back in the early 1990s, OrthoCo's chief technologist and key inventor, Dr. Corbin Roberts, created a body of intellectual property around the concept of making customized orthodontic brackets using automated treatment planning software.

OrthoCo employees referred to the project as "Star Wars," in reference to Ronald Reagan's Strategic Defense Initiative, the project that bankrupted the Soviet Union and led to its demise. OrthoCo had invested millions of dollars in developing Dr. Roberts' software, but never produced a meaningful product. Determined to get revenue out of their Star Wars project, OrthoCo's CEO threatened every new orthodontic technology company with a patent infringement lawsuit.

"Don't think the OrthoCo guys are your friends," Ruedger added. "If you show them what we are doing, they will steal it or sue us."

Hoffman nodded almost imperceptibly.

I understood his struggle. Like many doctors, he loved the attention lavished on insiders at a big company: the expensive dinners, the courting and shameless flattery. Being part of a special club appealed to sole proprietor orthodontists, mostly men who spend their days surrounded by female staff members with high school degrees. Executives at big companies like OrthoCo provided professional camaraderie and peer interaction that most doctors didn't have at the office.

We walked back to the hotel through the forest. Ruedger and Thomas, two meters behind me, argued in rapid-fire German. The wind picked up. Leaves scattered and swirled with each gust, shifting and changing shape in the darkness.

The pitch of Ruedger and Thomas' voices increased. I heard the word "OrthoCo" over and over again. Even though I didn't speak German, I knew they were having the same conversation I was having in my head.

What would we do if Hoffman reneged on our deal? Sue him? None of us had any money. We'd just quit our jobs.

Even worse, what if we started the company and OrthoCo sued us for patent infringement?

Hoffman had nothing to worry about. OrthoCo's European patents didn't contain any sticky claims. He ran a thriving orthodontic practice that printed money. No matter what happened, he would be fine.

If OrthoCo decided to get ugly, they would get ugly with our little company first. The fight would be ours.

I didn't sleep all night, and it wasn't due to jetlag.

The next morning, I joined Ruedger and Thomas downstairs. A red-cheeked hostess brought a pot of hot coffee to our table and invited me to the breakfast buffet with a sweep of her hand and a burst of German.

I grabbed a whole grain roll, a blob of peanut butter, two dried apricots and a slice of Butterkäse and returned to the table.

"Are you going to start this company with us or not?" said Thomas. "It's okay if you say no, but we need to know now so we can make a different plan."

"I agreed to stay at Mordix to get the severance package," I said. "My husband is unemployed. We need the money."

Ruedger challenged me. "Please tell us that you are committed. That you won't walk out when things get hard, because they will."

Could I make that promise in good faith? I didn't know if we would be able to raise money. I didn't know what would happen with OrthoCo. If it came down to sacrificing the company or sacrificing my family's well-being, I wouldn't pick the company.

But we hadn't reached that point.

Not yet.

"Yes, I'm committed," I said, unsure of where my words would lead me. Maybe one day I'd ring the NASDAQ bell, or maybe I'd beg a bankruptcy judge for leniency.

We went to Hoffman's office after breakfast and brainstormed a commercialization path, one that involved other doctors teaching courses using Hoffman's materials and a promise that we would monitor new doctors to ensure they followed Hoffman's clinical procedures.

As we walked through our roll-out plans, Hoffman offered suggestions, smiling more than he had the night before. It seemed our enthusiasm was contagious, because before we left his office, he agreed not to sign the OrthoCo letter.

To make the company a reality, we needed to form a legal entity, write a business plan and build a financial model and a pitch deck. But we couldn't do anything until we decided on a company name. I was tired of referring to it as "Newco." While driving back to Hannover, we tossed around different possibilities and landed on Oralign. It sounded dental and we aligned teeth.

When I arrived at my hotel, I went online and checked the U.S. Patent and Trademark office to see if Oralign was available. It was. I claimed it and then bought the URL.

Taking these small steps calmed me. Building Oralign would require many more steps, some small, some gigantic and some that would appear insurmountable at first glance. But I had to keep taking steps, even random ones, because if I did it long enough, a clearer picture would start to emerge.

On the flight home, I spoke the name aloud – "Or-a-line," "Ora-line," "Oraline" – as if this incantation would transform the word into a real company.

* * *

In October Roscoe started interviewing candidates for vice president of sales. He quickly narrowed it down to two, and in mid-November decided it was time for the other members of the executive team to participate in the process. He announced my resignation right before the Thanksgiving holiday.

The new sales vice president started in early December and I was tasked with briefing him. I'd brought on twelve customers since September and they were all in various stages of implementation. A big company guy like Roscoe, he seemed surprised that I wanted to talk in detail about the status of our new customers and the sales pipeline. During our transition meeting, he tapped a shiny tassel loafer on the corner of my desk and offered only a condescending half smile as I talked. He didn't even take notes.

After he departed, leaving a trail of Paco Rabanne cologne in his wake, I stared at the leafless trees swaying outside my window and thought about my immediate future.

The unknowns of Oralign made it hard to feel confident. When people asked me about the new company, I automatically reverted to pitch mode, but inside I fought an ongoing battle with panic.

As much as I loved the abstract idea of the company and the product, I didn't love the uncertainty of our reality.

Imagining hundreds of future scenarios and trying to mentally solve problems that had not yet occurred left me feeling overwhelmed. I did my best to maintain a myopic viewpoint, but I wasn't always successful.

Making lists helped, so I bought a small red notebook to carry in my purse. Writing down all the things I didn't know stopped the endless loop running in my head. Crossing items off the list gave me a jolt of excitement. I could see progress.

Talking to friends didn't help. A birthday lunch for a former colleague turned into a "Scared Straight" episode. One by one, my lunch mates recounted horror stories of start-up failures, friends who lost all their money and their parents' money, investor lawsuits and tarnished reputations.

"Did you know that ninety percent of start-ups don't survive the first year?"

"People a whole lot smarter than you have started companies and failed, what makes you think you can make it?"

"You've never been a CEO, why would anyone give you money?'

I had no answers to their questions. All I could do was smile, shrug and polish off a bowl of spicy cheese dip.

Right after Thanksgiving I'd called a friend who worked as a marketing director at Disney to tell her my plans.

She gasped when I said I was leaving my job to start Oralign with Ruedger and Thomas. "Do you even know how to start a company?" she said.

"No, but Ruedger and Thomas have done it before and I think I can figure it out."

"But you've only been working in dentistry for a couple of years. You're no expert."

"It's not nuclear fusion," I said, sounding defensive.

"What will you do if this doesn't work? This could ruin your whole career. You'll have a huge black mark on your resume. How will you ever get another job?"

I thought that I'd entertained every terrible thing that could happen if Oralign failed. Becoming permanently unemployable hadn't occurred to me.

How would I ever survive that kind of failure?

So That's a No

Dallas, Texas – January 2003

I didn't want to work from home, so before leaving Mordix I arranged for an office at a software start-up called Hireworks. I worked out a deal with the CEO, who gave me a furnished office, Internet access and a phone in exchange for help with marketing communications.

Hireworks sublet space in a building owned by a telecom company. They shared the lobby, bathrooms and kitchen with a start-up staffing company and a small IT services company. Entrepreneurial energy pulsed through the place.

On the first day, I discovered the staffing guys owned an Otis Spunkmeyer cookie oven. The smell of freshly baked chocolate chip and oatmeal raisin cookies wafted through the building three or four times a day. They usually made a few more than they needed for their client meetings and left them on the kitchen counter. Heaven.

Three years of working with Germans had given me an appreciation for natural light in the workplace so I chose a small office with two glass walls in the back of the building.

I commandeered two desks and oriented them facing each other. I hung Will's drawing of a pirate ship on the wall next to my phone, arranged three of my favorite family photos on the desk and bought two low-maintenance plants to round out the corners of the room. By the end of the first week, Oralign had a functional U.S. headquarters.

Hireworks' sales manager, a software company veteran named Kathy, sat across the hall from me. She worked the phones all day. Listening to her cajole, tell jokes, worm her way past gatekeepers and book orders inspired me.

I had an idea of how to sell the product concept and frame the financial opportunity to potential investors, but the only way to confirm my assumptions was to put it out there. I started by sending email announcements to all my professional contacts, letting them know about my new job as CEO of Oralign and explaining what we did. It felt weird, like I should add "April Fools" at the end of each message. Instead, I asked for referrals to any investors they knew who liked medical device companies or who might have a specific interest in dentistry.

One of the people I contacted was the head of research and development at Align Technology, makers of Invisalign. Ruedger and I had met the founders in the early days of Mordix. Because I thought of them as comrades in arms, their response surprised me:

Dear Lea,

I sincerely wish both of you success with the new venture. However, we would like to bring to your attention an issue with your trade-name choice "Oralign."

As you can appreciate, Align was highly concerned about this choice of name since it was confusingly similar to our trade-name Align Technology, Inc and its trademark Invisalign®. The name "Oralign" creates the perception of an association with Align and violates trademark and anti-dilution law. Therefore, please provide us with an assurance that you would use a name that was not confusingly similar to Align. Thank you for your prompt attention to this important matter.

> Best regards,
> Vice President of R&D

He copied their general counsel on the email.

So much for entrepreneurial camaraderie. Our first week in business and we were on notice for trademark infringement.

I forwarded the email to Ruedger and then called him. "I don't think it's a violation," I said.

"Change it," he said.

"I already registered the trademark and had business cards printed."

Our new logo looked elegant on the glossy cards. I'd even laminated several and attached them to my briefcase and suitcases.

"Kill it," Ruedger insisted. "It's not worth fighting about."

Our bank account held only a few thousand dollars, money that the three of us contributed when we formed the corporation. We couldn't afford a fight with Align and we didn't have much invested in the name except for a pile of corporate documents, a URL, a trademark application and my new luggage tags.

"Then we need to pick another name right now," I said. "I have to change the business plan and pitch deck before I can send it out."

I retrieved the list of names we brainstormed in Germany and scanned it for something that sound unique and didn't include the words "invisible" or "align."

"What do you think about the name Lingualcare?" I said.

"I like it."

Both the URL and trademarks were available.

"Buy them," said Ruedger, "and tell Align to call off the dogs."

I filed the name change with the Texas Secretary of State, then called our graphics guy for new logo designs. After I updated the executive summary and pitch deck, I sent a letter to Align about our name change. Now it was time to start dialing for dollars.

Unlike other times I'd raised money, this time I would be going in cold, raising dollar number one instead of dollar five million and one. I had no existing investors who could call their friends and make introductions.

I believed my best prospects were firms who knew me from Mordix. Those firms would likely call the Mordix guys for references on Ruedger and me, so before I contacted anyone, I called two Mordix board members and asked what type of reference I could expect.

Both assured me they would say good things. I didn't totally believe them, but it gave me a chance to recount my accomplishments at Mordix and reinforce the message that Lingualcare wasn't a competitor.

We needed two million dollars before the end of March, so I started dialing. Over and over I heard the same thing: "Nice to hear from you. Send me an executive summary." But they didn't give off any buying signals. Did our deal suck that much?

Sure, dental was a hard sell. One entrepreneur I knew always referred to dental as "the redheaded stepchild of medical devices," an apt description. Not many firms had experience with dental deals; there wasn't much innovation in the industry. And I'd always suspected that the topic of dentistry produced a visceral negative reaction in most people. I'd never heard anyone say, "I'm getting a root canal tomorrow and I'm so excited!"

After four hours of mediocre calls, I drove to Snuffer's Bar and Grill for a basket of their legendary cheese fries. They baked them in the oven with a mountain of shredded cheddar cheese, jalapeño peppers and chopped bacon, and served them with a vat of ranch dressing. I only ate at Snuffer's once a quarter as more frequent visits would lead to an early grave,

I mentally replayed the morning's calls. Something was off, but I didn't know what. I hadn't expected anyone to be giddy on the phone; professional investors never showed their hand. But I'd pitched worse deals than this one and gotten meeting invites.

Halfway through my fries, I decided that as soon as I got back to the office, I would call a junior partner I knew at a Boston firm whom I'd befriended during the last Mordix raise. His firm was too big for Lingualcare, they invested a minimum of five million dollars in the first round, but the junior partner grew up in Nebraska and we'd bonded over our mutual love of Cornhusker football.

He picked up on the second ring, and after a short discussion about the worst Husker season either of us could remember, I gave him the elevator pitch.

"I like the idea," he said. "But you're going to have a hard time getting money for a pre-revenue company. Everyone I know is in triage mode. Merger and acquisition activity is dead, and all the companies lined up to go public are on hold and burning cash."

The NASDAQ drop dominated the headlines, falling from a high of 5,048 in March 2000 to 1,335 in January 2003 and putting the tech industry into a death spiral. Not even the best Wall Street spin doctors could take a company public solely on hype anymore.

Until that moment, I hadn't factored in the trickle-down effect of the public market implosion on my own fundraising efforts.

"I can't look at anything new until we kick some of these kids out of the nest," he said.

Lingualcare had a problem.

I got up from my desk and went into the empty kitchen. Standing still, I listened for any movement in the hallway before I eased open the freezer door, reached into the Otis Spunkmeyer bag and grabbed two frozen blobs of chocolate chip cookie dough. I wrapped them in a napkin and then stole out the back door to the parking lot.

I paced back and forth in a small patch of sunlight and nibbled on the cookie dough. I'd fallen into fundraising in 1996, at a start-up that developed online travel software. The CEO had a good story, but didn't know how to package it, so I took it on. I had no experience raising money, but with the help of a junior associate at our lead investment firm, Austin Ventures, I wrote the company's first business plan, crafted a pitch deck and began giving presentations.

At first, asking strangers for millions of dollars felt decadent, like ordering crab cakes for lunch, but after several pitches it became second nature. We closed a five-million-dollar round in less than six months.

Since then, the hardest part had been identifying the right capital sources; scarcity of funds hadn't factored into the equation.

To that point I'd only called East Coast and West Coast firms, avoiding the local guys. I suspected that I'd been blackballed by Mordix investors but didn't know for sure.

The universe of early stage technology investors in Dallas was microscopic compared to Silicon Valley, New York and Boston. Most investment money in Dallas circled around oil and gas and real estate deals. The city boasted only a few venture capital firms. Unfortunately, most of them shared office space on the sixteenth floor of Two Galleria Tower. They also shared the same receptionist, the same restrooms, the same kitchen and the same conference rooms. If an entrepreneur got crosswise with one venture firm on the sixteenth floor, they would likely be blackballed by all the others.

Rather than call a sixteenth-floor firm, I contacted a local incubator, StarTech Early Ventures. Founded by a group of Texas venture capital firms in 1998, including several on the sixteenth floor, StarTech mentored early stage companies and helped them get financing. StarTech had made an investment in Mordix when they first came to the U.S., so Ruedger knew them well. Although we didn't need incubating – we already had a solid business plan and a product – we could certainly use their connectivity to venture capital.

I called StarTech's business development guy and offered to send him the Executive Summary.

"Don't worry about that," he said. "Just come over when Ruedger's in town. We are happy to look at your deal."

* * *

Pitching at StarTech felt great. Ruedger and I tag-teamed, playing off each other as we talked about the technology, the market and Hoffman's stellar clinical results.

We knew most of the people in the glass-walled conference room: the founder of StarTech, their technical analyst who mentored Ruedger and Thomas when they first came to Dallas, and StarTech's business development guy. Although the founder seemed removed, the business development guy and the technical analyst treated us like old friends.

When we finished the last PowerPoint slide, everyone clapped. After I sat down, all eyes turned to StarTech's founder. He leaned in, folded his hands in front of him and said, "Your presentation is impressive, but I talked to a board member this morning who feels Lingualcare and Mordix will be competitors. As we already have an investment in Mordix, investing in Lingualcare would be a conflict of interest."

I wanted to protest, but before I could utter a word, Ruedger said, "So that's a no."

"I like this deal, but we can't go forward," he said. "What I can do is introduce you to Ted at AV Labs. He can see you this afternoon at 3:00 if you're available."

Yes, we were available. We had nothing else to do but search for money.

That afternoon, Ruedger and I drove to Richardson, a suburb north of Dallas where software and telecom companies like Alcatel, Nortel, and Cisco had huge campuses. During the 1990s it became known as the Telecom Corridor, attracting start-ups and large companies alike. Just a few miles north of the Texas Instruments campus, the Telecom Corridor was a ghost town. Many of the new buildings constructed during the Internet bubble sat deserted and forlorn. Large signs proclaiming, "First Year Rent Free!!!" littered the landscape.

AV Labs was an accelerator backed by Austin Ventures, the largest venture capital firm in Texas. I knew most of the Austin Ventures partners from my time at the travel software company, but I didn't know Ted.

He greeted us with an appraising look and a firm handshake. "I'm excited to see what you've got," he said as he led us to a conference room that smelled of new carpet and stale coffee.

We ran through the pitch that we'd just given StarTech. Ted took notes and asked questions throughout the meeting, a good sign. When we played the time-lapse video showing how teeth moved with the new braces, Ted smiled with three quarters of his face.

"Send me over your full business plan and any market data you've got."

I stifled the urge to high-five Ruedger when we reached the parking lot. Maybe things were finally going our way.

It's Always Safer to Trash Someone

Dallas, Texas – February 2003

Ted and his enthusiasm vanished after three in-person meetings and a flood of document requests, leaving me with a weird mixture of paranoia and humiliation.

What had I done wrong?

Our meetings had all ended with a list of next steps. Ruedger spent a solid week documenting the manufacturing process in Bad Erlangen, quantifying costs and digging up research that supported our assumptions.

We proudly hit the send button.

Silence.

I called Ted's office repeatedly. His secretary politely took messages, but he never returned my calls. I left messages on his voice mail after hours. I called from the phone at my gym and from a friend's office, hoping he would answer the unfamiliar number.

I sent email.

I sent a letter on Lingualcare stationary via regular mail, then I sent another one via FedEx.

Nothing.

The confusion I felt over what happened with Ted shook my confidence. For the better part of a week I sat at my desk eavesdropping on Kathy, the Hireworks sales whiz. I envied how she let rejection roll off her, like water on a duck's feathers. She'd say, "thank you" and dial again within seconds. I willed myself to pick up the phone and pitch someone, anyone, to get back into sales mode, but all I could do was surf Internet shopping sites, look at clothes I couldn't afford and obsess about Ted.

Why wouldn't he call me back? Did the Mordix guys get to him?

Finally, late on a Friday night, I called Ted's voice mail and said, "Listen, if you hate our deal, just say so. Send me an email and tell me to fuck off. I don't care, I need closure."

He never called.

Ruedger pushed me to move on. "Call the Kingsleys," he said. "Let go of Ted."

Vincent and Chad Kingsley, two former Mordix investors and StarTech mentors, were a father and son team. Known to invest in all types of early stage technology deals, the Kingsleys had a reputation for being hard-nosed but fair-minded.

The origins of the Kingsley fortune were hazy and subject to speculation amongst members of the Dallas tech community. Some said they made their money on oil and gas leases in West Texas, others said they bought the rights to cellular phone territories on the East Coast before anyone understood the value of those rights.

I sent the Kingsley's an executive summary. The next day Chad, the son, called and requested a meeting.

We met on a Wednesday afternoon in February at their offices in North Dallas. As soon as I walked in, I noticed the dental degree from the University of Southern California dated 1912 hanging on the wall above Vincent's desk. He proudly told me it belonged to his mother, one of the first women to graduate from USC's dental school. I took it as a positive omen. Perhaps he had a soft spot in his heart for women who worked in dentistry.

Vincent had suffered a stroke a few years earlier, causing him to speak slowly and struggle to complete sentences. Despite this limitation, he drove the conversation and asked smart questions.

Red-faced, with thinning blond hair and angry lips, Chad nodded as his father spoke and asked questions about things I had already explained. Either his mind drifted or he didn't get it.

After giving them our pitch, I said, "What type of companies do you like to invest in?"

Chad said, "We look at everything."

"How much money do you want to put to work?"

"It depends on the deal."

Chad and Vincent concluded the meeting with two next steps – a business plan review and a discussion with "a guy we know."

They were the first angel investors I'd ever dealt with. While I understood how venture capital firms operated, I had no idea how vastly different angels were until I met the Kingsleys. The major difference became clear immediately – they had no defined process. I should have seen their vague answers about company profile and investment size as big red flags.

Chad and Vincent sent me random questions via email and offered no feedback. I didn't have the confidence or knowhow to grab control and steer them into a clear set of steps that would get us to a decision point.

After two weeks of random requests and sporadic communication, Chad called and asked me to meet with their family dentist, Dr. Martin. Although he was not an orthodontist, he treated aesthetically conscious adults in our demographic and they trusted him. I agreed to meet Dr. Martin after business hours the following week when Ruedger would be in Dallas.

For the meeting, Ruedger borrowed a product sample from Dr. Hoffman.

Unfortunately, it was a poor one.

In truth, it sucked.

Dr. Hoffman had glued a set of our custom lingual brackets to a clear plastic retainer and inserted a wire into the slots. The retainer was hollow in the middle and slipped over a plaster tooth model. The sample showed how the brackets conformed to the tooth anatomy; the backside and the front side of the bracket were both visible through the plastic.

Unfortunately, we had to spend most of the meeting explaining to Dr. Martin that our product wasn't a plastic retainer with

brackets glued to it, we glued the brackets directly to patients'
teeth like regular braces. When Ruedger showed clinical photos on
his laptop, it finally clicked.

After we left, the Kingsleys stayed behind to hear his
assessment. I hadn't eaten all day, so Ruedger and I drove across
the street to a Greek restaurant that served a killer lamb salad. The
hostess seated us in the corner by the front window. From my
vantage point, I could see Chad's car in Dr. Martin's parking lot.

"Why would he think we sold brackets glued to a plastic
retainer?" I said, venting the frustration that had built up during the
torturous meeting.

"That dentist will screw us," said Ruedger after ordering a beer.

"I thought he liked the product," I said, "once he finally figured
out what it was."

We both laughed.

Ruedger said, "Doctors like that have two faces. He told us
what we wanted to hear during the meeting, but he will tell the
Kingsleys something different. I saw it a hundred times in the early
days at Mordix."

"Why would he do that?" I said as I reached for the basket of
warm pita bread our waitress had just set on the table.

Ruedger shrugged and took a drink of his beer. "He doesn't
want to be responsible for them losing money. It's safer to trash us
than to endorse us."

I hated that Ruedger called it.

A week later, Chad invited me to their office. Ruedger had
already returned to Germany, so I went alone. The Kingsleys sat
across from me at a conference table in Vincent's spacious office.
Over Chad's shoulder I could see a line of cars crawling down the
Dallas North Tollway. I hoped the traffic would clear before I had
to head across town to get Will.

"Dr. Martin thinks this is a loser," said Chad. "He says that it's
only for rich people and celebrities."

"Plenty of adults pay a premium for Invisalign and we think they will pay for this, too."

"And your corporate governance is a problem," he added. "If we put money in, we won't be able to control the company."

"How much do you want to invest?" So far neither he nor Vincent had quantified their interest. For the right amount of money, we would give them a board seat, but we weren't going hand over complete control to the first guys willing to write a check.

Chad gave me a hard look. A vein running from his eyebrow to the corner of his receding hairline throbbed beneath his skin. He tapped the heel of his Gucci loafer against the chair leg. "The amount isn't the issue," he said. "We want control. Entrepreneurs can't be trusted."

I examined the pattern in the Chinese carpet, searching for the right words in the red and blue floral pattern. I wanted to defend my character, but I had no evidence to offer. Without a track record, what could I say to prove that I would never screw my investors?

Before I could respond, Chad charged forward. "We lost a company because the entrepreneur loaded up the board of directors with his friends. They increased the share pool and diluted the early investors down to nothing. Now it's a write off."

I tried to shift the conversation to a positive trajectory, pointing out the value of our patents and the consumer appeal of our product. I failed. Chad methodically tore down my house of cards. Gripping a legal pad filled with notes, likely compiled by his father, he questioned every assumption and number we'd give him. I wondered how many pages I could endure.

Vincent sat quietly, only chiming in when Chad got lost in the smoke clouds of his blitzkrieg.

"We don't think you can raise money. If another investor doesn't sign up, you will just waste our money," said Chad.

"Put your money in escrow," I said. "If we don't hit a five-hundred-thousand-dollar minimum threshold, you'll get it back." This was standard procedure. Why would he make it an issue?

"Who's going to run the company?" asked Chad, refusing to acknowledge the last answer I'd given. "You don't have any experience. You've never been a CEO before. Do you even know what you're doing?"

With that, he got me. I had no rebuttal. I waited a few seconds, then stood up and put my notepad and product sample in my briefcase. "Thank you for your time." I nodded at Vincent and did my very best to smile. I avoided Chad's hard eyes. "I'm sorry it didn't work out."

Chad offered a quizzical look. "Are we done?"

"I'm done," I said, heading for the door, willing myself to be out of sight before a tear hit my cheek. I tilted my head back to stem the flow of tears as I waited for the elevator to arrive.

I held my breath.

He was right. I didn't know what I was doing.

I was no CEO. What kind of CEO would listen to that bullshit for an hour, not realizing after the first five minutes that they never intended to write a check?

Why did they request the meeting? Did they find satisfaction in taunting entrepreneurs, like a cat batting around a mouse on the brink of death, watching it writhe a few more times before delivering the final blow?

I wasn't sure what felt worse, the silent treatment I'd gotten from Ted or Chad's verbal assault.

When I reached my car, I dialed Ruedger's cell number. It was almost midnight in Germany and he was probably asleep, but I called anyway. I needed to purge the image of Chad's angry face from my soul and tell Ruedger he'd been right about the two-faced doctor. More than anything I wanted him to help me reconstruct our house of cards, to tell me everything would be all right.

Voice mail.

I didn't leave a message.

* * *

The next morning, more bad news found me.

I woke up at 5:30 to go for a run and checked my email inbox before heading outside. A fund manager in Pennsylvania had replied to a message I'd sent a few days earlier.

I didn't know him. A friend of John's had introduced us and suggested he look at our deal, so I'd sent him an executive summary.

The fund manager's email said, "Introducing disruptive medical devices is difficult, expensive and will require a real CEO, at best you might be qualified to run marketing. You have no track record and your partners are engineers, therefore, professional investors will never fund you. That includes me."

My stomach churned as I walked out of the house and into the dark morning.

The first mile I beat myself up. What had I been thinking? How could two German engineers and some marketing chick from Dallas start a disruptive dental company? We had no credibility, no credentials.

The second mile I wanted to cry. Why did I think I could be a CEO? I had no real qualifications, only the chutzpah to claim the title. I was an imposter.

During the third mile, I started talking to the fund manager in my head, refuting his comments. What did he know? How was *he* qualified to judge *me*?

By the end of my fourth mile, as the early morning light flooded the horizon and I reached the bottom of the hill that led to my home, I'd crafted a response.

Sweaty and angry, I went into our home office and hammered out an email. I told the fund manager he didn't know anything about my abilities and was in no position to pass judgment. Then I wrote a long list of reasons why Lingualcare would succeed, thanked him for taking a look and hit the send button.

I printed a copy for John and left it in the kitchen, next to coffee pot. I wanted him to know the outcome of his friend's referral.

I stood in the shower with my eyes closed, allowing the rivulets of hot water to flow across my face. I hated how my encounters with Ted and Chad and Vincent and that stranger from Pennsylvania left me feeling like such a loser, like a beggar. Somehow, I had to learn to manage those feelings. If I continued to internalize rejection, it would paralyze me.

John was leaning against the kitchen counter with the email in his hand when I came in to get a cup of coffee. "This is the reason why you are a CEO and I'm not," he said, handing it to me. "I would have never written this."

I shrugged and said, "I'm sure it won't do any good."

"But at least you wrote it," he said in an insistent tone. "You didn't just roll over."

John left to help Will get dressed. I re-read the email while I ate my Raisin Bran. I hadn't held back. Defending myself against the faceless stranger from Pennsylvania made me feel better than I'd felt in months.

Before putting Will in the car to go to preschool, I checked my inbox and found a reply from Pennsylvania. It said, "You're right. You do have what it takes to be successful. If I had money in my fund, I would take a closer look at your deal."

What a jerk! Rather than admit that he had no money, he chose to tear me down, to make the rejection about the merits of me and my company.

Did he have any idea how devastating his first email had been? Did he know how fragile an entrepreneur's psyche was, how much courage it took to approach men like him, like Ted and the Kingsleys, hand extended, asking for money?

I had to stop swallowing whatever investors chose to feed me. Going forward, I would consider the sources of rejection more carefully, dig in and ask more questions, try and understand what was behind rejection rather than just running from it.

I knew there had to be money out there for Lingualcare. I just needed to find it.

Stumbling Horses Rarely Fall

Nebraska – 1982-1984

With no home to call my own and no parents to guide me, I dropped out of high school at the end of my junior year. I took the GED and college entrance exams in May, applied for admission to the University of Nebraska in Lincoln and got in.

Unprepared both emotionally and academically, I spent my freshman year going to football games and fraternity parties, skipping classes and drinking my way to academic probation. In May 1983, as my high school classmates graduated and prepared to leave for college, I returned to Hastings in disgrace.

My first day back, I landed a job cooking breakfast at the Clarke Hotel. It paid four hundred dollars a month.

I found a studio apartment in a females-only building. Pink stucco with a shared bathroom on each of the three floors, it was occupied almost exclusively by retired school teachers. My furnished second-floor apartment, about the size of a cigarette carton, cost a hundred dollars a month, all bills paid.

Although the cramped space, the beat-up furniture and the old lady smell in the hallways and bathroom had the potential to be depressing, I liked living there. For the first time since my father's death, I didn't have to rely on someone else for a place to live. It might have been crappy, but I could afford it.

The tight quarters made it impractical to have friends over, so I mostly drank alone.

I kept pint bottles of schnapps in my freezer, hidden behind the boxes of Geno's pizza rolls that I ate on my days off when I couldn't gorge on free hash browns and bacon at the restaurant. Sipping schnapps and singing along with the radio, I fantasized that I still had options, that this lavender-scented retirement home wasn't my destiny.

I wanted a big life, one that included traveling the world and experiencing places I'd read about. I wanted to be someone who accomplished important things, someone worthy of mention in a newspaper or, the pinnacle, *People* magazine.

How could I become someone important? Until I figured that out, I would spend my days making Denver omelets and my weekends hanging out with high school friends, drinking too much Budweiser, smoking too many Marlboro Lights and occasionally embarrassing myself.

And I would daydream.

On Memorial Day weekend 1984, I trekked down to the Harlan County Reservoir to go camping with a group of high school friends who hadn't made it to college. Most of the guys worked construction, or on family farms. The girls had dead-end jobs like mine, waiting tables and ringing up groceries at Safeway, distractions until they could score a wedding ring.

Someone tapped a pony keg. We roasted hotdogs, made s'mores and told high school stories, most of which involved running from the cops, ditching school and defying authority figures. The Eagles, Journey and REO Speedwagon provided the soundtrack.

Late on Saturday night, after several trips to the keg, I observed my friends around the bonfire, buzzed and smiling, kissing the edges of the firelight with their laughter. Everyone seemed content, except me.

In a moment of exquisite lucidity, I saw my future.

A future where camping trips like this would be the high point of my life. I'd come back year after year, maybe with a husband, a couple of kids and a pop-up camper, sip beer from red plastic cups, roast marshmallows while singing along with Steve Perry and fret about running out of charcoal briquettes.

I would never hear Big Ben toll the hour from the bank of the Thames or window shop at Harrods during Christmastime. I would never take a carriage ride through Central Park or eat a hot dog on a busy Manhattan street. I would never see Paris or Morocco or Tibet or Rio. I would live an unremarkable life in an unremarkable place surrounded by people happy to just get by.

Although I didn't know how to create a life worthy of a *People* magazine spread, a life that included matched luggage and big sunglasses, I knew with absolute, undeniable certainty that it would never happen in Hastings, Nebraska.

If I wanted a shot at a big life, I had to get out.

* * *

My mother married Wayne Macomber in June of 1982, four months after my father's death. A soft-spoken man with slightly bowed legs and a sardonic smile, Wayne owned a large ranch in Arthur County, population 435.

Wayne told Beth and me to consider the ranch our home. My mother, mellower than she'd been in years, echoed his sentiments. So, I spent Christmas in Arthur County that year and got to know his three sons and his daughter. We played cutthroat games of ten-point pitch and Yahtzee. We told jokes and stories until the wee hours, revealing more and more about ourselves as the hours passed. After four days in close quarters, I felt like I belonged to a family again.

During a visit at Easter, I'd overheard Wayne complaining about his lack of summer help. He had a short window to put up the hay he needed for winter. Normally two of his sons came home from college to work in the hayfields, but they had other plans for the summer.

Until my moment of clarity at the lake, it hadn't occurred to me that I should ask Wayne for a job. But suddenly it gelled. Working for Wayne could be my ticket out of Hastings. I wouldn't have to pay rent on the ranch. I could save money and go back to college.

I was totally unqualified. I didn't know how to drive a car with a manual transmission, forget about a tractor, and I could barely ride a horse. But I was willing to learn. And maybe Wayne was desperate enough to hire me.

As soon as I returned from the camping trip, I called him and asked for a job, explaining that I wanted to go back to college and I needed to save money.

"I can pay you six hundred a month," he said, "and you'll get room and board."

"Do you need to clear it with my mother?" I said.

"Nope," he said. "Get up here as quick as you can."

After giving my landlord a few hours' notice, I stuffed my possessions – mostly clothes and books – into Safeway grocery sacks and stolen milk crates and loaded my car. I stopped at the Clarke Hotel to quit my job and then drove four hours to the ranch.

The ranch entrance was twelve miles from the town of Arthur and required turning off Highway 92 near a picnic table, then carefully driving down a one-lane oil mat road. On the off chance two cars met, each driver had to move halfway off the road, a tricky maneuver when pulling a horse trailer or navigating around snowdrifts. The mile-long dirt road from the oil mat to the ranch house dissected several pastures, so I had to slow to a crawl and lay on the horn when a group of mean-eyed cows refused to leave the road.

Excited and a little scared, I parked my car in the yard and hauled my belongings down to the basement bedroom that would be my home, a walled-off corner with only a waterbed and a small rack to hang clothes. I had no idea if I could do the job, but Wayne had offered me a way out, the first step toward a different life, and I would make it work.

Wayne was a sink or swim kind of guy.

He gave me five minutes of instruction on how operate my tractor and mower before turning me loose in the hayfield. My first attempts at shifting gears ended with me sitting in the middle of the field, engine stalled. As Wayne didn't invest in batteries for hay tractors, I had to wait for him or my brother Robb to drive over with a heavy chain and pull start the tractor.

After a few days, I got the hang of it.

While I mowed, I daydreamed about college, wondering where to apply and what I should study. I wanted to be a writer, but not a starving artist; I didn't want a future that included another apartment with a shared bathroom. I didn't have the patience for teaching. The sight of blood made me sick, so nursing was out. The law seemed like an interesting profession, at least on TV, but as a high school dropout with a GED, law school seemed like a stretch.

One night after dinner, as I helped my mother clear the dishes, I asked what she thought I should do with my life.

"What about becoming a stewardess?" she said. "You'd get to fly for free."

I shook my head. "I want to be a professional."

"Joanne's daughter took welding classes over at the community college and she's making $9.75 an hour as a pipefitter," my mother said. "Welders can always find work."

I felt a rush of indignation. I wanted to say, "Thanks for encouraging me to aim high," but I stopped myself. My mother had never encouraged me to think big, so her responses should not have surprised me. Since my arrival, I'd avoided confrontations and wanted to maintain our détente. Instead of an angry retort, I said, "That's a good idea, I'll think about it."

* * *

During my first week on the ranch, I met a cowboy named Matt. He'd grown up in Arthur County, graduated from high school with Wayne's middle son and worked on a neighboring ranch. Until I witnessed Matt roping calves at a branding, I'd never seen a human connect so fluidly to an animal. I envied how Matt and his horse moved as one, communicating in a language of small gestures known only to them.

Ruggedly handsome, with the body of a running back, Matt was the manliest man I'd ever dated. He wore the standard cowboy uniform of Levi's 501s, pearl-buttoned shirts and hand-tooled leather boots. Matt met the world with a plainspoken vulnerability that made him approachable and wonderful.

I didn't tell him much about my past. It felt dishonest, only showing him my best side, but I wanted to be loved, if not for the person that I was, at least for the person I might become.

In the evenings, after dinner, I'd drive over to Matt's house and we'd go horseback riding. He was determined to improve my equestrian skills, to teach me the secret language. I doubted I would ever become fluent, but I loved those rides across the empty hay meadow, galloping side by side as the sun sank in the sky, with no destination in mind and no purpose other than to experience the joy of freedom.

When the sky darkened and the stars came out in force, we'd sit on his porch, drink beer, listen to music and try to identify constellations. With the Milky Way visible on clear nights, the star-filled Nebraska sky provided hours of entertainment.

At some point, we'd fall into bed and stay there until the alarm Matt set for midnight went off. I'd dress and drive home, carefully navigating the narrow roads and roaming livestock, to begin another day as a ranch hand.

* * *

On a Sunday afternoon at the end of August, I made the seventy-five-mile trip to North Platte, the nearest town that had a shopping mall with a bookstore.

I didn't know where I wanted to go to college, only that it should be somewhere warmer than Nebraska. Thumbing through the pages of Barron's Profiles of American Colleges, I scanned photos and descriptions, hoping one would jump out as an obvious choice. Near the end of the book, I noticed a photo of the University of Texas at El Paso (UTEP), formerly Texas Western College. It was located in the farthest corner of West Texas where the borders of Texas, Mexico and New Mexico converged. The photos showed a mountainous desert landscape with exotic buildings. The campus, described as a classic example of Bhutanese architecture, looked like it belonged in an episode of Kung Fu. I'd never seen anything like it in Nebraska.

Scanning the description, I saw that UTEP accepted applicants with GEDs, so I wrote down the address and phone number of the admissions office and returned the book to the shelf.

September on the ranch meant the end of hay season. Instead of driving a tractor for ten hours, I'd be doing many different things, including spending whole days on the back of a horse. Even though I'd been riding all summer with Matt, when it came time to work cattle, Wayne assigned me the oldest horse in the barn, a veteran cutting horse named Sam. Sam knew how to move cows without any assistance from me. Wayne instructed me to hang on, watch Sam's head because that's where we would be going next, and not fall off when he stumbled, which he did frequently.

"Can I ride a different horse?" I asked after a week of riding Sam. "His stumbling is driving me crazy."

"It's better to ride a stumbling horse," Wayne assured me. "They know how to catch themselves. Stumbling horses rarely fall."

Perhaps Sam and I were kindred spirits.

Every new task felt daunting: building fences, repairing equipment, pregnancy testing heifers – a process that required a glove that went all the way to the shoulder – and replacing the roof on the ranch house.

Just when I started to feel comfortable doing something, Wayne would throw a new task my way. The jobs changed daily, based on the weather, Wayne's inclinations and the fluctuating needs of hundreds of cows, calves, bulls and horses.

Our days started early, with breakfast at 6:00. That's when Wayne would make his pronouncement: "Let's fix that fence over by the road." or "We need to move those heavies (pregnant heifers) closer to the house."

We'd spend all day outside, regardless of the temperature or weather conditions. Inclement weather might mean a rain slicker instead of a denim jacket or insulated coveralls instead of a regular coat, but it never meant staying inside.

Wayne pushed me. Whenever I said, "I can't," he had a retort.

"I can't maneuver all those cows through that little opening."

"Yes, you can."

"I can't weld."

"Let me show you how."

"I can't back up the truck with a horse trailer attached."

"Sure, you can. *Stop*! Turn the wheel the other direction."

By the time I received my acceptance letter from UTEP in November, I could saddle up a real cutting horse a third Sam's age and move cattle from one end of the ranch to the other, operate every piece of machinery, connect and disconnect hydraulics without losing half the fluid, dig postholes and stretch barbed wire until my shoulders burned.

Sure, I made mistakes. Once, when a muskrat commandeered one of our livestock tanks, burrowing in and causing most of the water to drain out, I grabbed a shotgun from the rack in Wayne's pickup, waited until it popped its head above the water, took careful aim and pulled the trigger. I obliterated the muskrat, but in the process, blew a huge hole in the side of the tank.

"Next time try not to solve a small problem by creating a bigger one," Wayne said as he inspected my handiwork.

That's when he taught me how to weld.

My moment of truth came in mid-December, when Wayne's oldest son graduated from the University of Nebraska. Wayne, my mother, Robb and Lara went to Lincoln for three days. I was left to run the ranch alone, feed six tons of hay each morning, break ice on the wells and make sure no livestock died in his absence.

The trickiest job was starting the ancient and temperamental Ford tractor used to feed hay. This required plugging in an engine block heater overnight, hooking it to a battery charger, spraying ether into the carburetor and reciting an incantation while turning the ignition. If the tractor gods were smiling, it would start.

The first day, with a Canadian cold front driving the temperature into single digits, I killed the Ford more than a mile from the house. Listening to hungry cows mooing all around me, I cursed myself for breaking Wayne's cardinal rule: always park on a hill. That way, if you kill the engine, you can use gravity to restart it.

As no one would be coming to save me, I tied the flaps of my Elmer Fudd hat tight under my chin, put my head down and trudged back to the house. I called a neighbor. After lunch, she drove over and helped me pull start the old Ford with another tractor. Chores that should have been completed by noon sat undone until sunset, but no livestock died and I managed to get home in time to watch Jeopardy.

The next two days passed uneventfully. When Wayne returned on Sunday night and I delivered my status report, he said, "I never doubted you could handle it," and gave me a hug.

Pride brought a flush to my face, a sensation I'd almost forgotten.

In seven months, I'd gone from mediocre short-order cook to bona fide cowgirl and I had the calloused hands, wind-burned face and unattractive outerwear to prove it. Working with Wayne had taught me that if I put my fear aside, if I stopped obsessing about everything that could go sideways and focused on the task at hand, I could do almost anything.

On a cold morning in early January 1985, I packed all of my belongings into the ten-year-old brown Mustang II I'd bought after Barbara repossessed my Torino. As I stuffed the last sack full of clothing in the trunk, Wayne came outside and handed me an envelope.

"Be sure to stop at the bank when you get to Ogallala," he said.

The envelope contained a check for four thousand dollars.

"I can't accept this," I said, handing it back. The ranch operated on thin margins and four thousand dollars was a lot of money to Wayne.

He pushed the envelope into my jacket pocket. "If your dad were here, he'd be doing this. Since he's not, let me help you."

Wayne knew I only had enough money to pay for two months in El Paso, not enough to cover tuition, books and my room and board for the whole semester. I'd planned to get a job immediately, but even with a job, money would be tight. His four thousand dollars provided a much-needed safety net.

"I don't know how I'll pay you back," I said, my voice breaking.

"Just go and make a good life for yourself."

I Guess We Aren't Closing Today

Dallas, Texas – 18 March 2003

Finally, someone wanted to write us a check.

A week after the Kingsley debacle, Ruedger called with good news. "I presented our deal to Mr. Glasauer today and he likes it." His voice rose with excitement. I could hear the smile spreading across his face.

I'd met the infamous Mr. Gerald Glasauer in 2000, right after joining Mordix. He was an outspoken, unconventional German investor known for his theatrics. He had once blocked a shareholder revolt by showing up at an annual meeting with several large sacks of Euros and two burly security guards. He'd offered to pay cash on the spot to any shareholder who wanted out.

Ruedger said, "Like us, he's on the outside now. The European VCs don't want him in their deals. He's too controversial. He needs a big win."

Could there be an investor out there who needed us as much as we needed him?

It felt too good to be true, but I liked the idea of it.

"I'll come to Germany, just pick a day."

* * *

John drove me to the Dallas-Fort Worth Airport, speeding along Interstate 635 in our Volvo. He cycled through songs on the CD player, trying to find something that would take the edge off. Finally, he landed on Elton John's "Rocket Man" and put both hands back on the steering wheel.

"This is just irresponsible," he said. "George Bush is about to start a war and you want to leave the country. I can't believe you would put yourself at risk this way. You have a four-year-old son. What are you thinking? What if there are terrorist attacks?"

"I need to close a financing round now, because the investment environment will only get worse." I couldn't believe he was challenging me. Both of us knew what happened after the terrorist attacks on September 11th. John's company died and Mordix went on life support.

"Can't Ruedger do it? Why do you have to go?"

"It's bad enough that we're effectively a three-man show. If Ruedger goes alone, it will look like a one-man show. If he takes Thomas, it looks like two German engineers who don't know how to sell products in the U.S."

After I pulled my suitcase from the trunk and put it on the curb, I motioned for him to roll down the passenger side window. "If I don't make it back, be sure to enjoy the life insurance money," I said.

"That's not funny," he said as I walked away.

George Bush's shock and awe campaign began during my Atlantic crossing. The Frankfurt airport pulsed with the frantic energy of disrupted plans and anxious people. I made a beeline to the Admiral's Club on the second floor. They had shower rooms, an espresso machine and comfy chairs – an oasis where I could wait for Ruedger's train to arrive.

We planned to rent a car at the airport, find our hotel and drive to Schwaebisch Hall the next morning for a 10:00 meeting with Mr. Glasauer and his associate, Ronnie.

One hot shower, three cappuccinos and a bowl of spicy peanuts later, something happened that had never happened in thirteen years of frequenting airport lounges from Montreal to Cape Town and everywhere in between. I heard a familiar voice.

Dr. Derrick Wednesday, one of the most well-known orthodontists in the world, was talking to an agent at the service desk.

I followed the sound of his voice into the lobby. "Dr. Wednesday?" I said.

"Lea? Is that you?" He hugged me. The hug lasted just a few seconds too long. Despite being well into his sixties, Dr. Wednesday still enjoyed the ladies. "My trip to Moscow just got cancelled, so I'm going home. Let me get my ticket sorted out and I'll join you. I want to hear what you all are doing."

A charismatic speaker who lectured all over the world, Dr. Wednesday belonged to the original clinical group formed by OrthoCo in the early 1980s to promote and teach doctors the lingual technique. He had a brother and a nephew who also practiced orthodontics. My relationship with the Wednesday family went back to the spring of 2000. When I started at Mordix, I called several orthodontists in the Dallas area and asked if I could bring lunch to their office and pick their brains. Coming from the software industry, I knew nothing about orthodontics except my own terrible experience as a teenage patient. I wanted to learn as much about the industry as I could as quickly as possible. After I promised not to sell them anything, most agreed to meet me.

Near the end of that string of lunches, I went to see Dr. Wednesday. He taught me more about the fundamentals of orthodontics in an hour than I'd learned from all the other orthodontists combined.

He introduced me to his nephew, Dr. Sam Wednesday, who everyone called Dr. Sam. He was one of my beta testers at Mordix. Because of Dr. Sam's relationship with Mordix, I had hesitated to reach out to the Wednesday family after I left the company. I didn't want Roscoe to accuse me of poaching the customer base. But that day, five thousand one hundred and thirty-six miles from Dallas, all bets were off.

"I don't have to be at the gate for another hour," Dr. Wednesday said as he sat down next to me. "Show me what you have."

I opened my laptop and started Dr. Hoffman's clinical presentation. He sipped mineral water and asked questions. Most I could answer, for the others I made notes, promising to get the information from Dr. Hoffman and send it to him. He examined the final panoramic x-rays from the last clinical case. He took off his reading glasses and nodded. Film didn't lie. The tooth roots lined up perfectly.

"I've been waiting twenty-five years to see something like this," he said. "Congratulations, you guys figured out how to make lingual orthodontics work."

I could not suppress my smile. It was the first positive feedback I'd gotten from an American orthodontist or dentist since we started.

"What can I do to help you?" he asked.

I sank back in my chair and held my breath for a few seconds. So far, no one had offered to help us. What did I want? At the beginning of the conversation I'd just wanted validation, for someone important to buy into our concept.

"Will you help us get the word out?" I knew he wasn't practicing anymore, just lecturing.

"You bet," he said. "I'll mention it to Sam when I see him this weekend. I know he'd like to know more about it."

I couldn't have asked for a better outcome. Dr. Sam would be a perfect orthodontist for us to work with, and if his uncle recruited him instead of me, it wouldn't look like I was poaching a Mordix customer,

The hour passed quickly. I walked Dr. Wednesday to the exit to say goodbye. Just then Ruedger walked into the club rolling his suitcase behind him. He lifted his eyebrows and smiled when he saw me hugging the doctor.

"What was that all about?" asked Ruedger.

"I think we finally caught a break," I said.

* * *

We left early the next morning to drive to Glasauer's office in Schwaebisch Hall. As Ruedger negotiated the traffic, I squeezed the back of my neck with both hands and closed my eyes. Please, please let this work. We needed a miracle, one that involved operating capital. Maybe the meeting with Dr. Wednesday was an omen, a portent of good things to come.

Outside Würzburg, about halfway to our destination, we stopped at a rest area for coffee. Among the truck drivers and vacationers, I felt out of place, conspicuous in my black and white Chanel-wannabe tweed suit that I wore with a double strand of fake pearls. The skirt hit just above my knee, the jacket skimmed my hips. Black patent leather heels, black opaque tights and a black trench coat completed the look.

What does one wear when asking for large sums of money? I struggled with it whenever I prepared for a meeting like this. I wanted to appear professional but not matronly, fashionable but not frivolous, successful but not ostentatious. I needed to project confidence without seeming cocky. This outfit struck a good balance, I thought.

Maybe the skirt was too short.

We stood at a tall table next to the coffee bar. I sipped my Americano and scanned the rest area. On the far wall, a bank of video poker machines blinked and pinged. Two men sat on stools in front of them, sipping coffee, but neither appeared to be playing.

"Do you want part of my croissant?" Ruedger tore it in half, causing little flakes to fly all over the table.

"No, thank you," I said. I'd forgotten to put dental floss in my purse and did not want to show up with food stuck in my teeth. Fortunately, I had remembered breath mints to kill the coffee smell.

Ruedger touched my elbow and whispered, "Don't worry, Glasauer doesn't bite."

I smiled, lips pressed together, and nodded.

How many investor meetings had I led? Dozens. I'd pitched investment managers with multibillion-dollar funds in conference rooms larger than my college apartment. I'd enjoyed stunning views of Central Park and the Bay Bridge while being rejected by some of the brightest, highest-paid people on the planet.

But this felt different.

My Mordix severance money ran out at the end of the month. How would I pay the mortgage in April if we couldn't close today?

* * *

Mr. Glasauer and Ronnie welcomed us with firm handshakes.

Their cramped conference room overlooked a gravel parking lot and the highway that bordered it; traffic noise seeped in through a partially opened window. The scarred wood table and paper plate piled high with Swedish butter cookies didn't inspire confidence.

I gave Ruedger a long look.

Glasauer explained that the office was temporary, a favor from a friend. They planned to relocate in a few months.

Ronnie, dressed in a chalk-striped brown three-piece suit with a burgundy tie, resembled an old-school Swiss banker. His formal appearance reinforced the impression that he could be trusted with millions and millions of Euros. But he was German, not Swiss, and couldn't be older than twenty-five.

Mr. Glasauer, a trim, energetic man of indeterminate age, exuded confidence in his expensive pin stripes, Hermes tie and polished shoes. He smiled with his blue eyes and insisted on making cappuccino for everyone, including me, even though I told him I didn't want one. I sipped it, reluctant to refuse his hospitality.

From the start, our negotiation felt like a bullfight, running at each other and pulling back, waving the red cape to draw a reaction.

"We want to talk to you about a convertible loan," said Ruedger.

"We prefer a straight equity investment," Ronnie said.

Glasauer nodded. "Yes, equity and a million-dollar pre-money valuation. That's fair."

I ignored the million-dollar valuation trial balloon and moved straight to the presentation.

Ruedger and I had decided not to ask for an equity investment. We likely would not get a decent valuation for the company since we had no operating history. Instead we would propose a loan that could be converted to stock at the time of a larger financing.

The benefits, as I explained them to Mr. Glasauer, were threefold: 1) as a debt holder, he was first in line to claim assets if the company became insolvent; 2) the note included a discount of 25% off the price negotiated by a third-party investor when we closed a bigger financing; 3) he would receive the benefits of being an early shareholder, able to influence decisions while taking less risk.

The downside of not being an equity holder was tax related. If we went public or another company acquired us earlier than twelve months before he converted his loan to equity, he would have to pay ordinary income tax instead of capital gains tax. Given the stage of the company, this scenario was unlikely.

I gave the presentation.

Whenever Glasauer or Ronnie seemed lost, Ruedger stepped in and they argued in German until one of them remembered my presence, and then they reverted to English. I didn't mind the breaks. It gave me time to gulp mineral water and reorganize my line of attack.

Ruedger appeared calm, but I noticed that he'd eaten half of the butter cookies.

Glasauer kept pushing for an equity investment with a pre-money valuation of a million dollars. He wanted to put in two hundred and fifty thousand dollars and own twenty percent of the company post-money.

We reached an impasse.

Glasauer maintained his silence. He smiled at us from across the table, not speaking, just glancing back and forth at our faces. I knew this tactic – long silences made people squirmy, and more likely to concede. I shifted my eyes to the plate of cookies, unwilling to be manipulated.

But it worked on Ruedger. He stood up, jammed the convertible note agreement in his briefcase and said, "Well, I guess we aren't closing today." He snapped the lid closed with a finality that echoed through the small room and reached my bank account in Dallas.

What about my mortgage?

Glasauer leaned forward and grabbed me with his eyes. "How about lunch, Lea? I know a nice place not far from here."

The nice place was the Goldener Adler, a sixteenth-century inn perched on the edge of Schwaebisch Hall's historic Marktplatz. A meter-high gold eagle guarded the entry. To the left of the inn stood St. Michael's church, an imposing stone cathedral that dated back to the eleventh century, with wide semi-circular steps and enormous bells that chimed on the half hour. The Rathaus, or town hall, a baroque building topped with a gold dome, occupied the opposite side of the square.

A bright sun dominated the cloudless sky, but the temperature gauge in our rental car read only twelve degrees, fifty-four on the Fahrenheit scale. I almost objected when Glasauer asked the hostess if we could sit on the patio overlooking the Marktplatz, but remembered my looming mortgage payment.

Ruedger told me once that Germans loved sunshine. After a cold, gray winter they wanted to absorb every ray that fell from the spring sky, regardless of the temperature. Thankfully, I'd zipped the wool liner into my trench coat before leaving the hotel. I shivered until the waitress brought my coffee but didn't complain about the frigid metal chair with no cushion or the breeze that raised the skin on my legs. If Glasauer wanted to test my toughness, I intended to pass.

Ronnie recommended a special dish of the region, sautéed pork medallions with spätzle and grilled onions served with broiled green beans wrapped in bacon. Ruedger and Glasauer quickly follow his lead and ordered the same dish. I preferred salads for lunch, but salad felt like a wimpy choice, so I signed up for the pork medallions, too.

We chatted. No one mentioned the investment. Ronnie and Ruedger discussed the latest developments at Mordix. I understood only bits and pieces of the German conversation but got the gist.

Mr. Glasauer grilled me about Lingualcare's marketing strategy. He rocked back and forth in his chair and waved his hands while he talked. He knew many details of our business, having researched our competitors and studied their marketing campaigns. Clearly, his interest ran deeper than I'd originally thought.

By the time the food arrived, Glasauer's mood had visibly brightened. He joked about the old fountain near the edge of the patio where criminals were shackled and heckled as punishment for petty crimes during the Middle Ages. "Good thing they don't use it anymore," he said. "Half the investment managers in town would be chained to it."

Over espresso he agreed to rethink the convertible note. We decided to convene at his office in fifteen minutes.

While Ruedger made a phone call, I navigated the steps of Saint Michael's Church and pushed open the heavy oak door.

It smelled of incense and cold stones. Near the back of the church, a wrought iron rack with burning candles illuminated the murky darkness. To reach it, I had to traverse a large section of Plexiglas covering a pile of bones and skulls, the remains of monks buried centuries before. I found the display macabre and comforting at the same time – a reminder that many men had walked before me, and many more would do so after my bones turned to dust.

My fingers tingled with the cold as I deposited two Euros in a metal box, took four unlit candles from the tray beside it, and silently prayed as I lit them: one for my family, one for the company's success and two for Glasauer to sign the convertible note.

An hour later, he did.

Emergencies of the Prada Kind

New York, New York – April 2003

Glasauer's money arrived the first week of April.

To celebrate our transition into a real company, I hired our first employee, my sister Beth. Lingualcare needed someone to deal with the customers we would soon have. Beth had never managed customer support and didn't know anything about orthodontics, but she possessed great phone skills and had modest salary requirements for someone with a master's degree. Her last company had closed without warning and she needed a job.

Conflict of interest, complex emotions, inability to be impartial – these were all good reasons to avoid nepotism. But I knew from experience that early, unproven and under-funded ventures could not attract the best, most qualified people. Entrepreneurs hired whomever they could get, right or wrong. All the entrepreneurs I knew employed family and friends.

Before making the offer, I asked Ruedger his opinion.

"I like businesses with friends and family," he said. "I think they are more stable."

"Hopefully the whole sibling thing won't turn out to be weird," I said. "Don't forget this is the person who shoved my face into a litter box when I was six years old and forced cat shit into my mouth."

Although people would eventually figure out the relationship, our family ties were not obvious at first glance. Only eighteen months apart, we didn't resemble each other. I had blonde hair and my dad's crooked smile; Beth inherited my mother's dark hair and big green eyes. I stood five feet nine inches; Beth hovered closer to six feet. She had better hair, thicker and fuller than mine. Only the angle of our jaws betrayed our familial link.

Our offer to Beth included stock options in the company. Ruedger and I agreed that every employee should receive options regardless of their position on the org chart.

Along with bringing Beth into the company, I moved to a bigger office in the same building, one that could accommodate six desks and several rows of shelves. Maybe it was wishful thinking, but I expected to fill the desks soon.

A few days after Beth started, our first order arrived.

Dr. Lemond, a Park Avenue orthodontist I knew from my Mordix days, called me on my cell phone to tell me that he had a patient who wanted lingual braces. Beth and I hastily assembled a lab order form and a set of instructions and emailed them. When the package containing our first case arrived from New York, complete with dental impressions, we immediately sent it to Germany for manufacturing and celebrated with a box of Linzer cookies.

Five days later one of Hoffman's customer support people called to tell Beth they couldn't make braces from Dr. Lemond's poor-quality dental impressions.

Hoffman had been vocal about not wanting us to sell to U.S. customers. He believed that without training from him personally, even highly skilled orthodontists couldn't perform the procedure. Rejecting Dr. Lemond's impressions felt passive aggressive.

I called Ruedger.

"Don't make me reject our first case," I said.

"Let me see how bad it is."

A few hours later, Ruedger sent an email with photos of the plaster model poured from Dr. Lemond's impressions. Horrible. Bubbles in the impression resulted in big bumps on the teeth. Our promise of precise results relied on a precise representation of the teeth and this one didn't qualify. I would have rejected them, too.

I called Dr. Lemond and asked if he could take new impressions. "We can't promise perfect results if the impressions aren't perfect," I said.

"I don't want to recall this patient. If there are deviations caused by the impressions, I'll correct them at the end of treatment," he said.

I called Ruedger back and pleaded with him. "You have to get Hoffman to work with those impressions," I said. "We'll lose Lemond if you don't." This interaction would set the tone for how we worked with Dr. Hoffman's people going forward. We needed to have the final say with our customers.

When Ruedger called the next morning, he sounded weary. He shared only snippets of the conversation with Hoffman. "They will do it," he said. "The technicians can modify the plaster model and get close to the actual anatomical surface."

"How bad was it?" I asked.

"If Hoffman didn't think I was a complete idiot before, he does now," said Ruedger. "And he thinks Dr. Lemond is an idiot, and sloppy, and lazy, and that his case will be a disaster and ruin our reputation."

"You don't think the lab will sabotage it, do you?"

"No, they won't send out anything but their best work."

I hung up, pleased that we'd passed an important milestone. We had our first customer-related showdown with Hoffman and prevailed. I hoped it was not a hollow victory.

* * *

My next hire was a part-time clinical trainer named Cary. An orthodontic assistant by training, Cary had an air of quiet authority that grabbed people's attention but didn't make them feel intimidated. She had worked for me at Mordix, managing training and onboarding beta customers. I trusted she could do the same at Lingualcare. She agreed to travel with me to New York to babysit the first procedure.

Although we sent detailed instructions to Dr. Lemond's office along with a list of required materials, Cary suggested we buy the supplies also and take them with us. "I guarantee they won't have what we need," she said.

We booked tickets to New York and arranged to train Dr. Lemond's staff over the lunch hour prior to the procedure. In exchange for forty-five minutes of their undivided attention, we agreed to buy lunch for everyone.

Hoffman's regular training course took a day and a half, so distilling it into a meaningful forty-five-minute presentation created challenges. Cary and I spent hours reworking the PowerPoint slides, reducing the procedure information to the most essential points.

Before we left Dallas, Dr. Lemond called and told us that the patient's husband also wanted lingual braces. So, Cary packed a box of impression material from Germany, a product that would yield better results than what Dr. Lemond had used the first time.

We arrived at Dr. Lemond's office thirty minutes before the scheduled training. His waiting room, nice but not as plush as one might expect on Park Avenue, brimmed with patients, mostly adults. The receptionist ushered us into a small breakroom and pointed to a closet where we could leave our coats and suitcases.

"Where should we set up the slide presentation?" I asked.

"The reception area is the only room large enough to hold the whole staff, but we don't have a screen in there."

Cary and I exchanged glances. Before leaving Dallas, I'd printed handouts of the slides, just in case. Those would have to do.

Dr. Lemond's staff immediately connected with Cary. They sat in a semi-circle around her and listened attentively, eating sandwiches and rustling through bags of chips while she succinctly went through the material. By the end of our lunch she had them excited about working with our new lingual system.

At Mordix, I learned that selling to orthodontic assistants was as important as selling to the doctor. They had more face time with patients than the doctors did and were responsible for changing wires and elastics. In order for us to be successful, we needed to show them how to be successful with our product. No one wanted to look incompetent in front of a patient.

Before the training started, we learned that Dr. Lemond's schedule had changed and he would not be putting on the patient's braces. Instead his associate, Dr. Selnick, a young orthodontist who had recently joined his practice, would perform the procedure. Unfortunately, she knew nothing about our product and could not attend the training due to a personal emergency.

As the assistants picked up the Styrofoam cups and plates from lunch, Dr. Selnick breezed through the front door carrying a large Prada shopping bag. She brushed strands of long blonde hair from her pale, unlined face and offered me a quick nod as she strode back to her office.

I resisted the urge to ask about her Prada-related emergency.

The afternoon kicked off with the patient's husband, the one who also wanted to get braces. One of Dr. Lemond's assistants asked Cary to help her take the impressions since she was unfamiliar with our impression material. I joined them in the treatment room.

Our patient had the widest mouth I'd ever seen. The assistant scoured the cabinets for an impression tray large enough to accommodate him.

Cary noticed two missing teeth in his lower jaw. She told the assistant, "You might want to block those open spaces with wax before you put the tray in."

"We don't do that here," said the assistant, who finally located an XL impression tray.

She tried it in. It fit, but barely.

Cary showed her how to take a two-phase impression using the Polyvinyl Siloxane (PVS) material from Germany. She mixed phase one, put it in the tray and gave it to Dr. Lemond's assistant to push down over the patient's teeth. After three minutes, she took out the tray and filled it two-thirds full of phase two, a bright pink, fluid silicone meant to flow into the small crevices and capture tiny details.

Cary put a small dab of silicone on the instrument tray next to the chair so she could feel when it had hardened. After a few minutes, she checked it and gave the assistant a nod.

The assistant pulled up on the impression tray to remove it.

Nothing.

She pulled again, much harder this time.

It didn't budge.

She tried again, straining and using both hands. Panic showed in her eyes; she shifted them to Cary, then back at the tray, and shook her head. Without saying anything, Cary put on latex gloves and gave it a try. She pulled hard on the front of the tray while putting pressure with her fingers on the back, trying to break the seal.

Nothing.

The patient made an incoherent noise and raised his eyebrows.

The assistant patted his shoulder and said, "Don't worry. I'll just be a minute." Then she left the room.

I gave Cary a quizzical look.

She took off the latex gloves and threw them in the trashcan, motioned me over to the corner and whispered, "Those spaces where he's missing teeth have created a vacuum lock. That's why I suggested she block them with wax."

"How will you get it out?

Cary shook her head. "Somehow we need to break the seal."

I glanced at the patient's dental chart. He had two crowns in his lower jaw.

Great.

I flashed back to a terrible afternoon in the Mordix clinic two years earlier, when a dental assistant took an impression of my lower jaw while I had braces on. She did not remove the wire or block the spaces between the brackets with wax. After the impression material cured, she tried to remove the tray but could not get it to budge. The spaces between the brackets and wires had created a similar vacuum lock.

She tried to force the tray out. When I felt my dental crowns dislodging, I'd pushed her hands away.

Summoned by the frightened assistant, a handful of Mordix hardware engineers examined my mouth and discussed options for removing the tray, including using a pair of pliers that someone had retrieved from the maintenance closet. As I could not speak with a tray in my mouth, I grabbed a pad of paper and pen from the counter and wrote, in huge letters: *DOCTOR!!!*

One of the company's clinical advisors, an orthodontist with a practice in Highland Park, had just arrived for a meeting. An engineer corralled him in the waiting room and brought him to the clinic.

A soft-spoken man in his sixties, the orthodontist took one look at the situation and said, "Well, after thirty-two years, I thought I'd seen everything."

He used a high-speed hand piece to cut the plastic tray. It took all my willpower to keep from gagging when I smelled the burning plastic and felt hot shards hit the back of my throat.

Ten minutes later, he removed the tray and placed three dental crowns in the palm of my hand. Fortunately, a sympathetic general dentist had an office in our building. He immediately put me in a treatment room and re-bonded the crowns.

I hoped we weren't facing a similar situation here.

Dr. Lemond's assistant returned. "He'll be here in a minute," she said to the patient.

Cary said, "Did you try rocking the tray? Sometimes that helps to break to the seal."

The assistant took the handle of the tray and twisted it to the right and then to the left, back and forth, back and forth. It made a popping noise just as Dr. Lemond pushed open the door. She had gotten it out and the tray contained no dental crowns.

Hallelujah!

The assistant gave Dr. Lemond a thumbs-up and he left.

Fortunately, the patient only needed braces on his lower teeth, not on the upper teeth, so the assistant only had to take one impression.

Now the wife.

In the hallway I whispered to Cary, "I hope that wasn't a preview of coming attractions."

"Don't jinx me!"

"Be sure to let Dr. Selnick know if she's about to do something wrong," I said.

"Do you think I should have insisted on the wax?"

"You spoke up. The assistant didn't want to take your advice," I said. "But this is different. We need her to do it right. Dr. Lemond will blame us for a bad result."

"I know."

Anxiety tinged her voice. She would need to direct Dr. Selnick without it being obvious to the patient. It required walking a razor-thin line, one that subordinates always struggled with when teaching doctors.

Outside the operatory I pulled Cary to the side and said, "You can only control so much. If it's a disaster, then it's a disaster. We'll survive."

"I'm about to throw up," she whispered.

Inside the operatory an assistant prepared an instrument tray for the procedure. I noticed it did not contain anything on the materials list we'd sent the week before.

Without saying a word, Cary took the materials and sterilized instruments we'd brought with us from Dallas out of her bag.

Just then Dr. Selnick came around the corner.

"Okay, are we ready?" She flashed a gleaming smile.

"Do you have a few minutes to review the procedures?" asked Cary.

"The patient is right behind me," she said. "Can't you just talk me through it as we go?"

At Mordix I observed that most orthodontists fell into one of two categories: sticklers for detail who over-prepared and cowboys who operated on a wing and a prayer.

Dr. Selnick's attitude rivaled Wild Bill Hickok's.

She gave me an appraising glance and said, "It's going to be tight in here with me and two assistants, would you mind waiting in the hall?"

I did mind, but I left anyway, right as the patient arrived.

Ten minutes.

Fifteen minutes.

Twenty minutes.

Cary came out of the operatory wide-eyed. "We have a problem," she said. "One of the brackets on the lower jaw is missing and we can't find it."

"I don't know what that means," I said.

"She might have aspirated it."

No. No. NO.

Aspirating a bracket – i.e. sucking in into the lungs – was truly the worst possible thing that could occur during an orthodontic procedure. It was the only life-threatening outcome of having braces put on your teeth.

"Could she have swallowed it?"

"That's a possibility," Cary said, "but I think she would have choked."

"What's the treatment for inhaling a bracket?" I said.

"Surgery, you can't leave it in there."

Before I had a chance to think about what that sort of surgery might cost, the door opened and the assistant said, "We found the bracket hidden under her tongue. I don't know why she didn't feel it. Dr. Selnick needs your help putting it on."

"Thank God," said Cary and went back into the operatory.

I left the office, walked down Park Avenue toward 61st Street and breathed deeply, trying to dispel the adrenaline rushing through my body.

I could hear Hoffman's voice in my head.

I told you so.

I told you so.

I told you so.

Turning Your Worst Enemy into Your Best Friend

Bad Erlangen, Germany – May 2003

"Orthodontists are unreliable," said Ruedger. "We can't let them be the gatekeepers to our success. Your experience at Lemond's office is a perfect example."

Ruedger, Thomas and I were sitting in a café in Bad Erlangen, a few blocks from Hoffman's office. We had just signed a supply contract, something we'd been negotiating since Christmas.

Hoffman had agreed to produce our cases for cost plus fifteen percent. To get that price, we'd agreed to pay a higher shipping rate than his European customers. It wasn't ideal, but since we had no leverage, it felt like a win.

Outside, sunlight bathed the plaza, making the moss that grew in the cracks between the stones a brilliant green. People lounged on the wrought iron benches that rimmed the plaza, faces aimed toward the sky; others walked their dogs, stopping to chat in the warm afternoon sun.

The waitress brought me mint tea and a small dish of hard cookies that tasted like cinnamon-flavored cardboard. I was so hungry I dipped them in tea and ate them anyway. Although it was not quite three o'clock in the afternoon, both Thomas and Ruedger ordered beer.

"We should open our own clinics, like Hoffman," argued Ruedger. "If we own the clinics, then we own the patients and our destiny."

"Hoffman makes money at his clinic, because he's a *doctor*," I said, irritation creeping into my voice. "We aren't doctors. We would have to convince doctors to go into business with us, and I guarantee you they will want most of the money."

"What do you want to do?" Thomas asked.

"I want to sell products to orthodontists," I said, "like Invisalign and Mordix; run it as a service business."

Whenever we went to Bad Erlangen and Ruedger saw Dr. Hoffman's overflowing waiting room, he left feverish with envy. From the outside, treating patients appeared easier than hunting down and selling products to individual orthodontists.

I was immune to clinic fever. I felt more confident in my ability to sell products to orthodontists than I did in my ability to manage doctors and recruit patients.

Thomas offered, "What if we opened only one clinic in Dallas and used it as a training center? We could test the idea and see if it works."

"Do you have any idea how much it will cost to open a clinic?" I said.

"A few hundred thousand dollars," answered Ruedger.

"We don't have a few hundred thousand dollars," I reminded him.

"You're right," said Ruedger, "and we never will unless we have a business plan to sell investors."

Touché.

I owned the business plan, an ever-evolving document that seemed impossible to finalize because we could not agree on the narrative. "Let's run the numbers," I said. "Build a financial model for the clinics, one for direct selling and one that shows a combination of both."

A week later, Ruedger sent me a new financial model and called to sell me on the clinic idea. "We could build a clinic in a space big enough to accommodate our operations, design it so the clinic can be sealed off. If it doesn't work out, we can lease it to a dentist."

"According to your projections, we need to raise two million dollars to get through the first two years," I said. "Any thoughts on how we do that?"

"I'm relying on you," said Ruedger, the smile on his face apparent in his tone of voice.

He and I both knew that success on a spreadsheet meant that in some alternate universe where everything went exactly as planned, the idea might possibly work.

"Fine. I'll look at building a clinic," I said. "But in the meantime, you have to help me recruit orthodontists to try the product. Do we have a deal?"

He sighed. "Okay. I'm in."

Before Ruedger could back out of his commitment, I booked reasonably priced tickets to Hawaii and an inexpensive hotel near Waikiki Beach for the upcoming American Association of Orthodontists (AAO) meeting in Honolulu. We had missed the deadline for renting a booth, but I figured we could forage for potential customers on the show floor.

This AAO would be nothing like the Mordix days – no six-figure booth, no expensive giveaways and no big pre-show ad campaign. It would just be Ruedger and me wearing polo shirts stitched with the company logo, hunting for familiar faces in the crowded aisles and cajoling five or ten minutes of air time.

Our objective was to sell a training course to potential customers. After the near-fiasco in New York, I moved training to the top of the priority list. We would use clinical courses as a marketing tool, the way Dr. Hoffman did. Before leaving Bad Erlangen, I'd convinced Hoffman's now-wife Dr. Lilli Thalman to teach a course in Dallas and scheduled it for mid-July.

Ruedger met me at LAX and we flew to Honolulu together, both uneasy about presenting our new company to the world for the first time. On the way to our cheap hotel on Waikiki Beach, I drove down Kalakaua Avenue, past the big resorts and beach shops glittery in the fading light. I turned up the radio to sing "Gold Dust Woman," drowning out Stevie Nicks and ignoring the sideways glance from Ruedger.

Good things would come from this trip. I felt certain.

"Can we stop for a minute?" said Ruedger as we neared the public beach.

"Why?"

"Please, just pull over there and park." He pointed to a parking lot on our right. Before I could turn off the ignition, he slid out of the car.

Holding a signpost for balance, Ruedger removed his black leather dress shoes and gray wool socks, rolled up his Levi's and jogged toward the surf. The breeze pulled at his shirt as he stepped into the water, stretched his arms wide and tilted his head upward, toward the waxing moon.

I couldn't see his face, but I knew it wore a smile. His whole body wore a smile.

After dropping my high heels in the back seat, I tip-toed to the water's edge, bunching the extra fabric of my dress in one hand and pulling it to the side so the wind wouldn't grab it. Small waves rolled across my feet, white bubbles against the dark water, depositing bits of sand on my ankles. Closing my eyes, I breathed in the ocean air and for a few moments stood still, awash in possibility. We could do this.

As the tide shifted the sand beneath my toes, I opened my eyes and stepped forward.

* * *

"We think you are infringing our patents."

In the world of a technology start-up, these words constituted a nuclear strike.

Don Everson, CEO of OrthoCo, smiled as he dropped them on Ruedger and me, then added, "I wanted to make you aware of that."

The three of us stood in the middle of their gigantic trade show booth surrounded by hordes of OrthoCo salespeople wearing loud Hawaiian shirts and leis. Giant posters of smiling twelve-year-old kids with braces loomed overhead. Behind me a doctor on a small stage gave a presentation on facial symmetry to a half-circle of empty chairs.

Ruedger and I had gone to the OrthoCo booth to meet our friend Davis Marks, their vice president of business development, but Everson had pounced on us as soon as we walked up. Davis stood on the opposite side of the booth, back turned to us, talking to an orthodontist.

"Have you been to Hoffman's lab to see the manufacturing?" Ruedger asked.

Everson shook his head. "I'm going by what our development guys told me."

A compact man in his early fifties with ruddy, pock-marked skin, Everson wore rectangular wire-frame glasses that distorted the shape of his eyes, making them appear slightly reptilian. His close-cropped black hair looked abnormally dark, like he'd recently indulged in some Just for Men to cover the gray. He stood erect, hands on his hips, the posture of a high school football coach running a drill.

I'd met Everson three years ago when I'd visited the OrthoCo plant with Ruedger. He'd also started that meeting with, "We think you're infringing our patents." Perhaps it had become his standard opening line.

Being put on notice meant if we continued the alleged infringement, and a court ruled against us, we owed triple damages dating back to the notice date. Even worse, we were obligated to tell potential investors. Raising money with the threat of a patent infringement lawsuit was almost impossible. This could kill our business.

"I need a coffee," Ruedger said as we fled the booth.

We claimed an empty table in the cafeteria near the restrooms, far from the doctors sipping coffee and perusing the show guide. Ruedger stood in line while I guarded the company's assets, backpacks that held laptops, sign-up sheets for the Dallas course and a set of plastic teeth with braces glued on the back.

"Hey Lea." Davis Marks pulled out the chair across from me and sat down. He wore the same terrible Hawaiian shirt as his OrthoCo colleagues, and his black curly hair, shiny with perspiration, stuck to his forehead. He pushed it to the side as he arranged his large frame in the metal folding chair. "I apologize. I had no idea Everson intended to threaten you guys."

"Is it safe to be seen consorting with enemy?" I asked.

"He's just pissed off that Dr. Hoffman gave you a contract," Davis said. "We've sponsored Hoffman's courses in Europe for the last two years, paid for his marketing. That contract felt like a slap in the face."

Ruedger returned with two cups of coffee and a sticky bun. He sat the tray on the table and shook Davis' hand. "So, you have more good news for me?" Ruedger's lips smiled, but his voice did not.

Davis leaned forward and whispered. "I'm leaving OrthoCo. It hasn't been announced yet, so don't say anything. I took a job as president of Knightsbridge Orthodontics. I want to work with you. This lingual product is a winner. It could be bigger than Invisalign."

Now I understood why Don Everson had put us on notice.

He smelled money.

"I'll call you guys when I'm officially gone," Davis said as he got up to leave. "Don't freak out about Everson, he just barks loud."

The next day we shook off the OrthoCo blues and focused on our mission – finding prospective customers and selling the Dallas course. Since we only had one set of plastic teeth, we each took an arch and wandered the show floor, ambushing orthodontists who made the mistake of making eye contact.

For every five doctors that blew me off, one set his bag on the floor and examined the product sample up close. A few accepted the offer of an information package. At the end of the second day we ran out of data sheets and had to go to Kinko's to print more.

It felt like progress.

On the last day, right as the show opened, I spotted Dr. Sam Wednesday, nephew of the orthodontist I'd run into in the Frankfurt airport. He was standing in the coffee line looking hungover.

"Dr. Sam," I said, trying to catch his attention without screaming his name.

"Hey Lea!" He beckoned me to his spot in the front of the line and hugged me. "I was hoping that I'd run into you and Ruedger. My uncle told me about what you guys are doing. Can I see it?'

I handed him my half of the plastic teeth.

Despite being a man of small stature, Dr. Sam had a big presence. He exuded energy. It sounded like a cliché, but his smile literally did light up a room. Luminosity was a quality he shared with other members of the Wednesday clan. They practically glowed in the dark.

"I dropped out of the Mordix beta program," he said. "It wasn't the same after you left." He paid for his coffee without letting go of the teeth.

"Ruedger and I need a key opinion leader in the U.S., someone to teach courses," I said. "Any chance you would be interested?"

"I would love to try the product and take it from there," he said.

We agreed to meet in Dallas the following week. He promised to start recruiting patients immediately.

That night, I boarded the plane home with a stack of lead sheets and verbal commitments from fifteen orthodontists to attend our July training course in Dallas.

We'd accomplished our goal for the AAO, but I couldn't celebrate. All I could think about was Don Everson's threat of a patent infringement lawsuit and what that meant to our little company.

* * *

When I got back to Dallas, I went to the U.S. Patent and Trademark Office website to assess our situation. Back in my Mordix days I would have called the IP law firm and run up a twenty-thousand-dollar tab, but that was not an option.

I'd been around the world of technology companies long enough to know that when it came to patents, only two things mattered: priority dates and claim language. The priority date of a foundational patent could be extended to divisional patents and continuations in part. Most of OrthoCo's patents linked to a patent dating back to 1992.

As I waded through the claims, trying to understand exactly what they meant in relation to our processes, one question kept running through my brain. What did OrthoCo actually want? Did they want to shut us down? We were too small to pose a real threat. Or was this about ego and money?

I called Ruedger. "What if we partnered with OrthoCo?"

"Partnered how?"

"They wanted to distribute Hoffman's product in Europe. Why don't we ask them to be our distributor in the United States and pay them a sales commission on all sales?"

"What if they don't sell anything?"

"It doesn't matter," I said. "It gets them off our backs."

Together, we hatched a crazy plan.

Instead of fighting about the patents, we would ask OrthoCo to become our exclusive distributor. We would pay them a ten percent sales commission on everything we sold and in exchange they had to agree not to sue us for patent infringement. As an extra measure of protection, we would ask for a licensing agreement to fall back on in the event either party canceled the distribution contract. The licensing agreement would give us rights to the relevant patents for a predetermined royalty.

Ruedger said, "Are you sure you want to get into bed with these guys? I don't believe we've infringed."

"It doesn't matter. We don't have the resources to fight them. And as long as it remains unresolved, we can't raise money. We are dead as soon as Glasauer's money runs out."

I ran the idea past our corporate attorney.

"I've never seen a company turn their worst enemy into their best friend," he said. "But it's worth a shot."

At least Hoffman liked the idea. He set up a meeting with Don Everson, who would be in Amersfoort, the Netherlands at the end of June.

Now we just had to sell him.

When They Say "Yes," Leave

Amersfoort, The Netherlands – June 2003

Dr. Hoffman asked if I would drive him to Amersfoort while he worked on slides for the upcoming course in Dallas. Given my level of anxiety about the OrthoCo meeting, the idea of driving Hoffman's Ferrari on a road with no speed limit terrified me. I opted to ride with Ruedger in his Renault minivan instead.

Ruedger and I left the Wald Hotel right after breakfast, even though the meeting didn't start until 2:00. We exited the A30 at 11:30, found OrthoCo's Amersfoort office and then drove to city center to have lunch.

I doubted I could eat anything. The fear I'd been ignoring for days pulsed deep in my stomach.

What if they didn't want to work with us?

What if I was wrong about their intentions?

What if they wanted to shut us down out of pure spite?

Ruedger parked on a narrow street, two wheels on the curb. We walked in the direction of a church tower. In old European towns, churches usually anchored a central plaza and central plazas always housed restaurants.

Tall brick buildings with gray slate and orange tile roofs loomed over the cobblestone streets. Planters hung from the windows, ornate wrought iron boxes overflowing with fuchsia, lavender, gold, deep purple and white pansies. They softened the edges of the stone buildings and put a smile on the windowpanes.

The narrow street dead-ended into a huge plaza lined with cafés. We claimed a table for two under the bright green awning of a pizzeria. After we ordered, Ruedger opened his briefcase and pulled out a clear plastic sleeve with a document inside. He carefully removed it from the sleeve and handed it to me.

"You need to read this before we go into the meeting."

I flipped the pages one by one, going back to check the Appendix several times as I made my way through the document.

"Holy shit," I said. "Why didn't you tell me about this before?"

Ruedger smiled. "I knew it existed, but I wasn't sure if I could put my hands on it."

"What are you going to do with it?" I said.

"Nothing, unless they force my hand."

For the first time since Don Everson put us on notice at the AAO, I felt quivers of hope. Ruedger's document might save us.

* * *

We were parked on the street in front of OrthoCo's office when Hoffman arrived. He wasn't in the red Ferrari. Instead he had driven his other car, an old silver Mercedes station wagon he used for running errands. It was out of character, but maybe, just for today, Dr. Peter Hoffman didn't want to appear obnoxious.

"You ready?" I asked.

"No," he said as he straightened his tie and buttoned his suit jacket.

As we approached the glass double doors that would lead us into the lion's den, I leaned close and whispered, "Don't worry, Ruedger has a secret weapon."

We gathered in a large conference room. Juice, sparkling water and a plate of butter cookies sat in the middle of the table. On the OrthoCo side sat Don Everson and three of his European cronies. Ruedger and Everson lined up across from each other, both leaning back in their chairs.

Over lunch, Ruedger had explained that his relationship with Everson started in the early 1990s when Everson ran research and development at OrthoCo. Back then Everson and Dr. Corbin Roberts visited Ruedger and his boss, Norbert Geyer, in Berlin. Ruedger was running Geyer Medizintechnik, the company that would eventually become Mordix.

Because they were developing cutting edge software, an intra-oral scanner and wire-bending robots to automate one of the most time-consuming and inexact components of orthodontic treatment, Ruedger and Norbert only agreed to speak to Everson and Dr. Roberts after they signed a Non-Disclosure Agreement (NDA) with an appendix outlining the subject matters that constituted confidential information.

In 1994, when the USPTO published the first of OrthoCo's digital design patents, Ruedger discovered that much of the subject matter covered in the NDA had been turned into OrthoCo patent claims. When he checked the date of the patents, he realized they had been filed shortly after Don Everson's trip to Berlin.

Ruedger had the original NDA signed by Everson; that was the document he'd given me at lunch.

If we used it in court against OrthoCo, we would have a shot at invalidating their core patents. The web of divisional patents and continuations in part that they filed based on that initial priority date would tumble like dominoes.

Norbert had kept the original NDA on the off chance that Ruedger might need it someday.

Ruedger started the meeting by saying to Everson, "I spoke to Norbert this week. He asked me to give you his greetings."

Everson nodded and shifted in his chair.

None of the OrthoCo guys knew what Ruedger's casual remark meant, but I sensed a shift in the room.

I said, "After you put us on notice at the AAO..."

Everson interrupted me. "I never put you on notice."

Ruedger leaned in. "What would you call it, then?"

"I just wanted to make you aware that there might be a problem."

"The semantics don't matter," said Ruedger. "Legally what you did constitutes notice."

I continued. "We spoke to our attorneys and reviewed your claims. We do not believe our product infringes, but you've put us in a difficult position. Legally we have to disclose this to potential investors as a risk. Given the current investment climate, it puts us at an enormous disadvantage. So, we have a proposal."

I took the stack of documents that Ruedger and I had printed at Hoffman's office the night before and passed them around the table.

"Rather than spend money on lawyers, we would like to invest in our relationship and pay you to distribute our product."

Everson scanned the document. I knew what he was looking for. A sales guy at heart, he cared only about the money.

"We propose a 10% sales commission to be paid to you on every product sold. In exchange, we want your help with marketing and sales, and a written commitment that you won't sue us for infringement."

Ruedger jumped in. "We included a licensing agreement. If either party decides to terminate the distribution agreement, we want the right to license the relevant patents. And we'd like to define the royalty amount up front."

This was the part we were most worried about. Basically, we wanted OrthoCo to give us a get-out-of-jail-free card, a license to all their patents for a pre-defined amount and a promise to never sue us.

Everson glanced around the table at his team. They said nothing, obviously waiting for a cue from the boss. I held my breath, mentally begging him to say yes.

"We'll need to clarify some details, but in principle, I like it."

The other OrthoCo guys nodded.

For a moment, our little group at the end of the table sat frozen. I couldn't speak for Dr. Hoffman or Ruedger, but I had no expectation it would be that easy.

This was as good as it would get.

We needed to leave immediately.

I stood up. "Well then, we won't take any more of your time. I'll send you electronic copies of the documents and your general counsel can get back to us."

As soon as we got in the car, Ruedger and I called our IP attorney and told him the news. His laughter echoed from the small cell phone speaker as Ruedger navigated Amersfoort's narrow streets, trying to keep up with Hoffman who drove his old Mercedes as if it were a Ferrari.

"I can't believe you guys did it. We had long odds on this one."

I wanted to laugh, shout and cry all at the same time, partially from relief, partially from disbelief.

Could it be true? Could we have turned our worst enemy into our best friend? Could we now tell investors our IP was clean and the largest orthodontic company in the world wanted to be our exclusive distributor?

Ruedger entered the autobahn behind Hoffman. A few kilometers outside the city he followed him into a rest area with a Shell gas station and a small restaurant. We walked inside the Shell station, turned to look at each other and started laughing and hugging.

"I never thought they would go for it," said Hoffman.

"In and out in less than fifteen minutes," said Ruedger. "Unbelievable."

Hoffman bought ice cream for all of us, milk chocolate coated Häagen-Dazs bars covered in chopped almonds. We stood next to the bright blue ice cream freezer and ate while Ruedger told Hoffman the Norbert story.

I enjoyed the ice cream, perhaps the best I'd ever tasted, and didn't allow the calorie count to scare me into throwing it away half eaten.

We would live to fight another day, and that was a victory worth savoring.

If You Dig a Hole and Fill It with Water, Frogs Will Come

Dallas, Texas – July 2003

Beth and Cary were in charge of the logistics for our July training course. They chose to hold it at the Cooper Aerobics Center, a clinic, fitness center, research institute and conference facility in North Dallas. Dr. Thalman would teach the classroom portion there on Friday. On Saturday everyone would go to Dr. Sam's office for a live patient procedure.

On Friday morning, I arrived at the Cooper Center an hour before the official start of the course and found Beth in the second-floor meeting room, stacking course materials on the sign-up table and arranging name badges in alphabetical order. The room had been set up classroom style, with three rows of tables and twenty-four chairs. A large white screen stood next to a podium in the front of the room.

"Have you seen Dr. Thalman this morning?" I said.

"Cary went to get her," said Beth.

I heard Cary's muffled voice on the stairs followed by a heavy thud. "Help!"

I rushed into the hallway and saw Dr. Thalman on her back, immobile, on the landing with Cary crouched next to her, one hand under her neck.

"What happened?" I said, taking the stairs two at a time.

"She passed out."

"They have doctors across the parking lot at the Cooper Clinic." I turned to Beth. "Go over there and bring back someone who can help."

Dr. Thalman's eyelids fluttered and opened.

"Sorry, I got dizzy," she said.

"Do you need a doctor?" I asked.

"No, no, I'm okay." She pushed herself up with her elbows and leaned against the wall. "I haven't had anything to eat in a couple of days, so maybe a piece of fruit or some yogurt would be good."

I didn't need to ask why she hadn't eaten in a couple of days. She still maintained her runway model figure, a state incompatible with regular food intake.

Cary brought her an apple and a bottle of water and stayed to make sure she was okay.

I went outside to help Beth put up signs with big red arrows near the entrance to direct course attendees to the right building. My hands shook from the adrenaline rush as I pushed them into the soft ground.

"What else can I do to help?" Beth asked after we'd finished.

"Could you force feed Dr. Thalman a bag of mini donuts?'

Beth laughed. "You hold her down, I'll stuff the donuts in her mouth."

I loved my sister.

When Dr. Thalman started her presentation, nineteen orthodontists and one dental hygienist became the first dental professionals to attend a Dr. Hoffman-sanctioned lingual orthodontic training course in the United States. Many hailed from Texas, but others had come from Florida, Connecticut, California and New York.

Dr. Thalman kept them engaged for almost six hours with an information-packed presentation that included many patient treatment photos I hadn't seen before. Even though Dr. Hoffman had been reluctant to allow us to sell in the U.S., he'd invested some serious time and effort in making our first training course the best it could possibly be.

She wrapped up at four o'clock. Despite the long day of lecture and discussion, the participants lingered, asking questions and eating cookies, healthy ones chock full of seeds and dried fruit.

I hoped their enthusiasm would translate into orders.

On the second day, Dr. Thalman played the role of orthodontic assistant during the live procedure. All the doctors crowded around the treatment chair in Dr. Sam's office to watch as Dr. Thalman explained the clinical procedure step-by-step.

Dr. Sam couldn't contain his excitement, flashing that high wattage smile as the patient got out of the chair. He asked me to stick around afterward to talk privately.

As he tidied up the operatory, he said, "In Hawaii you mentioned needing someone to teach courses and lecture. I'd like to volunteer."

"Fantastic," I said.

We needed U.S. doctors to teach courses. Without them, we could not build a business independent of Dr. Hoffman.

"This thing is going to be huge," he said.

I nodded. We believed that, too.

"Ruedger mentioned that you might be opening a clinic in Dallas. Are you still planning to do that? Have you lined up anyone to treat patients there?" he asked.

"No," I said. "We haven't gotten that far."

"Well, I'd be interested in looking at that, too."

We shook hands and I promised to follow up.

After the course, we began receiving a steady stream of orders. Doctors who hadn't been able to attend contacted Cary and requested private, in-office training. Most called when they had a patient already lined up, so Cary trained right at the chairside during the procedure.

With orders coming in, I hoped Ruedger would abandon the idea of building a clinic. But he still believed that patients would drive adoption of the product, not doctors. When I mentioned that Dr. Sam wanted to work at our yet-to-be-built clinic, Ruedger amped up the pressure.

"When I'm in Dallas next week, let's look at potential clinic sites, see what is available."

Reluctantly I agreed.

I called a friend from my software company days, Judy. Her husband worked for a large real estate development company. Over dinner one night, she had mentioned that his firm leased space to new companies. They often accepted stock in exchange for rent and buildout if they liked the company's prospects.

Judy had their leasing agent show me a property that occupied the corner of a popular shopping center and had signage to Beltline Road, one of the busiest streets in Dallas. Inside, it had honey-colored parquet floors and huge windows that flooded the space with natural light, offering views of a tree-lined creek on the other side of the parking lot.

Large enough to accommodate a small orthodontic clinic and our corporate offices, the building was a five-minute drive from my house and only ten minutes from Will's school.

Judy's husband offered us a great deal: six months free rent, free buildout and stock for rent if we paid cash for the taxes.

Ruedger made a trip to Dallas to check it out. He loved the space and the deal. "We won't do better."

We were having lunch at a restaurant in the same shopping center as the proposed clinic. It was mid-afternoon on a Wednesday and the place was jammed with potential orthodontic patients.

"They want us to sign an eight-year lease," I said. "Who knows what's going to happen over the next eight years? And we don't have money to buy clinic equipment."

"Let's just do it, start right now and figure out the rest as we go."

His excitement crept over to my side of the table. I imagined myself sitting next to the big picture window with a view of the creek, watching patients come into the clinic and leave with beautiful smiles on their faces.

"My friend Norbert told me that if you dig a hole in the ground, fill it with water and plant a few flowers, eventually frogs will come," said Ruedger. "We need to dig the hole."

"I like the location," I said.

I knew that proximity to my home should not be a consideration. As the CEO, I was supposed to make impartial decisions based on what was best for the company. But I liked the idea of being close to home and Will's school. A shorter commute would definitely reduce my stress level.

"Okay," I said.

"Are you sure?"

"No, I'm not sure at all, but I don't have a better answer."

We celebrated with crab cakes and a brownie sundae.

* * *

After we signed the clinic lease, I hired a fractional CFO named Scott to help me find investors and prepare proper financial statements. I liked Scott. He wasn't a typical buttoned-up CFO. A former rock musician, Scott refused to take himself too seriously and was unafraid to call bullshit.

"We need dental equipment for the clinic," I told him on the phone one day. "Do you know anyone who does equipment leases for underfinanced, extremely risky ventures?"

"The banks are hurting right now," he said. "With the telecom crash and the markets going to hell, there might be someone out there willing to make a deal."

He promised to look around and get back to me.

I hired my friend Judy to manage the clinic buildout. From our software days I knew her to be a solid project manager, organized and efficient. She offered to work for stock. How could I refuse an educated, experienced person willing to work for free?

But part of me knew better.

Judy thrived on drama. At our prior company, she had spread negative gossip about everyone from the CEO to the receptionist. I hired her anyway, believing that because we were friends, she would behave differently.

The trouble began almost immediately.

She hadn't even been at the office a week when she called me while I was in Germany to complain about Beth. Apparently, Beth had sent letters to doctors with just their names on the envelopes, no doctor titles.

"These people went to school for years, spent tens of thousands of dollars on their education and expect to be addressed properly," she said, her voice quivering with irritation. "Beth should know better. You need to say something to her. This is just the sort of mistake that can kill the business."

"I'm sure it will be fine," I said from my hotel room five thousand miles away. It was after eleven o'clock and I needed sleep. Ruedger and I had an early meeting with Mr. Glasauer in the morning.

"Did you see her new purse?" Judy asked.

"Her purse?"

"She bought it at a thrift store. It has an owl embroidered on the front. So tacky!"

"Where are you going with this?" I said, not connecting the dots between a botched mailing and a secondhand owl purse.

"I'm just wondering if she's the right sort of person to handle customer care," said Judy. "She has to deal with educated, sophisticated people."

Should I feel ashamed that my sister shopped at thrift stores and liked eclectic handbags?

"I'll talk to Beth tomorrow. I'm sure it was an honest mistake," I said and ended the phone call before Judy could make any more negative comments about my sister.

Despite my exhaustion, I couldn't sleep. I kept replaying the conversation with Judy. What could she possibly have against Beth?

Beth had an empathic soul. In high school, she had collected a ragtag group of friends, social outcasts whose only common trait was their misfit status. One girl, the greasy-haired daughter of a baker whose countenance reflected her steady diet of sausage rolls and kolaches, came to school every day in sweat-stained, flour-dusted clothes, reeking of yeast and body odor. Rather than shun her, like her classmates had, Beth befriended her.

Beth did her hair and make-up. They shopped. The baker's daughter embraced deodorant. She glowed.

How could Judy say negative things about my kind-hearted sister? Did she expect me to fire her?

A week later, when I was back in Dallas, I drove over to the clinic to check on the buildout. The contractor had just finished framing the walls, and for the first time, the proportions of each room became real.

I immediately noticed that our conference room was too small. It felt claustrophobic. I asked the construction manager to get me an estimate for moving one of the walls two feet and adding a large window on one side. He was nice about it. Apparently, I wasn't the first client who couldn't judge room size by blueprints alone.

Before going back to the office, I walked across the parking lot to check out my new neighbors in the shopping center. I perused the menu at an Italian restaurant, peered in the window of a hair salon and walked into a small tea shop. They sold beautiful tea sets, pots, cups and a wide selection of specialty teas. I admired a set from Russia with hand-painted rural scenes. It had a price tag larger than my monthly salary.

A man came from the back of the store and greeted me. "Can I show you something?"

"My company is moving in across the parking lot," I said. "I just wanted to introduce myself and see what you sold here."

He smiled and nodded. "Yes, yes," he said. "I met the owner of your company a few days ago. She came by to warn me about the construction noise."

"You met the owner?"

"Julie or Judy, I think."

I didn't correct him, just thanked him and left.

Why would Judy tell him she owned the clinic? I drove back to the office, feeling more confused than angry. I didn't understand Judy's motivations, but I knew they couldn't be good.

En route, my phone rang. I hesitated when I saw Judy's name, but answered.

"Did you tell the construction manager to move the wall and add a window to the conference room?"

"Yes," I said as I maneuvered my car onto Beltline Road.

"Was there a reason you didn't inform me?"

"I was going to tell you when I got back to the office."

"Moving the wall isn't a problem, but it will cost five hundred dollars to add that window. *Five hundred dollars!* And you need to clear it with the real estate company. They have to approve the budget."

"I'll pay the extra five hundred dollars," I said.

"You still need approval. They pay first and charge you for the overrun. But the construction manager won't go over budget without their permission."

"Can you call and get their approval?" I asked. Irritation crept into my voice.

"This is about Ruedger, isn't it?" Judy said in an accusatory tone.

During the planning phase, Ruedger had insisted every workspace have natural light. That's why we added big windows at the top of the walls that separated the clinic from the waiting area and my office from the open work area. It would cost more, but Ruedger and I both agreed that access to natural light made for a happier workplace.

"No, it's about me wanting a window in the conference room."

After she hung up, I called Ruedger to tell him about my conversation with the tea shop owner and the unpleasant phone call with Judy.

"She wants your job."

"No, she doesn't."

"Yes, she does," Ruedger said. "She wants to be the boss, either by making you her puppet or undermining you. Get rid of her."

"I can't believe you're saying that. She's my friend," I said.

"She's not your friend," Ruedger insisted.

Was she?

I would find out soon enough.

You Gotta Pay Bernie to Get to Barney

Dallas, Texas – August 2003

As the clinic buildout moved into high gear, and the need to buy dental equipment became more immediate, I continued my search for investment money. We hadn't yet finalized the OrthoCo agreement, so our story for investors was still fuzzy.

Phil Romano wasn't helping our cause.

Anyone who has ever eaten at a Fuddruckers or Romano's Macaroni Grill has had at least a peripheral encounter with Phil Romano. He made a couple of fortunes in the restaurant business, but he made a much bigger fortune with a medical device.

Back in 1985 Romano invested $250,000 for 30% ownership in a partnership to develop the Palmaz-Schatz stent, a device that kept arteries open during surgery. Rumor had it that Phil made more than $160,000,000 in patent royalties from that investment, a 650x return.

When *D Magazine* published an article about Phil's success, suddenly every investor in Dallas wanted to talk about medical devices. Scott set up meetings with private investors all over town. After going to the first meeting alone, I asked Scott to accompany me to the others. I didn't know if there was power in numbers, or if having a man on my side of the table did the trick, but the meetings had a more positive tenor when I didn't have to face a room full of people alone.

Scott and I pitched more than a dozen firms that invested primarily in public markets, real estate, oil and gas leases and retail, all businesses with well-known metrics and risk profiles. We quickly concluded that although people wanted to talk about medical device investments, they lacked the confidence to sink money into something they didn't fully understand.

We moved on to the investment bankers.

Until I started Lingualcare, I thought investment bankers were all Wall Street guys like Gordon Gekko who did IPOs, leveraged buyouts and multibillion-dollar mergers. As I searched for financing sources, I quickly learned that investment bankers came in all flavors and textures. And a wide variety of people claimed the moniker.

Legit investment bankers had Series 7 licenses regulated by the Financial Industry Regulatory Authority (FINRA). FINRA published a searchable database so clients could verify their banker's license was in good standing.

The maybe-ok-but-leaning-toward-shady ones usually did not have Series 7 licenses. They used the title "investment banker," but they acted as finders, guys who made introductions in exchange for a portion of the proceeds. Their fees ran between five and ten percent, and they didn't get paid until funds flowed.

Ruedger and I decided to try a banker who Scott knew, one of the guys who didn't have a Series 7 license. His name was Craig.

A jovial man wearing the largest gold and diamond encrusted Rolex I'd ever seen, Craig met with Scott and me at his office in North Dallas, a tall smoked glass structure with windows that offered a stunning view of downtown. The man and the setting reeked of success.

"I think your best option is to skip the traditional VCs and go directly to dentists," Craig said. "I know a guy who has an investment group in Florida with dentists and doctors who love deals like this. I guarantee they'll be interested."

Craig didn't ask for any cash up front, just five percent on the back end, so I decided to give him a chance. We had minimal downside. He might waste our time, but the upside could be enormous.

I signed Craig's contract and sent him the business plan and pitch deck so he could forward it to the guy in Florida.

A few days later he called. "Bernie, my friend in Fort Lauderdale, can set up the meeting with the dental group, but there's a fee. He needs five thousand dollars."

"How many people are in the group?" I said. "And what's their track record in investing in companies like ours?" I was willing to pay if we had good odds of closing a deal.

"Let me get back to you on that," he said.

Three days later Craig called me back. "It's not actually Bernie's group," he said. "Bernie knows this other guy, Barney. It's Barney's group. Barney's fee is twenty-five hundred and Bernie wants twenty-five hundred to introduce us to Barney. If you want to get in front of the dentists, you gotta pay Bernie to get to Barney."

Bernie and Barney?

Was this a Marx Brothers skit?

I said, "Let me get this straight. I'm supposed to pay twenty-five hundred dollars to be introduced to someone who may not even be legitimate, and another twenty-five hundred to a guy who knows some dentists who may or may not be interested in investing?"

"Bernie assured me that Barney is the real deal." He added. "And if the dentists invest, Barney and Bernie want a couple of points on top of the five you're paying me. We can negotiate that later."

The whole thing sounded sketchy. "I'm not paying money for introductions. Aren't there other groups we can talk to?"

Craig promised to get back to me. A month went by and I didn't hear from him. I sent a termination letter.

As our bank balance dropped and the need for dental equipment loomed, I spent ninety percent of my waking hours obsessing about getting money into the company. I constantly did internet searches for possible investors, attended networking breakfasts and investment forums and asked friends and acquaintances for referrals. Anxiety became my new best friend.

I had one offer on the table that I hesitated to take. I hadn't even told Ruedger it existed because it came from a man who broke my heart when I was 29 years old.

I'll call him Mr. Kryptonite.

We dated for almost five years. I wanted to marry him, could not imagine a life with any man other than him, even though our long-distance relationship had seen its share of ups and downs, more downs than ups if I had to be honest. But the ups surpassed all of my prior relationships. Our frenetic passion overshadowed the darker times.

And then, one sunny afternoon in February of 1995, I received a phone call.

I was working at a graphics software company in Dallas as the managing director of Latin American and the Middle East. I'd just returned from a trip to Argentina and was filling out an expense report when my phone rang.

"Lea, I've got a call for you," said the receptionist. She transferred it without identifying the caller.

It was Mr. Kryptonite's wife.

"I hired a detective to follow him," she said in a matter-of-fact tone. "He uncovered the apartment my husband was renting in Berkeley. Your letters were there, and the phone bills with calls to your number."

I'd put the phone on mute right after she identified herself as my boyfriend's wife – the woman I thought he'd divorced years ago – and puked in my gray plastic trashcan. My stomach heaved as her voice droned over the speaker. All the little bits of his life that hadn't made sense immediately coalesced into an ugly picture.

How many times had he lied to me? Thousands. He had lied to me at least two or three times a day, every day, for years.

"Does he know that you know?" I asked.

"Yes," she said. "I confronted him this morning. He denied it until I put your love letters on the table."

I wanted to evaporate.

I muted the phone as another wave of nausea send me to the trash can.

"He hasn't called, has he? Obviously, he's too much of a coward to face you," she said. "If he ever gets the balls to pick up the phone, I hope you'll have enough self-respect not to answer."

That five-minute call catapulted my life into a Jerry Springer episode. WOMEN WHOSE BOYFRIENDS ARE LEADING A DOUBLE LIFE. STAY TUNED.

It took six months to reassemble myself. I slept too much, smoked too many Virginia Slims and stopped eating. I dropped from a size eight to a size four, something I'd aspired to for years, but felt too miserable to shop for all the great clothes size four people wore. I hid from friends, ashamed to answer simple questions like, "How are you?" and "What's going on?"

When Mr. Kryptonite finally called, I listened to his voice on my answering machine, willing myself not to pick up the receiver, but I did.

Pathetic.

I'd like to say the relationship ended there, but that would have been too tidy for a Jerry Springer episode. After his wife filed for divorce, Mr. Kryptonite showed up in Dallas with a big diamond ring and a torrent of promises. As badly as I wanted to salvage the five years I'd invested in him, I could not marry a man capable of immaculate deception.

We stayed in touch.

He made millions at an Internet company before the dotcom bubble burst, and then moved into venture capital, getting richer by the day.

When I started Lingualcare, I sent him an email telling him about the new company. He offered to invest, to help me out. I told him I'd let him know if we needed the money but hoped we never would.

Now we did.

I called my friend Sharon, who had helped me survive my first two bouts with him. Somewhat ashamed, I told her about his offer.

"Take his money," Sharon said. "He has a karmic debt to pay."

"But then he's back in my life."

"Are you susceptible to his charms?"

"No," I said with a conviction that didn't feel entirely solid.

"Then take the damn money," she said.

Taking his money meant withholding information from John. John hated Mr. Kryptonite for hurting me and hated him even more for achieving financial success despite his character flaws. John seethed with the injustice of it.

Sharon helped me rationalize that, too. "What John doesn't know won't hurt him. This is business. You need to think like a man. A man wouldn't hesitate. Take the money."

I waited a few days to tell Ruedger about Mr. Kryptonite's offer, walking out of the office to make the call. I didn't want Beth to overhear. She, of course, knew all about Mr. Kryptonite and had no love for him – no one in my family did.

"We have an offer on the table for a two-hundred-thousand-dollar investment," I told Ruedger as I paced the length of our building.

"That's great news," he said. "Who is it? Do they want to participate on the same terms as Glasauer?"

"It's an old friend of mine," I said, "and yes, he's fine with the convertible note. I'm just not sure that I want him in our deal."

"Why not?"

I sucked in a deep breath. "He's an old boyfriend. It didn't end well."

Ruedger said, "It's up to you, but don't compromise yourself. We don't need the money that bad."

But we did need the money that bad.

I called Mr. Kryptonite. "Would you be willing to form an entity to use as an investment vehicle?" I said, fearing John would see his name on our investor list and have a conniption.

He didn't ask why. He knew. "Sure, if that's what you want."

The following week he sent me the investment paperwork. Instead of naming his investment entity after one of the sports teams he loved, he chose the name of a casino in Las Vegas, a place where we had an amazing date in 1991 – a night forever seared into my memory.

I signed the paperwork, ignoring my trepidation. I'd made plenty of relationship mistakes in my life. I hoped this wasn't one of them..

When Everything Stops Working, Go

El Paso, Texas – 1984

I didn't go to Texas alone. Matt followed me south. Through a friend, he'd got a job on a large ranch outside Lubbock. It was a seven-hour drive from El Paso, but it was closer than Nebraska, and we could occasionally see each other on weekends.

Right after registering for classes at UTEP, I went to the university's employment office. I wanted a waitressing job, or maybe something on campus, but there was only one job posted on the job board that day: errand runner at a downtown law firm.

I had no idea what being a runner would entail, but I called the number anyway and scheduled an interview for the following day.

My wardrobe didn't include any law-firm-appropriate clothes. After I mentioned it over dinner in the cafeteria, two guys from my dorm floor volunteered to drive me to the nearest mall with a Dillard's department store. There, I confessed my situation to a saleswoman in the clothing department. I had eighty dollars to spend and no idea what to buy. She took it as a personal challenge, and helped me find a skirt, blouse and shoes on sale.

The day of my interview, I exited the elevator on the eleventh floor of the Texas Commerce Bank building, unsteady on my new high heels. I immediately felt intimidated. The furniture, oriental carpets and paintings in gilded frames in the lobby looked like something from the set of *Dynasty*.

A UTEP student named Nancy, the firm's head runner, collected me from the lobby and walked me back to meet the legal administrator. She noticed my awestruck expression as I took in the well-appointed offices, the bullpen of secretaries and men in expensive suits. "Don't let them scare you," she said. "They put their panties on one leg at a time, just like the rest of us."

Even though my prior experience as a fry cook and ranch hand hardly qualified me for the job, Nancy and the administrator liked my Midwestern work ethic and hired me on the spot. I'd make $4.50 an hour and would be paid $.20 a mile for anything I delivered in my car.

Working for thirty-five articulate, educated, ambitious bosses with little tolerance for mistakes took all the courage I could muster. Deadlines were etched in stone and the lawyers never finished projects early. I frequently had to speed across town to get a client's signature and then make a mad dash to the courthouse to file it. Every other document in the runner's basket bore the bright red RUSH stamp.

In addition to client work, all of the runners did personal errands like make bank deposits, pick up kids from school, take cars to the repair shop and buy gifts for their spouses. I got to know many of the lawyers personally, and quickly discovered that Nancy had been right, they were just people with families, problems and quirks.

Even the senior partners made a point to ask about classes, my exams and how I was adjusting to life in El Paso. The secretaries and paralegals confided in me, telling me about their love lives and frustrations with their temperamental bosses. I was doing something important and felt proud to be included in their ranks.

The new associates, all recent law school graduates, were only a few years older than the college-aged runners. They frequently included us in their happy hour plans and trips to one of Juarez's famous steakhouses, where prime cuts of beef cost less than a hamburger in El Paso. Hanging out with them, I saw what life could be like if I finished college with strong grades and went to law school. The gap between the life I had and the life I desired narrowed. A path materialized.

I attended classes in the morning and worked in the afternoons. My drinking accelerated. The blackouts got worse. Many times, driving to a club with a group of friends, I'd feel cold fear in my stomach as I contemplated the night ahead. But it never stopped me from going out. And once I started drinking, if I had money in my purse or someone buying me drinks, I could not stop.

The real trouble started that Thanksgiving.

Matt invited me to spend the holiday with him and I decided to make the drive north. We'd been exchanging letters, and calling when we could afford it, but it had been four months since we'd seen each other, and I was anxious about the trip. I still loved him, but I couldn't resist good-looking guys after I'd consumed five or six gin and tonics at an El Paso nightclub. Flirting and dancing often evolved into more, and the guilt nagged at me. Matt deserved better.

As I pulled into the ranch, I hoped I'd feel that fluttering in my stomach, the excitement I'd felt back in Nebraska. But that night, when he emerged from the bunkhouse, waving and smiling in the headlights of my approaching car, dread washed over me.

Why did I feel so bad? Was it because I'd been hanging out with slick clubgoers who drove BMWs and had lost my taste for hard-working cowboys with Chevy trucks? Or was it the shame of seeing Matt beam at me, unaware that I was no longer the wide-eyed girl he'd taught a secret language?

That night, after Matt fell asleep, I got up, went to the kitchen and drank beer until I passed out.

The next day Matt made me breakfast, jalapeño and cheese omelets, his specialty. He took me horseback riding and showed me his favorite vistas on the ranch. We celebrated Thanksgiving with his bosses and co-workers, eating and drinking too much wine, and then falling into bed the way we used to back in Nebraska.

But the wine didn't help.

Our intimacy left me sad. I had forfeited the right to Matt's love back in March, when I'd allowed a stranger to buy me drinks, and then kissed him, openmouthed, as we swayed to "I Want to Know What Love Is." That stranger had been the first of many.

I had no right to sleep beside Matt, to steal his warmth, to smell his hair and share the heavy quilt he'd brought from home.

The right thing to do was to leave.

Before Matt awoke on Friday morning, I packed my duffle bag, left a note on his dresser and drove back to El Paso. The note said, "You deserve better. Please forgive me."

The month of December passed in a blur. I went out three or four nights a week and barely made it to class in the morning. I managed to take my final exams and go to work but no matter how hard I pretended to be fine, I couldn't shake the sick dread I'd picked up over Thanksgiving.

I felt like a terrible person. A failure.

Matt and I didn't speak after Thanksgiving, but he wrote letters declaring his love. Maybe we should get married. I could go to college in Lubbock. He would take care of me, help me fix whatever was wrong. He pleaded with me to write back.

But I didn't, because I had no answers.

Something inside me felt broken.

And my liquid repair kit no longer worked.

* * *

December 29th, 1985.

The day after the Sun Bowl game between Arizona and Georgia, my roommate and I went to a bar where we met several college football players in town for the game. I started flirting with a good-looking blond, an all-American defensive back with an unbelievable smile.

We danced fast, then slow. He kissed me.

As the night progressed, we migrated to a bar in Horizon City, Texas. We drank, played pool, dropped quarters in the juke box and sang along to "Tiny Dancer," my favorite song.

My recollections ended after I ordered my first Long Island iced tea. Apparently, I drank three.

My next memory was waking up in a hotel room next to a naked man whose face I could not see. My clothes, shoes and purse lay in a pile on the floor below me.

How had I gotten there?

Where was "there"?

Suppressing my panic, I slid onto the floor and dressed quickly, praying that the naked man would not wake up before I could get out the door. Panic pushed my heart against my rib cage as I slowly turned the doorknob and slid through a sliver of light into the hallway. The sheets rustled as the door clicked close.

I found my car parked in front of the glass exit door.

The sky shifted from black to yellowish gray as I drove away from the El Paso Airport Hilton. I squeezed the steering wheel in an attempt to steady my shaking hands. How had I gotten to that hotel? Who was the man in bed with me? Was it the all-American? What had happened to my roommate?

When I arrived at our apartment, she told me.

I'd almost killed her and the two football players when I crossed the center line of a highway and entered the path of an eighteen-wheeler. A last second swerve averted the accident. We ended up on the side of the road, in the grass. She insisted that one of the guys drive and drop her at a friend's house. I left with them. The rest she didn't know.

Overcome by an urge to throw up, I went into the bathroom of our small apartment and heaved until my stomach emptied. After I washed my face and rinsed the bile from my mouth, I raised my head, but I could not meet my own eyes in the mirror. I sank to the floor and sobbed. All I wanted to do was return to the last place I'd felt safe.

The ranch.

It took thirteen hours, driving north and east across the New Mexico desert and the plains of Eastern Colorado. I stopped only for gas and coffee. When I arrived at two in the morning, the house was dark. Our springer spaniel greeted me, offering a low growl, a sniff and a lick on my palm.

Without rousing my mother and Wayne, I crept down to the basement and crashed in my old waterbed, which was ice cold. I turned on the heater, but knowing it would take forever to warm up, I opted to sleep in my clothes in old sleeping bag on top of the mattress.

I heard the phone ringing upstairs as I slipped in and out of sleep. I awoke sometime in the late morning to my mother screaming my name and pounding on the door of my room.

"Nancy and your roommate called this morning. They told me everything. You're an alcoholic and your life is out of control."

I covered my head with a pillow and waited to hear her retreating footsteps. How could my friends have ratted me out? How could they have destroyed my only safe haven? I crawled out of the sleeping bag, grabbed my still-packed duffle bag, then climbed the stairs and went out the front door before my mother could stop me.

Snow fell sideways from a slate-colored sky, building drifts against the barbed wire fences and clinging to the horses' manes and tails. My feet sank into it and cold wetness seeped in through the fabric of my Keds.

A thick layer of ice and snow coated my car. A search of the glove box and trunk produced no ice scraper, an implement unnecessary in West Texas.

I crossed the yard to the machine shop and procured a smooth piece of wood, sturdy enough to break the ice, and a pair of insulated leather gloves. They were stiff and smelled like grease, but they'd do. Emerging from the shop, I found Wayne standing next to my car.

He wore no coat, just jeans and a flannel shirt, black rubber overshoes and a bright orange hat with ear flaps. His hands were stuffed in the pockets of his Levi's. From his expression, it was clear that my mother had told him about the phone call.

Wayne knew the truth about me.

Thick snowflakes fell on his bifocals. He took them off and wiped each lens with a clean white handkerchief while I attacked the ice, trying to get a purchase point without breaking the windshield.

"I've never asked you for anything, have I?" he said in a low, calm voice.

"No."

"Well, today I need to ask you to do something for me."

I stopped chipping, but shame prevented me from looking him in the eye.

"I want you to go to treatment for thirty days, get yourself sober," he said.

The words hung in the cold air, heavy like the wet snow piling up around us.

I could have said no to my mother. I could have said no to Beth, Robb, Lara, my grandparents, aunts, uncles, cousins, friends, boyfriends or my employer. But I could not say no to Wayne.

He loved me like a father.

And I loved him.

"Okay," I said, "I'll go."

Avoid Heat Miser

New Orleans, Louisiana – September 2003

I had to go to New Orleans.

After two months of back and forth between our lawyer and theirs, we signed the distribution and licensing agreements with OrthoCo on the last day of August. To kick off our new relationship, OrthoCo's business development manager suggested that I attend an upcoming orthodontic meeting in New Orleans and work in the OrthoCo booth.

New Orleans was my least favorite city in the United States. I wasn't into mud wrestling, étouffée gave me indigestion and I hated jazz. Add in oppressive humidity and the city became a little slice of hell.

Wanting to minimize my time there, I flew in the morning of the meeting and took a cab to the hotel where the conference was being held. I'd spend one night, and then fly home the following evening.

My cab driver smiled as he loaded my bag, a row of gold teeth catching the sun. He wore a sweat-stained guayabera shirt and battered huarache sandals that revealed heels in desperate need of a pumice stone. We made our way downtown in his white mini-van, dashboard covered in religious paraphernalia. I especially liked the plastic Virgin Mary perched on top of the New Orleans Saints flag. She swayed back forth as we zig-zagged through traffic on the way to the Hyatt.

The OrthoCo booth occupied prime real estate, a large corner space right next to the entrance of the hotel ballroom. I knew their Dallas rep from my Mordix days. He introduced me to the other sales guys working the booth, young men with fresh haircuts and decent suits. There were very few customers roaming the aisles, so

I took the opportunity to brief everyone on the deal we just signed with their company.

The Illinois rep, a young kid with wide green eyes, pulled me aside. "I have a perfect guy for you. He's a little wacky but has five offices in the Chicago metro area and loves trying new products. He's all over Invisalign."

The rep called the Chicago doctor on his cell phone. When he hung up, he said "He wants to try it. I'm going to send you his contact information so you can follow up."

I could have hugged him. We'd hoped that OrthoCo would provide a shortcut to customers. This was exactly what we needed.

The continuing education sessions ended at noon and the doctors came to the exhibition hall for lunch. I talked non-stop for two hours. The OrthoCo reps brought me a steady stream of doctors and handed out our brochures. By the time the afternoon sessions started and the hall emptied, I had a stack of solid leads.

As I made notes on the lead sheets, OrthoCo's Houston sales rep approached me. His eyes jumped back and forth across the booth, looking at everything but me. "Hey, um, I just talked to Richard, you know him right, our vice president of sales?"

I nodded. I knew Richard. He muscled my friend Davis Marks out of OrthoCo. Rumor had it he was now gunning for the CEO job currently occupied by Don Everson. Richard and I had shaken hands a few times at industry events, but that was the extent of our relationship.

Richard had a reputation for terrorizing his sales team; miss a month's sales goals, expect an hour of screaming, miss a quarter's, find a new job.

"Well, um, he's downstairs, in the bar, and he wants to talk to you."

"Sure," I said. "I'll go now."

Upon entering the bar, I saw Richard in a small booth, crouched like a hyena, berating a sales rep. Although I couldn't hear the conversation, his bright pink face and wild hand gestures spoke volumes. The rep gripped the arms of his chair, poised to spring up the second Richard dismissed him, which he did a few seconds later with a curt wave.

"Richard," I said, crossing the room and extending my hand for him to shake.

He ignored it.

"Sit," he said and pointed at the seat across from him.

I awkwardly dropped my hand.

He pulled a copy of the contract from his laptop bag and tossed it on the table. "I don't know whose bright idea this was, but nobody told me about it until yesterday."

"Okay."

"I heard you were talking to my sales reps," he said. "You told them specifics of this agreement. Is that true?"

"Yes…" I said hesitantly.

"Well, let me set you straight. I didn't sign this and I'm not going to do ONE FUCKING THING that defocuses my sales force. Do you understand? And you have NO business telling my guys ANYTHING without talking to me first."

I fought the urge to bolt out of the chair and flee like a startled gazelle. But CEOs didn't run and hide when someone screamed at them. Did they?

I picked up the contract, thumbed to the back page and pointed to Everson's illegible scrawl. "Your boss signed it. I'm only doing what he agreed to."

Richard tore the contract in half and threw the pieces on the thick brown carpet. "That's what I think of your contract," he said jabbing a finger toward a torn page to emphasize his point. "You can sit in the booth for the rest of the show with your lips zipped or take a cab to the airport, I don't give a rat's ass, but stop talking to my reps and don't expect any help from me. You got that?"

As I looked into his angry face, trying to maintain my composure, my mind pulled up an image of Heat Miser, the antagonist from *The Year Without a Santa Claus*, my favorite childhood holiday TV special. While Richard ranted, his face growing redder and redder, Heat Miser's anthem started to play in my head. *"He's mister Heat Miser, He's mister sun, He's mister heat blister, He's mister hundred and one."*

"Do you understand me?" Richard said. His voice, pitched high with antagonism, snapped me back into the moment.

My legs trembled as I rose to leave. I wondered if they sold voodoo dolls in the gift shop. Maybe I could buy a Richard doll and stick needles in its eyes.

"Lea…" he shouted as I exited the lounge.

I reclaimed my corner of the booth, acknowledging the pitying glances from the OrthoCo reps with a tight smile.

They continued sending doctors to talk to me during the afternoon coffee break, defying Richard's directive. The regional sales manager even invited me to join his team for dinner at Brennan's. Knowing that Richard would be there, I declined. But I appreciated the offer. His decency stood in stark contrast to Richard's viciousness.

The next morning, after a night of fitful sleep, I arrived at the booth to find Dr. Gene Guidry, a friend of Dr. Hoffman, sitting at one of the sales tables eating a bagel and drinking coffee. He tilted his head in the direction of the OrthoCo banner. "What in the hell are you doing in this den of vipers?"

"We did a deal with them."

"Hoffman told me," he said. "You must be desperate."

I glanced across the booth. The OrthoCo guys glared at Dr. Guidry. They knew he didn't intend to buy anything – he lectured for a competitor – and they resented him using their sales counter as his personal picnic table. But he was an orthodontist, a sacred cow in their world, so they would not do anything to offend him.

Dr. Guidry finished his coffee, collected his beat-up leather satchel from the floor, winked at the OrthoCo guys and walked out of the booth, leaving the remains of his half-eaten bagel for someone else to clean up.

Before he rounded the corner, he turned to me and said, "Nothing good comes of consorting with deceitful people."

I thought about his words all the way back to Dallas.

* * *

The smell of garlic and onions greeted me when I came in through the garage door and entered the kitchen. I hadn't eaten anything on the flight from New Orleans, and my stomach gurgled audibly.

Will and John sat at the dining table, bent over bowls of spaghetti. On the stove, a large pot of his mother's famous tomato sauce simmered alongside a skillet brimming with meatballs. Every few months, John cooked up a double batch. We'd have it for dinner, then fill glass containers with the leftovers and freeze it for later. The sauce tasted even more garlicky after a few weeks in cold storage.

I hugged Will and gave John a kiss on the cheek, then filled a bowl with spaghetti and a few extra meatballs.

"I have good news," said John. "I got a job offer today."

He'd been talking to a major advertising conglomerate about a consulting job for the last month. The week before he'd interviewed at their Chicago office.

"That's great!" I said. "How long is the contract?" I'd been praying that John would get an offer. Our family desperately needed the money, and John desperately needed a purpose. It had been almost eighteen months since his company had been sold. He'd done two consulting projects; both had paid well, but neither had lasted very long.

"It's not a consulting gig," he said as he put down his fork. "They offered me an executive position in Chicago, starting the first week of October."

It took a few seconds for the words to sink in.

"I can't move to Chicago," I blurted out.

"No one is asking you to move," he said. "I'll be there Monday through Friday and come home on the weekends."

"But how is that going to work? How am I going to travel? What about Lingualcare?" I pushed back from the table. My appetite had disappeared.

"Why are you making this about you? You should be happy for me. You've been nagging me to get a job for months.

"A job in Dallas…" I began, but John cut me off.

"I don't have the luxury of picking the city." He threw his napkin on the table and stood up. "Do you want me to turn it down? Because if you do, I will. But then you better figure out a way to make more money because right now we're underwater."

"Mom, can I watch *Bob the Builder*?" Will's small voice cut through our anger.

I'd forgotten he was sitting at the end of the table.

"Yes," I said. "Why don't you watch the TV in Mom and Dad's bedroom?"

I waited for Will to disappear into the hallway, then lowered my voice, not wanting to freak him out.

"I'm not trying to make this about me, but I have obligations, too," I said as I moved to the sink and started rinsing dishes.

"You're not the CEO here," John said, sweeping his hand toward the living room. "It's not your decision."

His words stung. Was he angry that I was a CEO, albeit of a barely functioning enterprise, and he was not? Did he resent me for leaving my high-paying job and exposing our financial vulnerability?

Before I could offer a retort, John walked over to the sink and put his hands on my shoulders. "I don't know how it will work, but I can't go on like this," he said. "I need to get my career back on track."

That night, as John snored softly next to me, I cried. How would I manage Will, the house and Lingualcare on my own? I could barely manage to squeeze a trip to the dry cleaners and a haircut for Will into the same week. Doing it without John's help would be impossible.

Lingualcare would fail.

And then what would I do?

* * *

Near the end of September, Ruedger came to Dallas for investor meetings. Driving back to the office after our first unsuccessful meeting we stopped at the Starbucks on Beltline Road for lattes.

"John is effectively moving to Chicago," I said, digging in my purse for sunglasses. We were sitting outside and the umbrella did little to block the afternoon sun. "He's dumping the day-to-day responsibilities on me."

I slipped Ray Bans over my eyes and turned to face Ruedger.

As worried as I was about the aftermath of John's decision, part of me felt relieved that he would be out of the house. At some point, I wasn't sure exactly when, I'd stopping loving John and started managing him. Instead of being my confidante and lover, he'd become another item on my to-do list.

My phone vibrated in my purse. It was Scott.

"I think I have someone who will loan you the money for that dental equipment," he said. "Can you meet me at three o'clock?" He gave me directions to the bank. "And bring that price list you got from the dental company."

Ruedger and I met Scott in the bank parking lot a few minutes before the meeting.

"Listen, these guys are new to Dallas," said Scott as he opened the front door to the bank and held it for Ruedger and me. "They started in Lubbock and are trying to expand. They're hungrier than the average bear, so they're willing to deal. But they won't do it unless they like you. It's all going to come down to the relationship."

The banker's secretary ushered us into a conference room with a gleaming wood table and new-smelling leather chairs. She offered water. No espresso. No butter cookies.

The banker came in and extended a big palm to shake my hand, then Ruedger's and finally Scott's. His accent said East Texas, his suit screamed Men's Warehouse. He looked more like a Baptist preacher than a Dallas banker.

"I'm so glad to meet you all," he said. "Scott told me about your situation and I think I can help."

He sat across from me and leaned over the table to see my laptop screen. He squinted and nodded as I presented an overview of the company. I hoped to impress him with our potential, since our reality left a lot to be desired. I explained our need for an equipment lease, with a minimum amount of money down, and the dental equipment as collateral.

"We loan money to lots of dentists," he said. "Most are a good credit risk because they need that equipment to practice their profession. They get out of school with a pile of debt, and they're highly motivated to be successful, highly motivated."

I knew where he was headed.

"You, on the other hand, don't have that same motivation. This is just a business opportunity. So why should I take a chance on you?"

Scott jumped in. "These guys have investors in the deal with deep pockets. And I would definitely categorize them as highly motivated."

"Would one of your investors be willing to guarantee the lease?"

"No," I said.

"Someone needs to give a personal guarantee," the banker said as he opened his bottle of water and took a long swallow. Droplets fell on his chin and he wiped them away with the back of his hand.

Ruedger shook his head, almost unperceptively.

At the company before Mordix, Ruedger faced a bankruptcy action because he gave personal guarantees. Last-minute maneuvering saved him from a legal mess that would have ruined him and his family. He swore he would never personally guarantee anything again.

"What if we make a larger down payment?" I asked.

The banker checked the proposal from the dental equipment company. The total came to a little over a hundred and fifty thousand dollars.

"We can go ten percent down with a personal guarantee," he said, "or fifty percent down without the guarantee."

No way could we afford to put seventy-five thousand dollars down for dental equipment.

He turned to Ruedger. "Are you a U.S. citizen?"

"No."

He turned to me. "You live in Dallas, right?"

I nodded.

"You'll need to sign the guarantee."

We thanked him for his time and reconvened in the parking lot.

Scott said, "You're not going to get around that personal guarantee. I talked to several other banks and they all said the same thing. And on top of the guarantee, they required an even bigger down payment, at least twenty-five percent."

He pointed to the bank's logo on the side of the building, a big red buffalo. "These Lubbock guys will work with you if you get in trouble. Hell, they do agricultural loans. They're used to people getting in trouble. If you're serious about starting up that clinic, you need to take it. You won't swing a better deal anywhere else in Dallas."

"John will kill me," I said.

"Only if you tell him," said Scott, with a big smile.

"I would sign with you," Ruedger said, "but they don't care about me. If something goes wrong, they will knock on your door."

"Cheer up! There's no debtor's prison anymore," Scott said as he squeezed my shoulder, "so the worst thing that happens is John divorces you and your credit's trashed for seven years."

We all laughed at that.

A hundred and thirty-five thousand dollars was more than my mortgage, but we couldn't run a clinic without dental equipment. It seemed like the only way forward.

"Have him draw up the papers," I told Scott. "I'll sign the guarantee."

Hopefully John would never find out.

* * *

In December, I decided to retire from my position as head of sales and hire Kathy, the girl who sat across the hall from me at Hireworks. Since Lingualcare had started advertising in trade magazines, our customer base had grown significantly. The ads generated more leads than I could manage.

After listening to Kathy cold call for almost a year, I already knew her style, work ethic and tenacious, yet friendly approach to customers. I didn't worry that she knew almost nothing about orthodontics or dentistry; I'd learned it fast and figured she could, too.

Ruedger teased me about hiring a fourth woman into the company. "I think you are discriminating against men," he said. "Be careful that we don't get sued."

At most technology companies, it wasn't uncommon to see a ratio of five men to every woman. Maybe I was subconsciously trying to even the score.

Beth, Cary and Kathy quickly banded into a tight circle. Cary took the lead on teaching them about orthodontics and how to deal with doctors and staff. I heard them talking about their families, sharing beauty tips and planning activities outside of work. They formed the core of our little operation.

And then there was Judy.

As soon as she entered our shared office with her appraising eyes and tight-lipped expression, the tension level spiked. Beth, Cary and Kathy stopped chatting and limited their conversations to business-related topics.

At times Judy oozed sweetness, bringing all of us Linzer cookies from a popular French bakery, cooing over Cary's new riding boots and inviting me to her famous Christmas party, where she introduced me to her friends as "a brilliant entrepreneur."

Behind my back she complained to Scott.

"Yesterday at lunch Judy told me that you are incompetent," he said.

Scott and I were in his Suburban, driving back from an investor meeting. I was already feeling down because I knew the firm we'd just visited wasn't a good fit. The managing partner had only taken the meeting because of his relationship with Scott.

"According to her, you're too inexperienced. You need adult supervision." Scott laughed and shook his head. "I'm telling you, that woman is a piece of work."

"If she thinks that, why is she still at the company?" I said.

"She's bored, got nothing to do at home but rearrange her sofa pillows."

I smiled, thinking about Judy in her pristine mini-mansion on the golf course, expertly plumping pillows and positioning them just so. Scott had nailed it.

"I'd let her go," said Scott. "But it's your call."

Scott dropped me off at the office. Before pulling away, he rolled down his window and said, "Hey Lea, watch your back."

Redemption Comes in Many Forms

1986-1992

The law firm had my back.

When I called Marianne Berry, the firm's legal administrator, to tell her that I was checking into rehab and ask if she would hold my job, she said, "Yes, you can come back when you complete the thirty-day treatment program."

The following day she called me to tell me that she'd spoken to the executive committee and the firm would pay for my treatment. "We are all rooting for you," Marianne said.

I hung up the phone, not believing what I'd heard. Why would the law firm pay for my rehab? I wasn't a partner, an associate or even a paralegal who billed by the hour. I dwelled at the bottom of the law firm food chain. I felt humbled by their generosity.

Three days later I voluntarily committed myself to the 30-day addiction treatment program at the Ogallala Community Hospital.

The director of the program, a former bull rider named Gregg, met me at the front door of the hospital. He stood with his hands on his hips, giant rodeo belt buckle glinting in the sunlight.

He told Wayne, "I got her from here. You can go on home."

After dropping my duffle bag in a yellow-green room with large windows, Gregg brought me into his office to complete the pre-treatment assessment.

"You ever black out?" he asked.

"A few times."

"How many is a few?" He looked up from his yellow legal pad with a raised eyebrow when I didn't respond.

"I don't know," I said.

"That sounds like more than a few," he said.

I had never actually counted, but as I mentally scrolled through the last few years I realized that I'd blacked out at least twenty or thirty times. But I wasn't going to tell him that.

He put down his pen and leaned back in his chair. "I don't think you can get sober," he said. "You're smart, young and pretty. Life still looks shiny from where you sit."

"It's not that shiny," I said, remembering the events that landed me in his office.

"How old are you?"

"Twenty."

"Just wait fifteen or twenty years, after you've lost a few jobs and probably a few husbands. Wait till your skin turns yellow and you bloat up like a balloon because your liver doesn't work right." He puffed out his cheeks and held his hands above his midsection, sweeping them from side to side to bring home the point about bloating. "That's when people are motivated to get sober."

I wasn't sure how to respond. Was this some weird attempt at reverse psychology? Or was he already setting the expectation that I'd likely fail?

"I don't know if I'm an alcoholic," I said. Even though I suspected that I might be, I still clung to the hope that my drinking would decline once my circumstances improved, when life didn't feel so scary.

He leaned across his desk. "Why don't you try not drinking for a while and see how you feel?"

There were only three other people in the treatment program besides me: the son of a local dentist who had gotten hooked on his father's pharmacopeia, a woman about my age who liked to cut herself, and a sixty-five-year-old cowboy with nicotine-stained fingers who'd almost frozen to death when he passed out in the alley behind his favorite bar on New Year's Eve.

My first day in group therapy, after I'd given the short version of why I was there, the old cowboy turned to me and said in his raspy voice, "I probably spilled more beer than you ever drank," and then laughed until he started coughing and hacking up the remnants of the last thousand packs of cigarettes he'd smoked.

Compared to him I was a neophyte.

The routine at the hospital consisted of private sessions with Gregg, group therapy and occasional excursions to Walgreens or to Nelson's Dairy Crème, where I'd gotten my first job at age twelve. The soft serve dip cones at Nelson's were the best in town.

As instructed, I read the AA Big Book and wrote in the journal Gregg provided. But instead of honestly assessing my drinking, I spent most of the group sessions cherry-picking reasons why I wasn't an alcoholic. I'd never stolen from my family like the pharmacist's son. I'd never spent a night in jail like the cowboy. I'd never been committed to the psyche ward like our resident cutter. My list of "terrible things that happened while drinking" couldn't compete with the lists compiled by my fellow inmates.

Maybe I wasn't an alcoholic.

When I thought about not drinking, it was like thinking about being dead – a totally abstract concept. I couldn't imagine a life without alcohol. I'd never kissed a guy, danced or been intimate without a solid helping of liquid courage.

What would I do if I didn't drink? The weekends would hold no meaning. I'd never be able to ring in the New Year at a big party or drink green beer on St. Patrick's Day or participate in wedding toasts and backyard soirées. How would I meet men? Wasn't I too young to be an alcoholic? Maybe I was just a heavy drinker, going through a bad phase.

But by the end of the third week, four realizations cracked the façade of my denial and the truth began to seep in.

The first came in the form of a question. If I wasn't an alcoholic, would the thought of not drinking bother me this much? The logical answer was no, it would not.

Second, Gregg said something in our private session that resonated: holding on to resentment was like taking poison and expecting the other person to die. He highlighted his point by adding, "If you keep drinking because you're angry about what all those people did to you, then you're the loser. Except for your dad, they are getting on with their lives. If you don't sober up, you'll end up dead, in jail or insane. Is that what you want?

No. I hated to lose. And I hated the idea of Barbara and her son reveling in my self-destruction.

Third, the increased frequency of blackouts scared me. Even when I wanted to drink in moderation, I could not. I had no control. Gregg made me write about how I felt that morning when I woke up at the El Paso Airport Hilton. As I committed that experience to paper, my stomach churned with fear. I never wanted to feel that way again.

Finally, during that third week in the hospital, we took a trip to the cowboy's ranch for our Wednesday excursion. He was concerned about his chickens. A neighbor had promised to feed them, but he didn't trust the man.

I would never forget the sight of that old man standing in front of the barn, in a frayed flannel shirt, stooped over with his back to the wind, clutching an almost empty burlap sack in one hand, reaching deep inside with the other, scratching the coarse fabric to loosen the last bits of chicken feed clinging to the side. His hand-rolled cigarette bobbed up and down as he called to his flock, five scrawny brown hens and a shiny-feathered black rooster, the last occupants of his once prosperous ranch.

In our group sessions, the cowboy talked about his five ex-wives, the six kids who no longer spoke to him and his family ranch. Back in the 1960s, his place had been one of the largest cattle operations in the county. But twenty-five years of bad decisions and neglect had whittled it down; only a house in need of a paint, a listing barn and a handful of chickens remained.

Gregg constantly preached about alcoholism being a one-way road to places most people didn't want to go, but it wasn't until I sat on the sagging porch of the cowboy's house and watched him feed his chickens that it became real.

I saw my future in the bent form of that old man.

That evening, after a dinner, I went to the hospital chapel. The AA Big Book said that if you asked God to remove your desire to drink, he would. I doubted if an all-powerful benevolent God existed, and if he did, he probably didn't care much for me.

But that night, I faked it.

I prayed.

I asked God to remove my desire to drink, and I promised that if I got another chance to build a life, I would not waste it.

The next day, in the group circle I said, "My name is Lea and I'm an alcoholic."

Back in El Paso, I attended AA meetings and hung out at the AA clubhouse in my free time. Occasionally I'd go out to bars with my friends. As the designated driver, I became more popular than I'd been when I drank. But drinking club soda for hours and hauling drunk people from one bar to another quickly lost its allure.

My AA sponsor explained that long-term sobriety depended on my willingness to undergo a searching and fearless moral inventory of myself, to admit and make amends for the things I had done to others and to forgive people who had harmed me.

I found the first part cathartic; once I started admitting my transgressions and making amends, it got easier and easier. I hadn't realized the emotional toll that secrets exact on the keeper, or how much energy I'd spent managing the tapestry of excuses and lies I'd told during my years of drinking.

Forgiveness was much harder. My mother, Barbara, her son, my father. How could I forgive the things they'd done?

Over a cup of bitter coffee at a pancake house near the AA clubhouse, I told my sponsor, "I can't forgive them. I can't say what they did to me is okay."

My sponsor said, "Forgiving and condoning are not the same thing. The act of forgiveness doesn't erase their sins, but it will save your life."

I leaned back in the booth and shook my head. "I don't know how to forgive," I said. "I say the words, I write them in my journal, but I don't mean any of it."

"You have to pray for them, it's the only way."

She instructed me to make a list of everything I wanted in my life, my professional and academic goals, vacations, material possessions, relationships and experiences I wanted to have.

"For the next sixty days, before you go to bed, pray that the people who hurt you get the things on your list," she said. "Pray for them one at a time and say their names when you do."

I poured sugar in the coffee, trying to make it more palatable, and considered the assignment. I doubted it would work.

"I don't think I can pray for them and mean it," I said.

"You don't have to mean it," she said. "Just do it and keep doing it until that changes."

I prayed.

When I prayed for my father, I pictured him alive, sitting across from me at Daylight Donuts, flashing his crooked smile as I told him all the wonderful things I wished for him. That make-believe conversation always evoked tears. I imagined him holding my hand, the way he had when he walked me to kindergarten, and gently squeezing my fingers before letting go.

My sponsor had been right. As I prayed, my anger morphed into something that more closely resembled pity. I began to see my tormentors in a different light, as sick people in need of help rather than monsters. They wrestled with demons of their own. I felt profoundly grateful that I didn't inhabit their skin.

* * *

Because the spring semester at UTEP had started while I'd been in the hospital, I worked full-time at the law firm for several months.

Marianne, the firm's administrator, took me on as a pet project. We hadn't been close before I went to rehab, but upon my return, she assumed the role of mentor-mother-protector and took every opportunity to teach me how to navigate the world.

A professional woman who had risen through the ranks in a male-dominated profession, Marianne graduated from college during WWII, divorced an abusive husband in the 1950s and raised her daughter as a single, working parent.

She didn't take crap from anyone.

Her advice ranged from, "Always polish your shoes, scuffed shoes are an outward sign of internal sloppiness," to "Never join women's organizations, women have no power, go where the men are."

She told me to stand tall with my shoulders back, to never buy black umbrellas because men would steal them, to give money to beggars because it might be me standing on the corner someday, to not wear white shoes before Memorial Day, to floss my teeth daily, to never give up my ability to earn money because money was the currency of freedom, to avoid skirts that accentuated panty lines, to only date men who were crazier about me than I was about them, to rinse out my nylons in the sink after each wearing, to hold my emotions in check in the workplace, and to love myself fiercely. "If you don't love yourself, honey, no one else will."

I stayed sober.

I graduated with honors from UTEP in May 1989 with a degree in Political Science and a nomination for Top Ten Seniors.

After seeing the day-to-day realities of a lawyer's life, I chose not to go to law school. I longed to see the world, not be confined to a dusty library, so I applied to the Thunderbird School of International Management and was accepted for the 1989 summer session.

Thunderbird, a top-rated international business school, was the right launching pad for someone intent on working abroad. Since more than half the students hailed from other countries, simply being there counted as an international experience. I took the maximum number of hours possible, borrowed more money than I thought I'd ever be able to repay, and graduated in August 1990.

During my last semester, I accepted all the interview invitations that came my way, talking to companies that sold soda flavorings, financial services, consumer goods and commodities. I was leaning toward commodities trading when, a month before graduation, I received a call from a software company in Berkeley, California regarding a marketing job.

It was July and 115 degrees in Phoenix. I'd never been to California, so I took the interview more as a break from the heat than out of a genuine interest in working at a software company. To my surprise, I immediately connected with the CEO, a serial entrepreneur who, over a plate of the best Thai food I'd ever tasted, convinced me that his company could defeat Microsoft in the operating system business. It speaks to my naiveté that I bought into his story.

That company was Geoworks. They offered me a decent salary and stock options, and I took it.

Before driving to Berkeley, I returned to El Paso to pick up some boxes I'd stored in Marianne's garage. On my last day, she insisted on taking me shopping to buy clothes for my new job. I had barely enough money to rent an apartment, only one suit and a few dresses and blouses that could pass for professional clothing.

"We need to get your ready for work," she said in a tone that did not invite discussion. "I'd like to buy you a few things as a graduation gift."

Marianne's "few things" turned into an entire wardrobe with accessories, jewelry and shoes. She helped me select all the pieces I'd need to for ten days without having to wear the same outfit twice. Like Wayne with his four-thousand-dollar check and the law firm partners who'd paid for me to go to rehab, Marianne saw someone in need and chose to help.

She sent me into the world with just the right armor, knowing that self-confidence was the best protection a girl could have.

* * *

In 1986, Wayne and my mother left the ranch and moved to her house in Ogallala. Her mood swings and violent outbursts had worsened, and Wayne thought living in town, closer to her friends, would help.

He turned over the ranch to his middle son and became a long-haul trucker. It gave him the chance to see the country after spending years confined to a small patch of ground.

The geographical cure didn't work. In the spring of 1989, Wayne and my mother separated.

Around the same time, my mother got into a horrible fight with my youngest sister Lara, then a high school senior, and threw her out of the house. When I ventured to Ogallala for Lara's graduation, I found both Lara and Wayne living in the same row of efficiency apartments a few blocks from my mother's house.

I did not speak to my mother for more than two years, going through graduate school and the move to California parentless.

The incident with Lara and her decision to divorce Wayne served as fresh reminders of my mother's destructive capabilities. I wanted no part of it. It seemed like she needed to test those she loved, to see if they would stand by her no matter how horribly she treated them. Three husbands and four children had flunked the test, and she found herself alone, for the first time in twenty-six years.

My mother started a nonprofit, a crisis intervention organization for victims of domestic violence in Western Nebraska. She sent me long letters describing her work with battered women and children and the men's anger management classes she taught. Somehow, through that process, she learned how to manage her own anger.

Wayne divorced my mother, but he didn't divorce me or my siblings. We stayed in each other's lives and avoided the topic of my mother. He remarried a few years later, to a wonderful woman named Marilyn and she became part of our family too.

In the early 1990s, my mother discovered radical Christianity, joined Aglow International and became a warrior for Christ. She began praying for our family and going to church after years of avoiding organized religion. Her shelves groaned under the weight of prayer books. The raging monster of my childhood transformed into a Sunday morning greeter.

She asked for my forgiveness.

I gave her another chance.

* * *

My two years at Geoworks got me hooked on start-up software companies. I would work for three more in the nineties, rising from a junior marketing person to a vice president before my thirty-third birthday. I learned to write business plans and pitch investors while working for an internet start-up in 1996. By the time I landed at Mordix, I had helped raise more than twenty million dollars in venture capital.

And I got to see the world.

My jobs took me to all fifty states, to Europe, the Middle East, Africa, South America and the Pacific Rim. I stood on Cape Point in South Africa, where the Indian Ocean met the Atlantic, had dinner on the shore of Lake Geneva, walked on the beach in Rio, shopped at Harrod's, jogged through Central Park, hiked down the Haleakalā volcano in Hawaii, rode on top of a bus through the jungle in Belize, bought earrings at the gold souk in Dubai, took a train through the Andes to Machu Picchu and explored a gold mine in South Africa. I did more and saw more than I'd ever envisioned during those long days in the hayfields.

I loved the start-up technology world, the complexity, the pace, the smart people and the ability to win through building a better mousetrap. Who you were today didn't dictate who you would be tomorrow. Technology companies offered forgiveness to those who had stumbled, opportunities for those with good ideas and redemption for those willing to take risks.

Finally, I'd found a place to thrive.

It's Only Crazy If It Doesn't Work

Dallas, Texas – January 2004

Ronnie and Mr. Glasauer thrived on pushing the boundaries of convention. At the end of our first year in business, they requested that Ruedger and I come to Schwaebisch Hall. They wanted to discuss a new financing option they were evaluating for companies in their portfolio.

My mother volunteered to stay with Will since John was out of town. Our relationship had improved over the years. My mother still had control issues. Rather than tyrannize my siblings and me with violent tantrums, she passed along directives from God, an annoying but manageable situation. I maintained my boundaries, but I didn't keep her away from Will. I wanted him to have a grandmother.

Ruedger and I made the trip to Schwaebisch Hall at the end of January.

Ronny and Glasauer had abandoned the dinged-up offices by the highway and moved into a beautiful historic building not far from the Marktplatz and St. Michael's church. As had become our habit, Ruedger and I stopped at St. Michael's to light several candles on the way to the meeting. I lit an entire row of small votives for an increase in sales and, on the way out the door, dropped an extra five Euros in the offering box for good measure.

Glasauer greeted us with cappuccinos, a heaping plate of butter cookies and an interesting proposal. "I think many of the small shareholders in our current fund might be interested in buying your stock," he said. "We want to make a direct offer to them."

I tried to think through the consequences of selling our shares to the public. In the U.S., the Securities and Exchange Commission

(SEC) prohibited the sale of shares in private companies to non-qualified investors, people with less than a million dollars in assets and annual income of less than two hundred and fifty thousand dollars. I didn't know how it worked in Germany, but they had to have similar protections.

Glasauer seemed to anticipate my train of thought. "As long as the shareholder is not a U.S. citizen and doesn't have a bank account in the U.S., then it's not a problem. The SEC regulations don't apply."

"What about German regulations?" I said.

"We aren't selling shares in a German company, so the German regulations don't apply either." He smiled and winked at me, then took a sip of his cappuccino.

Clever.

Ruedger and I left their offices after agreeing to think it over. We promised to come back in the morning with a decision.

"You know this is a crazy idea," I said as we turned the corner to the Marktplatz. Small trucks lined both sides of the open square where a farmer's market was in full swing. The smell of fried onions filled the air.

"It's only a crazy idea if it doesn't work," said Ruedger. "And I don't think it will cost much to find out."

There was a difference between my legal obligations as a CEO and what I considered to be my ethical obligations as a person. Lingualcare was a high-risk investment. Should we be selling shares to small, unsophisticated shareholders?

As we walked back to the hotel, I thought about the potential pitfalls of a quasi-public offering, including being sued in a foreign language and institutional investors shunning us because we had too many small investors on our cap table – the list of all shareholders and the number of shares they owned. But we needed money to support our growing business, and at that moment I didn't have a better or faster way to raise it.

Over plates of pork medallions and spätzle at the Golden Adler, Ruedger and I debated what to do.

"Ronnie admitted that Glasauer hopes we will sell enough shares to create a market, and then float a much bigger public offering later in the year," said Ruedger.

"It's too early," I said. "We're not big enough. We don't have the infrastructure to support it."

"It didn't stop the dotcom guys," said Ruedger. "At least we have a product that works."

He had a valid point.

I switched gears. "How are we even going to deal with hundreds of small German shareholders?"

We needed two million dollars. Without a minimum purchase amount, we could potentially have hundreds of shareholders. How would a professional investor react to that? They equated more shareholders to more risk. This could make our already hairy deal look like a giant fur ball.

"Do you have a better solution?" asked Ruedger.

"No," I admitted. "This just seems extreme."

"Glasauer will guarantee half a million toward the offering because he knows preparing for it will consume a lot of time, time we can't spend looking for other investors."

"Could this trigger the convertible notes?" I said, finally seeing a bright spot in what looked like a murky, bubbling cauldron of risk.

"Yes."

We'd used convertible notes, debt instruments, for all the investments so far. An equity investment of more than half a million dollars would trigger the notes and convert those debt holders to stockholders, improving our balance sheet.

After dinner, I called our corporate attorney, explained the situation and asked the only question that truly mattered to me.

"Can I go to jail for this?"

"No," he said. "It's perfectly legal if no one is a U.S. citizen or has a bank account over here. Make sure they sign a statement to that effect when they execute the subscription documents."

The next morning, we shook hands with Glasauer and went to work on the offering. According to Glasauer, the key to a successful offering was an impressive-looking brochure. He had people to write the marketing copy, in German, and compile all the disclaimers. They tasked Ruedger and me with producing charts, graphs and photos.

When I got back to Dallas, I hired a photographer who came to the clinic and photographed Ruedger and me in our best suits, hands fully visible to prove our honesty. We commandeered all the employees, contractors and friends of the company to pose for pictures, some in dental chairs, others filling chairs in the clinic waiting room or at desks looking focused.

By the time Mr. Glasauer and his marketing agency finished making the brochure, it looked so impressive I would have bought more stock in the company if I'd had the money.

The offering yielded a million and a half dollars, enough to keep us afloat for another year. It also added almost three hundred shareholders.

Ruedger sanitized the cap table by inserting one line that said, "German Shareholders" and put the long list of names in a linked worksheet. When an investor dug in during due diligence, they would find the three hundred German shareholders, but hopefully it wouldn't scare anyone away at first glance.

When You See a Fine Line, Walk It

Dallas, Texas – February 2004

We opened the clinic in late February with Dr. Sam and his father as our resident orthodontists. They agreed to give us one half-day per week to start, Friday afternoons. The elder Dr. Wednesday would serve as his son's backup on the last Friday of the month when Dr. Sam taught orthodontic classes at his alma mater.

In exchange for Dr. Sam's commitment, we offered to pay him cash for all the services he performed on our behalf and gave him a pile of stock options.

During the negotiation, it concerned me that most of his questions revolved exclusively around money. He asked how much he could expect to make in the clinic each month, what I thought the stock options would be worth and if we would increase his lecture fees once our sales grew. He had his sights set on a new lake house and hoped we would provide the means to buy it.

Walking a fine line, I answered his questions as best I could. Yes, I think the clinic *could* be successful and you *could* make lots of money. Yes, the stock *could* be valuable. Yes, we *could* pay more money for lecturing as the company grows. Sure, you *might* make enough to buy a new lake house.

I feared he didn't hear the qualifiers.

Ideally, Dr. Sam would join the team because he believed in our mission, to help change the status quo. Given the uncertain trajectory of a start-up company, I feared that if he was only in it for the money, we would disappoint him.

* * *

Ruedger came to Dallas for investor meetings after our clinic grand opening. While he was in town, Judy pulled him aside for a confidential conversation.

Ruedger held the title Chairman of the Board, so technically I reported to him. Judy approached him on that level. She told him I was too young and inexperienced to be running the company, that it would be best to put her in charge and make me her subordinate. She cited multiple instances of my incompetence and provided Ruedger with a file folder containing "evidence."

That day, I arrived at the office after 1:00. I'd volunteered to make homemade pizza for Will's Montessori class and had stayed to clean-up. Flexibility was one of the few perks of my job, allowing me to occasionally act like a mom who didn't work.

Ruedger told me about the meeting as soon as I dropped my briefcase on the desk, erasing the happy glow I'd brought back from the classroom of kids who had devoured my pizzas.

Despite the warning from Scott back in December, Judy's blatant betrayal shocked me. I sank into my office chair and rubbed my forehead with my fingertips. "How could she do that to me?"

Ruedger closed the door to our shared office. "She wants your job," he said, holding back the "I told you so" portion of the sentence, which I appreciated.

"What exactly did she say?" I asked. "What was in the folder?"

"It doesn't matter," said Ruedger. "She's gone and I shredded the folder."

"She's gone?

"I fired her."

"You what?"

"I fired her," he said in an even tone. "I took her keys to the clinic and her laptop and told her to empty her desk. She drove away fifteen minutes ago."

I contemplated calling Judy to tell her I was sorry, even though I wasn't. Could we still be friends? Did I even want to be friends? What had I done to deserve that kind of betrayal?

"Do you think there will be any backlash from the real estate guys?" I said, immediately going to the worst possible scenario.

"If anyone knows what she's like," said Ruedger, "her husband does." He added. "And just for the record, I think you are doing a perfect job."

* * *

In conjunction with opening the clinic, I hired my friend Katrina, a part-time PR and marketing person I'd worked with in the early 1990s. She immediately got us two local news segments and coverage in several regional newspapers and engaged a direct marketing agency that specialized in targeted mailings to create patient demand.

A week before our mailing was scheduled to drop, I received a call from the owner of the marketing agency. "You have a problem," he said. "I know Dr. Sam and his dad. They don't advertise. I faxed your mail piece over to their office this morning. His dad told me under no circumstances could we send it out."

"I'll get right back to you."

I pulled the contract from my file cabinet and searched for the marketing clause. It clearly stated that he agreed to help us market the clinic. Maybe he hadn't read it before signing it, but his initials graced the bottom of each page.

I called Dr. Sam.

"Hey Lea! How are you?" he said with a cheeriness I didn't share.

"Our marketing agency talked to your dad this morning about the clinic mailing. Your dad told them not to send it because you don't advertise."

"Yeah, that's right. Dad doesn't think it's professional."

"You signed off on the mailer." I said. I had the paperwork on my desk and his signature was on the back page.

"I was in kind of a hurry when Katrina showed me. I didn't realize my name was on it."

I had to bite my tongue. Not only was his name on the mailer, his picture was on it too. The professional headshot he'd provided occupied a quarter of the postcard.

"Can you just remove my name?"

I explained that in Texas a clinic couldn't legally advertise medical or dental services without including the name of the doctor in the advertisement.

"Well, then I guess you need to cancel it."

"We've already paid for it," I said. "Six thousand dollars up front."

"My next patient is here so I have to run," he said. "I know you'll figure it out."

I made a decision that I hoped I would not regret later. I told Katrina to print the postcards without Dr. Sam's name and photograph, to just use the clinic information.

She frowned. "You know we're not supposed to do that, right? It's not legal."

"We won't do it again, just this one time." I crossed my fingers and toes, hoping the postcard would not be delivered to a medical professional who would report us to the ethics board.

The mailing brought in leads, but not enough. Katrina and I struggled to fill the schedule. Dr. Sam also refused to talk to his referring dentists about our new clinic. He didn't want to poach patients from his other practices.

Katrina changed tactics. She focused on marketing our product instead of the clinic directly, advertising the Lingualcare System in local health and beauty magazines and including the clinic phone number in the call to action.

It was a fine line.

Technically we were advertising our product, not a medical or dental service. When a patient called to find a doctor in their area, we referred them to our clinic first, or to another orthodontist in Dallas if the clinic wasn't convenient.

Despite our efforts, Dr. Sam constantly complained about the lack of patient flow. He'd given up his Friday afternoons and the schedule was rarely full.

Month after month, the clinic lost money. The product sales side of the balance sheet looked much better. I wished I'd held my ground and not given in to Ruedger's clinic fever.

"How are things in Berlin?" I asked Ruedger one day in late May.

By my tone of voice, he knew something was wrong.

"What is it?" he said.

"I hate this clinic."

"Come on, Lea, we just opened a few months ago. You need to give it time."

"We have to start looking for the next big investor. We need more revenue to get a decent valuation. But instead of focusing on product sales, I'm worrying about how to get the next patient into this clinic and keep Dr. Sam from walking away because he'd rather play golf than waste his Friday afternoons here."

"You sound like you're ready to write it off," said Ruedger.

"We had six patients scheduled for today," I said. "At the last minute, Dr. Sam's assistant called in sick. Cary had an on-site training scheduled in Houston, so she couldn't cover. I had to call a placement agency and pay a fortune to get a substitute."

"What do you want me to do?' he said.

"I want you to come to Dallas and find patients for this fucking clinic. I want you to deal with the people who don't show up, and with Dr. Sam's weird habits."

"What weird habits?" he said.

"You don't want to know."

I wished I hadn't let that little bit of information slip. Just thinking about it made me feel icky. I didn't want to talk about it, especially with Ruedger.

"Tell me," said Ruedger.

"He spends a lot of time in the men's room." I said.

Ruedger laughed nervously. "Okay, and…?"

"Last Friday Cary came into my office and told me that we had patients waiting in two chairs. Dr. Sam had been in the men's room for more than twenty minutes." I continued, "She went into the clinic office to pull up a patient chart and the browser was open to a nasty porn site."

"No."

"I checked the browsing history. It was full of porn sites and websites for hooking up with people for one-night stands," I said. "He didn't even attempt to cover his tracks."

Not wanting to confront Dr. Sam and create a situation where he might leave me with no orthodontist to treat patients, I'd simply sent out a warning email to everyone in the company, including our contract employees and Dr. Sam. I said that starting the following Monday, our IT group was installing monitoring software on our server, and any website deemed "inappropriate" would be flagged and I'd get a weekly report. I reminded them of the policy in our employee handbook – misusing the company's network was grounds for termination.

Neither of us said anything for a moment.

"Do you hate me for making you open the clinic?" said Ruedger.

"No."

Maybe.

I'd Rather Pour Beer

Dallas, Texas – August 2004

Richard Riley kept his promise. He ignored our agreement and forbade the OrthoCo sales reps from mentioning our product to their customers. Of course, this didn't stop OrthoCo from cashing the commission checks and it didn't stop me from telling investors about our distribution partnership with them.

I focused on the positive. We no longer had to contend with the threat of an IP lawsuit, and the one customer lead they gave me at the New Orleans show, the Chicago doctor with five practices, turned out to be a cash cow. Every month he ordered more than anyone else.

Our doctor marketing campaigns were working well. The call to action was free online training, and we had a steady flow of new customers. The online training wasn't as comprehensive as what Dr. Hoffman offered in Europe, but we compensated by sending a clinical trainer to the doctor's first procedure.

Orthodontists who saw themselves as entrepreneurs turned out to be our best customers. They actively looked for new technologies that would give them a competitive edge when recruiting patients.

As our sales grew, I fantasized about other ways we could spend the OrthoCo commission payments: hire more sales reps, rent larger booths at the regional trade shows and boost our advertising. But until the IP threat went away, we would have to pay.

In August a gift arrived, unexpectedly, from the U. S. District Court for the Central District, Southern Division. As part of ongoing litigation, the court granted Align Technology's motion for summary judgment, declaring the patents OrthoCo held over their heads (and ours) to be invalid due to lack of enablement.

Davis Marks, formerly of OrthoCo, now President of Knightsbridge Orthodontics, forwarded the press release to me. The subject line read: *CALL ME.*

Lack of enablement – I'd never heard that term before. I didn't know what it meant in the context of patents, so I searched the Internet and learned that lack of enablement meant the patent holder had not made the invention described in their patent work. Moreover, no one else "skilled in the art" had demonstrated they could make it work either.

I emailed the press release to our patent attorney and followed up with a phone call.

"If the patents are invalid, they can't come after us, right?" I said.

"That's right," he said, "but if the court reinstates them on appeal, then they can assert the licensing agreement and request a royalty."

That's all I needed to know. We owed OrthoCo sixty days' notice to terminate and their lack of performance provided sufficient grounds. "Write them a termination letter today," I told him. "I want to end that agreement as soon as possible."

He stopped me before I could hang up. "Have you spoken to Thomas this week?"

"No. Why?"

"We have an upcoming deadline for a Canadian patent application. I expected to have a draft from him on Monday but have not received anything."

"When is it due?"

"Friday before 5:00 Eastern."

It was already Thursday in Berlin.

"If we don't file on Friday, we can't file at all," said the lawyer. "That particular deadline is written in stone."

I considered asking the lawyer to pull an all-nighter, but it would cost thousands of dollars. Surely Thomas had done the work; he must have forgotten to hit the send button.

Even though it was past midnight in Germany, I called Thomas. His cell phone went to voice mail. After leaving a message, I fired off a detailed email asking about the status of the Canadian patent application and letting him know we *had to* file by Friday. I copied Ruedger and the patent attorney and flagged it as urgent.

We wouldn't die without a Canadian patent; we only had two customers in Vancouver. But as a start-up technology company, intellectual property determined a large part of our value. We needed every patent we could get.

Ruedger called as I was driving home. "Thomas is freaking out," he said. "Hoffman kept him busy all week with European patent filings and he forgot about Canada."

"Why is he more concerned with Hoffman's patents than ours? Who's paying his salary anyway?" I said.

"You need to give him a break. He's stressed out. His wife filed for a divorce."

I immediately regretted my sarcasm. Thomas had only been married two years. Why hadn't I heard that he was having problems?

"We'll get the Canadian filing in on time," said Ruedger, "and when it's done I'll talk to Thomas about prioritizing."

The next morning Thomas called as I was packing Will's school lunch. Because we were running late, I almost didn't answer.

"Hey," I said, zipping the lunch box with the phone squeezed between my ear and my shoulder. I motioned for Will to head for the garage and handed him the lunch box.

"I submitted the Canadian patent application a few minutes ago," Thomas said. "I'm sorry. I've been distracted and I let it slip. That should have never happened."

"No harm, no foul," I said, sounding too much like a lawyer and not enough like a friend. I wanted to ask about his wife and express my sympathy for what was happening in his life, but he didn't give me a chance.

"Lea, I'm going to resign. My last day will be August 31st."

"That's not necessary. We all make mistakes." I checked to see if Will had buckled his seatbelt, then put Thomas on my speaker phone and maneuvered my car out of the garage.

"This company is killing me," he said, his voice tinged with sadness.

I had no argument to counter that statement.

"The stress is too much for me. I need to do something else."

If I were a good person, I would sympathize with my friend. He'd lost his marriage. His world was turning inside out. But I didn't feel sympathy, I felt anger.

The three of us started Lingualcare together, as a team. Thomas' defection would look terrible to investors. They would see it as a vote of no confidence from an insider. And what about the workload? Who would pick up his responsibilities? Thomas had been working on software development, manufacturing optimization and troubleshooting problems at Hoffman's lab.

And then it hit me – the equity. Thomas owned the same amount of founder's stock that Ruedger and I did. He could walk away, leave all the heavy lifting to Ruedger and me, and receive the same financial reward.

As soon as I got to my office, I closed the door and called Ruedger. "Is Thomas going to leave, or is this a knee-jerk reaction?" I said.

"He's done."

"Have you thought about his stock?" I said, hoping that he wouldn't find my question as predatory as it sounded.

"We need to get it back."

"Exactly," I said. "How do we do that?"

"We ask him," said Ruedger.

"He has no incentive to give it back."

Ruedger and I debated the possible scenarios. We had no leverage, but we both agreed that Thomas was fair-minded, not greedy. Perhaps we could appeal to his sense of fairness. He didn't deserve to keep his all of his founder's stock if he wasn't going to fulfill the obligations of a founder.

I'd foreseen this possibility two years ago but had done nothing to cover the potential downside. Neither had Ruedger. He didn't believe Thomas would bolt again.

When we'd conceived Lingualcare, the three of us agreed it would take a minimum of five years to build the company. We were eighteen months into this venture, so it seemed only right to ask Thomas to return two-thirds of his stock.

Over the weekend, Ruedger and I drafted the agreement we should have drafted in 2003. It stated that any founder who left before twenty-four months had to give back two-thirds of his or her stock. If a founder left before forty-two months they had to give back one-third.

Ruedger and I signed it.

Monday night Ruedger met Thomas at the same Italian place where we'd struck our original deal. He hoped the difficult conversation would be easier after a heavy meal and three or four beers. Ruedger called me after he left the restaurant. "Thomas signed the agreement."

"Was it bad?"

"He didn't see it coming, but once I put it on the table he accepted the logic," Ruedger said. "He would expect the same from you and me if we skipped out early."

What would I tell the employees? They loved Thomas.

Dr. Hoffman adored Thomas, he only tolerated Ruedger and me.

How would Thomas' departure impact the company's dynamics? What would it be like without him to provide a voice of reason or a deciding vote when Ruedger and I disagreed?

"I'm freaking out," I admitted.

Lingualcare was still fragile. We had big plans and not many people to help us accomplish them. With Thomas' departure there was one less competent warrior to charge into battle alongside us.

"Don't freak out today," said Ruedger. "Freak out tomorrow"

We both laughed. It broke the tension.

"I need to tell the employees. Wish me luck."

I rose from my desk and paced, looking out the window at the parking lot. The trees on the other side swayed as heavy gray clouds, moving across the sky, blocked the sun and deepened the green of the leaves. I mulled over how to break the news, wanting to frame Thomas' departure in the best possible light. I didn't want the team to lose confidence in our mission.

Before I could find the right words, Thomas sent a goodbye email to the whole company. I heard it ding in my inbox, opened it and had barely finished reading it when Cary knocked on my door.

"Should I be worried?" she said, succumbing to the age-old belief that the smartest rats abandoned the sinking ship first.

Choosing my words carefully, because I knew they would be repeated to everyone in the company and probably most of our customers, I said, "Thomas isn't leaving because there's something wrong with Lingualcare. He's under tremendous personal stress and needs a break."

"Did you know he's going to bartend at a hotel?" Cary said.

"You talked to him?" I said, caught off guard.

"He called me before he sent the email."

I launched into the best pep talk I could muster, rattling off a long list of milestones we'd reached. She nodded as I spoke, conceding that we'd come a long way since that first procedure in Dr. Lemond's office.

I hadn't heard about Thomas' post-Lingualcare plans. Bartending would lower his stress. Maybe he'd even get free drinks. But what did that say about Lingualcare's prospects? Was pouring beer and polishing glassware more enticing than being an executive at a start-up company? Had he lost confidence in our dream of becoming multimillionaires, deciding to settle for the contents of a tip jar instead?

After Cary left, I thought about the daily stress that plagued Ruedger and me. The constant hunt for money, dealing with Hoffman's mercurial moods – one day he loved us, the next day he despised us – and constantly pretending that everything was going according to plan when it wasn't. The word anxiety didn't have enough syllables to properly convey the constant inner rumblings that stalked me day and night.

Sometimes I felt more like an illusionist than a CEO. Pay no attention to that dwindling bank account behind the curtain...

I didn't have much time to dwell on the subtext of Thomas' leaving because, unfortunately, his departure wasn't our most pressing problem. Back in June, we had started missing delivery dates and the problem had continued to snowball. August was the worst month for on-time deliveries we'd ever had.

As Hoffman's European business grew, he pushed our orders to the back of the production line, shipping orders for his high-margin European customers first. On top of that, U.S. Customs frequently stopped our packages for additional inspection – fallout from September 11th, 2001.

In an orthodontic practice, time was money. If a doctor had a patient scheduled for a procedure and the product didn't arrive on time, they would have to reschedule at the last minute and might not be able to fill the appointment slot.

We had to make a change. With our exclusive OrthoCo partnership about to end, I called Davis Marks. He had been sending me regular updates on his progress at Knightsbridge and suggestions about how we could work together. I was most interested in his company's manufacturing facility in Mexicali, Mexico. Davis told me they had unused manufacturing space and a highly skilled dental labor force.

"How long will it take you guys to get out of the OrthoCo agreement?" asked Davis.

"Sixty days," I said. "We already sent the termination letter. But our biggest issue is manufacturing, not distribution."

"What's going on?"

"We have no ability to impact our manufacturing costs or our delivery dates," I said. "And we have currency risk. It's a bad optic for potential investors."

The Euro, which had once been our friend, had turned on us. It was $1.05 back in early 2003, but by mid-2004 had risen to $1.35. As a small company with limited cash, we could not hedge the currency market. I downplayed the risk when investors raised it as a concern, but I knew the days of buying in Euros and selling in dollars needed to end.

"Next time Ruedger is in the country, come to California, meet Bart, our new CEO, and we'll take you to Mexicali to see the plant. We can talk about a deal."

The thought of no longer manufacturing in Germany brightened my mood. I hated relying on Hoffman's goodwill and scrambling when packages got sucked into the black hole of U.S. Customs. Having our factory two time zones away instead of seven, and being able and optimize our cost of goods and reach profitability, would transform the company and give us access to a whole new spectrum of investors.

I also liked the idea of working with an experienced team who understood the orthodontic market. Being a CEO is a lonely business. Having partners to collaborate with and who would bring new ideas to the table would give Lingualcare a much-needed boost.

A deal with Knightsbridge looked like a silver bullet.

You're the One Who's Going to Jail

Mexicali, Mexico – September 2004

Ruedger had never been to Mexico, or any third world country for that matter, and he nervously scanned the landscape as we drove down a dirt road, past half-constructed cinderblock houses, emaciated stray dogs and battered pick-up trucks.

"Are you sure you know where you're going?" he asked.

"This is the right street," I said, pointed at a street sign.

We passed a woman in a bright pink apron hanging a freshly killed chicken from a clothesline in her front yard. Blood poured from its headless neck. Ruedger put his hands over his face and then pushed his fingers through his hair. I waited for a snarky comment but he said nothing.

Having toured several German factories, notably a spotlessly clean Mercedes-Benz plant in Stuttgart where they stamped the Mercedes three-point star on the sugar cubes at the coffee bar, I understood Ruedger's frame of reference. Most German factories were clean, clean, clean, open, bright and filled with natural light. They were located on well-tended streets or next to green fields, not on dirt roads lined with cinderblock shacks that moonlighted as butcher shops.

"Look, there's a Bosch facility," said Ruedger, pointing at a modern-looking building a few blocks away with a large red Bosch logo painted on the side. His face visibly brightened at the familiar brand.

"You would be surprised at how many international companies have plants in Mexico," I said, trying to put a positive spin on the dusty landscape. "Mexico is known for high quality handwork. All the orthodontic companies have plants here, including OrthoCo."

I spotted a bright blue concrete building with a Knightsbridge logo and pulled into the parking lot. Two smaller buildings, with a basketball court in the center, made up the complex.

The aroma of Mexico hit my nose as soon as I got out of the car. It smelled like every third world country I'd ever visited, an unmistakable combination of diesel, propane, wood smoke, dust and rotting food.

Sean Guthrie, Knightsbridge's vice president of operations, greeted us as soon as we walked through the front door. Tall and fit with brown hair and a graying moustache, Sean wore sensible shoes and a Blackberry clipped to his belt. Like Davis Marks, Sean was an OrthoCo alumnus.

He ushered us to a freshly painted room with a chipped wood veneer conference table and metal folding chairs. "The new conference room furniture hasn't arrived yet, so we're improvising," he said as he pulled out a folding chair. "You guys want coffee?"

Ruedger always said yes to coffee. Because of my intimate familiarity with the microbes that lived in Mexican water, I hesitated.

Sean seemed to read my mind. "We make it with filtered water," he said.

"I'd love some," I said.

We sipped our coffee while Sean told us about the changes underway in the factory. "We can compete with major orthodontic manufacturers," he said. "Including my old friends at OrthoCo."

His phone rang and he left the room to take the call. When he came back he said, "Davis and Bart got a late start from Carlsbad, but they are on their way. Do you want to take a quick plant tour while we wait?"

We followed Sean into a wide, brightly lit, open space that housed rows of large computer-controlled machines. The new vinyl floors and freshly-painted walls gleamed. The workers wore matching baby blue smocks over their street clothes along with hair nets and safety glasses. Sean handed us white lab coats and safety glasses at the door.

Machines hummed. Spanish music drifted through the room. The room smelled of oil and disinfectant.

Ruedger peppered Sean with questions. I listened, nodded and tried to look impressed as Sean showed us each manufacturing line and explained its function. I had no ability to judge the value of the machines, only the relaxed faces of the employees. If working there made them happy then it couldn't be too bad.

At the far end of the manufacturing floor, we entered a smaller room with long tables occupied mostly by women. Some welded tiny brackets under brightly lit magnifying glasses, while others performed quality assurance, inspecting the parts against a large schematic tacked in front of each workstation. Sean stopped, took a just-welded bracket from the pre-inspection bin and put it in my hand.

"Since I took over down here, our rejection rate has dropped eighty percent," he said. "Our quality rivals OrthoCo's."

He led us through the company cafeteria, loud with lunchtime chatter, past a white door with a red cross painted on it. Sean stopped in front of the door and said, "This is our medical clinic. We pay a doctor to come in two days a week and provide free medical care to all of our employees and their families."

Ruedger smiled at me and winked. He liked it.

I'd been skeptical an hour ago as I'd driven over the international bridge and navigated the dirt road to the facility, expecting to be disappointed. But as we walked outside, across the basketball court to a smaller building, I felt excited. These guys were underdogs, like us, and like us, they were itching to prove they could compete with companies twenty times their size.

Sean unlocked the steel door and we entered a musty, cavernous room with peeling paint and an exposed ceiling. Bare bulbs cast circles of light on a concrete floor stained with rust and oil. "This used to be a storage area," he said. "I know it doesn't look like much, but from what I know about Hoffman's operation in Germany, I think it's big enough to accommodate your manufacturing line."

Ruedger paced the length and width of the room and peered into the dark corners. He took in the details, and then he planted his hands on his hips and nodded. "I like it," he said. "I think it's perfect."

I didn't have the imagination needed to mentally transform this dirty storeroom into a German-style manufacturing facility, but I trusted Ruedger's judgment. If he liked it, I liked it.

Sean deposited us in the conference room and went to find Bart and Davis.

After he closed the door, I said, "I'll bet we could drop our cost of goods in half down here."

"Can they find engineers and dental lab techs with the skills we need?" said Ruedger.

I didn't know the composition of the local talent pool, but more than a million people lived in Mexicali. There had to be forty or fifty CAD engineers and dental technicians who needed work.

Before we could discuss it further, Bart and Davis arrived.

An investment banker by trade, a legitimate one who went to MIT and worked on Wall Street, Bart had run several companies and led turnarounds like the kind needed at Knightsbridge. He was in his early forties with white-blond hair, blue eyes and teeth so perfect they had to be veneers.

Bart got straight to the point. "We'd like to put together a proposal for distributing your products in the U.S. and doing your manufacturing."

There was a sharp knock on the door.

Sean got up to answer it. A woman came in carrying a platter piled high with carne asada tacos, cans of Coke and plastic containers filled with fresh guacamole and pico de gallo.

"I hope you don't mind," said Sean. "I ordered lunch for us."

Ruedger grabbed a taco from the platter.

I hesitated, even though the meat smelled fantastic.

Davis nudged me. "Don't be afraid. We order from this restaurant all the time. No one has ever gotten sick."

The tacos tasted as good as they smelled.

After grabbing a second taco from the platter Ruedger asked, "Would you consider investing in the manufacturing line in exchange for equity? You purchase the equipment, we reimburse you with Lingualcare stock, and then we agree to buy product from you at a fixed price."

Bart nodded. "Absolutely."

Before the last taco disappeared, the five of us had talked through the equipment and types of skilled workers needed to manufacture our product in Mexico and outlined deal points so we could start working on a contract.

I thought a manufacturing partnership made sense. But I would not sign up for another distribution agreement like the one we'd had with OrthoCo.

Since the manufacturing discussion had consumed most of our time, Davis and I scheduled a phone call to discuss marketing and sales.

As Ruedger and I sat in traffic on the international bridge, waiting to cross back into the United States, I thought about the path to independence that Knightsbridge had proposed. A smile crossed my face. I tapped my fingers on the steering wheel in time with the music on the radio. If it worked, our business would look completely different in a year. How great would that be?

A little boy of about eight or nine ran up to my window and held up a box of individually wrapped Chiclets, bright-colored little rectangles glinting in the sun.

"Chicklet! Chiclets!" he yelled as he placed his small palm against my window.

I rolled down the window, handed him a five-dollar bill and shook my head when he reached into the box to give me a handful. His face lit up and he ran to the next car.

I didn't want any Chiclets, I just wanted to share my joy.

* * *

That night, back at the Westin in the Gaslamp Quarter, Ruedger and I met at the hotel restaurant for dinner. Over a plate of antipasti and a basket of bread, we discussed the possible implications of doing a deal with Davis and Bart.

The cases Dr. Hoffman produced for us consumed manufacturing capacity he could use for his own, higher-revenue cases, so in theory he should be happy to get rid of us. But both of us worried about Hoffman's reaction. Would he make the transition hard? Would he help us or impede us? Worse, would he stop manufacturing our cases while we built the factory in Mexico?

Before the main courses arrived, I asked the question that had been rolling around my brain since we walked the factory floor with Sean. "Do you know how to make the product?"

Ruedger squinted at me.

"Let me rephrase that," I said. "Last time I was in Bad Erlangen, Hoffman had not documented his manufacturing processes in detail. Has that changed?"

"Six weeks ago, I hired a consultant to go there and write work instructions. I knew we would need them to establish a quality management system for the FDA. So yes, I know how to make the product."

Rather than feel happy because the consultant's work would make it much easier to transfer production, I felt angry. How could he have hired an expensive consultant without telling me?

"And you were going to tell me…when?"

"She's working for stock right now, it won't cost any money for a while," he said, as if that should be the end of the discussion.

"Why didn't you tell me?" I asked

"Because I knew you would freak out."

I had been aware for the last year that we needed to invest in a formal quality management system to meet FDA's guidelines for Good Manufacturing Practices. When Ruedger first told me about the requirement, and his estimate of a thirty-thousand-dollar price tag to put one in place, I argued against it. After all, it was Hoffman's responsibility. He was the manufacturer. No one was complaining so his quality controls must be sufficient.

At that time, we didn't have the thirty thousand dollars, so I swept it to the side. I thought Ruedger had also, but apparently not.

"She isn't charging us any money?" I asked, pushing him to make a full disclosure.

"You think this is optional? It's not optional. It's the law. It's your law." His voice rose and his cheek muscles flexed. "If the FDA audits our operations and we don't have a robust quality management system, we're in trouble; they will shut us down."

"But you said the FDA rarely inspects businesses that make Class I devices." We made orthodontic braces, not cancer drugs or pacemakers. Surely the FDA had bigger fish to fry.

"You just sent OrthoCo a termination letter. If they decided to make our lives miserable, they could call the FDA with an anonymous tip and we'd have an inspector at our office in a week," he said, holding his beer in a white-knuckled grip.

That point did not seem particularly relevant since he'd hired the consultant several weeks before I'd sent the termination letter, but he was right, reporting us to the FDA was definitely in OrthCo's playbook.

"I talked her into working for almost nothing, to help me out, to help us out. Yes, at some point you're going to have to pay her, not thirty thousand, maybe only fifteen and some stock. You should thank me, not give me a hard time."

"We don't have fifteen thousand dollars to spend on that," I said in a voice too loud for the hushed restaurant.

Ruedger raised his voice to match mine. "You're the fucking CEO. If the FDA shows up and finds us in violation, you're the one going to jail."

I felt like the breath had been knocked out of my lungs.

"Then you can have the fucking job back!" I threw my napkin down on the plate and left the restaurant.

On the elevator, I started to shiver. Had it been cold in the restaurant? My hands felt icy. I couldn't catch my breath. I tried to breathe deep, but the tightness in my chest only increased. When I got to my room I turned on the shower, undressed and stood under a hot stream of water.

Was this how it happened? The descent down the slippery slope? What would I tell the jury? Yeah, I knew it was iffy, but I thought the odds of being caught were slim, so I decided to do it anyway.

I won't get caught. Was that what my father had thought?

My legs didn't want to hold me anymore. I slid down the wall to the floor of the shower and pulled my knees to my chest. Despite the temperature of the water, I still felt cold inside, like no amount of heat could make my body warm again.

Then the sobs hit me, erupting from a place deep in my interior. I hadn't sobbed like that since the night my father died. My body shook, harder and harder as each scary thought rolled through my brain.

Jail. Financial ruin. Death.

Water pooled around my feet as images from my past and future swirled through my mind – my father sitting on the living room sofa, calmly telling me the FBI had tapped our phones; me standing in the hospital corridor numbly absorbing the news of his death; me alone in a jail cell, crayon drawings and photos of Will taped to the cinderblock walls above a narrow bunk bed, and my former Mordix colleagues gossiping about my downfall over decaf lattes at Starbucks – my carefully constructed life destroyed as irreparably as my father's. Was this the price of wanting to be somebody?

Through the hiss of the shower, I heard my cell phone ring. It was late in Dallas; John would already be in bed. It had to be Ruedger. Maybe he was calling to apologize. Maybe he was calling to check on me. Maybe he wanted to continue the fight.

He'd lost confidence. He no longer trusted me; that's why he'd been forced to go behind my back and hire the consultant. He had done the right thing when I would not.

I thought about Thomas. Maybe he'd resigned because he'd lost faith in me. Maybe he saw through my thin veneer of confidence, glimpsed the scared little girl disguised as a CEO. No wonder he walked away from the stock. He knew I lacked the power to make it valuable.

I stayed in the shower a long time, grateful for the seemingly endless supply of hot water. When I finally caught my breath and the sobs subsided, I stood up and turned off the water.

The display on my phone said I'd missed nine calls from Ruedger. I didn't want to talk to him, but I also didn't want to let him think I'd cut my wrists in the shower, so I called. A phone rang in the hallway.

"Are you outside my room?" I said as I looked out the peephole and saw him sitting against the wall opposite my door.

"I'm so sorry, Lea. I'm so sorry. I made the jail comment to get your attention, not to scare you to death. After you left the restaurant I remembered the story about your father and I felt like an idiot."

"It's okay, I deserved it," I said.

"Did you mean what you said about quitting?"

"Yes."

"Can we talk about this in person? Will you meet me in the lobby bar or at the pool?"

"The pool. Give me fifteen minutes."

Ruedger sat perched on the edge of the deep end, pants rolled up to his knees, bare feet dangling in the water, shoes and socks on the lounge chair behind him. He was drinking a beer. It reminded me of Hawaii, of him pulling off his shoes, running across the beach and standing in the surf staring up at the stars, exuding joy. But he didn't look particularly joyful as I sat next to him, cross-legged.

He handed me a small bottle of Perrier.

Ruedger never offered me alcohol. He'd noticed I didn't drink within a few weeks of meeting me, unlike friends I'd known for years who still offered me wine whenever I came over for dinner.

"You can't quit," he said. "I can't do this without you."

"You did it before, at Mordix," I said.

"I got kicked out of Mordix," he said. "I know how to write patents and build products, but not how to lead a U.S. company."

"Will you visit me in jail?"

"Stop."

"I'm in over my head," I said.

"You assume that if you don't know something, it makes you a loser," he said, looking down at the water and making small circles with his foot. "So you ignore what you don't understand, and fight me when I bring it to your attention."

I hated that he was right. Revealing my ignorance made me feel vulnerable to attack. But who did I think would lead the charge? Ruedger? So far, he had done nothing but support me, mistake after mistake.

"I can't believe you committed so much money without saying one word."

"I knew you would freak out."

"Better to ask forgiveness than permission?" I said.

"Having a quality system is a cost of doing business," said Ruedger, "like payroll taxes. You must pay them even though you might not want to. Would you skip paying the IRS?"

"Of course not," I said. Few things scared me more than the IRS.

"You can't skip this either."

Why was I so unwilling to admit my mistakes? Maybe because most rules felt more like guidelines to me, especially when ignoring them didn't cause injury.

I suspected my father had felt the same way. He'd probably believed that breaking a few banking laws and using the U.S. Post Office to do it wouldn't harm anyone. He probably didn't think of it as fraud, just a temporary measure to cover his cash shortfalls.

"What do I have to do?" I said.

"Stop giving me a hard time and pay the invoice when she submits it."

"Okay."

"Does this mean you're not quitting?" Ruedger asked, smiling at me.

"Ask me tomorrow."

* * *

The next morning, I woke with an emotional hangover and a heavy sense of shame. What the hell had I been thinking?

Tired, puffy eyes stared back at me in the Westin bathroom mirror as I tried to apply mascara to my swollen eye lids.

My cavalier attitude had to go, especially when it came to government regulations.

When I got back to Dallas, I cancelled two direct mail campaigns scheduled for the end of the year and earmarked the money to pay the German consultant. I sent Ruedger an email to that effect and hoped he would never mention that night in San Diego again.

We worked out the deal points with Knightsbridge and forwarded drafts of the contracts for legal review.

Davis and I negotiated a marketing and distribution contract that gave Lingualcare the ability to sell independently and only pay

Knightsbridge for sales their reps closed. It also included a clear termination path for nonperformance.

Before we could sign the contracts, Ruedger and I had to tell Dr. Hoffman. Breaking the news would have been easier if Hoffman hadn't been in emotional turmoil. Through Thomas, I learned that he and his wife had split up after she had a public affair with a German rock star.

Hoffman learned about her transgression while standing in line at the local supermarket. Out of the corner of his eye he saw a picture of his wife getting out of a helicopter. He picked up the tabloid, the German equivalent of the National Enquirer, and saw the inside spread with photos of her and the rock star, arms around each other, and a detailed story about their new relationship.

Thomas bought the tabloid too. He scanned the article and sent it to me. I couldn't read German but didn't need to; the pictures told the whole story. There was even one of Dr. Thalman in her orthodontic office canoodling with her new lover.

What was going on?

Effectively 50% of our founding team were getting divorced. Given the state of my relationship with John, it could easily shift to 75%. Was it the nature of the start-up environment, the stress and demands on time and focus? Or was it personality driven? Were obsessive, restless people more inclined to start companies and suck at relationships?

Divorce, financial ruin, career derailment, debilitating anxiety – when would the glamorous part start?

* * *

Ruedger and I made the trek to Bad Erlangen at the end of November. Hoffman asked us to meet him at his house instead of the clinic, so we drove there from the Hannover train station.

"Are you worried?" Ruedger said as he navigated the winding road that cut through the forest surrounding Bad Erlangen.

"He can't force us to buy from him," I said. "All he can do is make it painful during the transition. In the worst case he stops delivering, but I don't see him doing that. He still needs our help with software development."

For the past two years, Ruedger and Thomas had refined the manufacturing software to reduce design time and lower costs. After Thomas' departure, we'd hired a new programmer to continue the work. Software development was an ongoing project and Hoffman did not have the in-house expertise to manage it.

"Hoffman's in a bad place," said Ruedger. "He thought he was having a heart attack a few weeks ago, his blood pressure was dangerously high." We turned down Hoffman's street and parked a few houses from the corner. "Be as nice as you can."

I'd psyched myself up for an ugly confrontation and prepared a sheaf of documents detailing the missed delivery dates and overall negative attitude of his lab people. During the flight across the ocean yesterday I'd formulated arguments in my head and tested them against an imaginary Hoffman. But I didn't want to attack him while he was down.

When I got out of the car, sans documentation, I had to look up and down the street a couple of times before I realized that Hoffman's German-style house was gone. In its place stood an enormous, half-constructed modern home.

I looked at Ruedger and raised my eyebrows.

He pulled on his heavy coat and said, "He was building a palace for his wife when she took off with the rock star."

The only portion of the original house remaining was the garage, which had an apartment above it. Ruedger and I climbed the steps and knocked on the door.

Hoffman greeted us with a smile and ushered us into his small kitchen. He poured wine for himself and Ruedger and offered me a sparkling water.

We toasted.

"As you can see," he said, waving in the direction of the new house, "my life is a mess."

Ruedger said, "Is there anything we can do to help?"

Hoffman confessed that he was in a tight spot financially. High growth in Europe had forced him to expand his manufacturing facility and buy new machines. At the same time, his house project had turned into a money pit, and he was staring down an expensive divorce.

"Christmas is coming and I don't have money for employee bonuses," he said. "If I give nothing, my people will think the company is in trouble and maybe they will start looking for new jobs." He tipped his glass and drank the rest of his white wine, then refilled it.

"We're tight on money, too," I said.

Ruedger fixed his gaze on the stem of his wine glass, avoiding eye contact with Hoffman, as if he anticipated something unpleasant.

Hoffman took another drink of his wine and said, "Thomas told me last year you gave shares of Lingualcare to your employees for a Christmas bonus. Would you be willing to give shares of Lingualcare to five or six of my top people?"

I considered telling him that we would do it if he agreed to help us transition to the new manufacturing facility, but that seemed callous.

Ruedger inclined his head my direction and lifted his eyebrows.

We had plenty of options remaining in the pool. And what did I care about a few more German shareholders? We already had several hundred. I nodded in agreement.

"Yes," said Ruedger. "We will do that."

"We can give you 3,000 shares," I said.

Hoffman smiled and raised his glass.

Over dinner at a nearby pub, Ruedger broached the subject of moving our manufacturing to Mexico. Although we sat upstairs, far from the crowded bar, we had to raise our voices to be heard above the din. Hoffman and Ruedger lapsed into loud German. I tried to follow along but gave up after a few minutes.

Ruedger switched back to English. "I explained that letting us go is cheaper than investing in more machines and people to produce our products on a cost-plus basis. His ROI is better when he produces full-priced products for his customers."

The waitress brought us a bowl of fried potato wedges and a selection of dipping sauces, sweet and sour, barbecue and yogurt with herbs. The discussion stopped for a few minutes as we dug into the pile of greasy potatoes.

Hoffman said, "I'm worried about the quality. I trust you and Ruedger, but I don't know these people in Mexico."

"No one cares more about quality more than we do," I said. "We won't ship products that aren't as good as, or better than, what you make here."

A few seconds later he nodded. "Then it's okay with me."

Could we produce products at the same quality on day one? Maybe not, but we had to move, and with a little time I knew we would get there.

That's Just How It Is

Dallas, Texas – January 2005

We'd raised enough in the German offering to live until the end of summer, depending on our sales and how much we invested in marketing. Scott and I started calling potential investors at the beginning of the year, arranging meetings and polishing the pitch deck. I presented at the Southwest Venture Conference and at healthcare investment conferences in Houston and Irvine. I attended a slew of networking events and gave my card and an elevator pitch to anyone who even remotely looked like they had money.

I heard many forms of "no" – we don't invest in healthcare, you're not profitable, you're too small, you're too early, you're too late, the valuation is too high, I like it but my partners don't, call me in six months, I'll get back to you, let me pass it along to a friend of mine, maybe when we close our next fund, that's fascinating – but I never heard "yes."

After months of no progress, I decided to give the world of investment banking another try.

I hired a guy named Ryan who worked for a small boutique firm in Dallas. They did deals across several industries, including healthcare. I had Scott check the FINRA database and confirm that Ryan had a Series 7 license in good standing.

After hearing our pitch, Ryan suggested we consider a bigger deal. "Have you guys ever thought about combining with Knightsbridge?" he said. "They are already a public company. You could effectively borrow their operating history and do a secondary offering on the public market. It would be cheaper than venture capital."

On the surface, it sounded like a good idea. As a public company, Knightsbridge would bring liquidity to our investors. They also had a manufacturing plant, sales infrastructure and a large customer base. We had a cool, high-tech product and a great story that could boost the value of a traditional manufacturing company.

Ruedger and I took the idea to Bart and Davis and we started talking about possible terms. The discussion stalled around valuation, ours relative to theirs, and who would lead the new company. I didn't want to work for Davis and he didn't want to work for me.

In the middle of the negotiation process, Ruedger traveled alone to California to meet with Davis and Bart about purchasing manufacturing equipment for the plant in Mexicali. While he was there, they suggested that Ruedger move to California and become CEO of the combined company. To entice him, they said the new company would give him an interest-free loan to buy a home in California so he could move his family.

Ruedger said, "What about Lea?"

Bart said, "We'll figure out something for her."

I had to give Bart credit for creative thinking. He killed the Davis-versus-Lea-as-CEO debate by throwing Ruedger into the mix.

Bart had no desire to run the company full-time, but as Ruedger's rabbi, he could use his influence to guide it. Ruedger, being a technical guy, would be open to Bart's business advice and push it down to Davis and me, if I still had a role. And Bart knew that Ruedger could influence Thomas, who was still a large shareholder, as well as Glasauer and the smaller German shareholders – more than enough votes to make a merger happen.

Brilliant.

When Ruedger told me, I immediately wanted to confront Bart about his treachery. Ruedger begged me not to.

"They think they can divide us," he said. "If you confront Bart, they will know I told you and we will lose insight into future schemes."

"I should act like nothing happened?" I said, incredulous.

"Yes," he said. "The relationship will implode if you don't."

The aftermath of that incident left me feeling more vulnerable than usual. I had trusted the men who smiled at me across the conference table in Mexicali, the men who inquired about the health of my son and shared their vacation photos, the men who swapped stories over dinner and shared desserts. I considered them friends and didn't understand why they would betray me.

Ruedger insisted it was not personal. "It's just business," he said. "You can't take it personally."

It felt personal.

It felt terrible.

The only thing that helped was weightlifting. I started going to the gym, in the evenings when I could get a friend to stay with Will and on the weekends when John came home. I thought making my body stronger would make me feel less vulnerable. Although the paranoia never completely left me, I dropped a dress size, and that was cause for celebration.

* * *

In parallel with the Knightsbridge discussion, Ryan lined up investor meetings for me in Dallas. I didn't want to delay the fundraising process while we talked about a potential merger; it was best to keep all options open.

My first meeting was with a general partner at a mid-sized healthcare VC based in Florida. The firm made two-to-five-million-dollar investments all over the Southeastern and Southwestern United States and already had two portfolio companies in Texas: one in Dallas, the other in Houston. From Ryan's description, he sounded perfect.

In the hallway right before the meeting, Ryan whispered, "When we get in there, don't stare at his glass eye."

"He's got a glass eye? Which eye is his glass eye?"

"I don't remember which one it is, but you'll know it when you see it."

Even though the conference room occupied a corner of a downtown high-rise that afforded a spectacular view, I couldn't see anything other than the investor's left eye, the one that never moved.

At the end of the meeting, the man with the glass eye said, "I like you and I like your product, but we invest in companies with at least five million dollars in annual revenue." He stood up and shook my hand. "Please keep in touch and let me know when you get close to five million."

After he left I confronted Ryan. "If you had asked, he probably would have told you about the five-million-dollar threshold upfront. We wasted his time and ours."

"I take every meeting I can get, even if the company only loosely fits the investor's criteria," he said. "They might say no now, but yes later. Or they might like the technology so much they make an exception. He was downtown for another meeting anyway, so it was no big deal for him to come by."

I understood the numbers game, but each time I pitched, I left bits of myself on the table, bits I'd never get back. I couldn't detach myself from the enterprise. Every time I heard, "Thanks, but no thanks," I physically felt the rejection. It burned in my chest.

The following week, Ryan called and asked me to meet him downtown at the offices of a new investment firm that had just opened in Dallas, a CAPCO fund.

Ryan explained to me that the CAPCO program had recently been approved by the Texas Legislature. CAPCOs raised money from insurance companies that did business in Texas. In exchange for their investment, the insurance company got a tax credit. The state required CAPCOs to invest in economically distressed areas to create jobs.

On the way to the meeting, Ryan said, "If he asks if you'd consider relocating to South Dallas, say yes."

"We can't put a clinic in South Dallas," I said, "but we could potentially have our corporate offices there." I didn't want to work in South Dallas and face the hellish commute through downtown, but Lingualcare needed money, so I would keep an open mind.

Ryan and I arrived early to find the CAPCO guy unpacking boxes. He wore jeans and sneakers. Large cardboard cartons lined two sides of his office, and the leather furniture smelled like it had just escaped from a Chinese container ship.

The CAPCO guy started the meeting by handing the deal memo back to Ryan and saying, "We only invest growth capital in low-risk businesses, no high tech, no health tech." He added, "I agreed to the meeting because I'm new in town and am interested in connecting with the entrepreneurial community. If you know any CEOs running more traditional businesses who might consider relocating to South Dallas, please give them my card."

He pushed a card across the table in my direction. I put it in my briefcase and checked my watch. We'd been there less than three minutes, perhaps a record for the shortest investor meeting of all time. I pushed back my chair, ready to leave.

"Do you have kids?" he asked.

We spent the next thirty minutes talking about his newborn daughter, the pros and cons of different strollers, my son's Montessori school, and his wife's search for a trustworthy babysitter. Before leaving, I promised to email him the phone number of a reputable nanny agency.

"Well, that was a waste of time," I said on the way back to the car.

"Not for him, he's going to get a nanny out of it," said Ryan, laughing.

"Do you think he discusses jogging strollers with the male CEOs who come in looking for money?" I said.

Ryan shook his head. "Lighten up. If the nanny thing works out, he'll definitely remember you."

After several more unproductive meetings with Ryan's contacts, I sent Mr. Kryptonite our product pitch deck and deal memo and asked him to take a look. If our messaging was horribly wrong, he would tell me.

He called me that evening as I was driving to pick up Will from a birthday party at a nearby bowling alley.

"Your message is fine," he said. "The pitch deck is not the issue."

"What's the issue?" I said.

"You're a woman."

I let the words hang in the air.

Finally, I said, "Seriously?"

"I'll let you in on a secret. When female CEOs pitch a deal that we like, the first discussion we have after she leaves is what role we could put her in," he said. "It's this unspoken thing. No one wants a female CEO."

"How can you just discriminate like that?"

"It's not discrimination. Every start-up goes off the rails at some point. We're forced to have hard conversations with the CEO, and no one wants to yell at a woman. It would be like abusing your mom or your sister."

"That's ridiculous," I said.

"I'm not defending it. I'm just telling you the reality. How many female general partners have you met at firms you've talked to?"

"None," I said.

"What else can I tell you?" he said. "That's just how it is."

That's just how it is.

I'd heard those words before.

* * *

When I was nine years old, I dreamed of becoming a professional football player.

An avid Miami Dolphins fan, I insisted on being Larry Csonka during recess football at Longfellow Elementary. Reprimands from my mother over torn clothing and dirty shoes did nothing to dissuaded me from channeling my inner Larry Csonka three times a day. I loved the feel of the pebbled leather in my hands and the rush each time I outmaneuvered boys bigger than me to score a touchdown. And let's face it, no one cheered for girls who played Barbie Dreamhouse.

In 1974 the world was in flux. Billy Jean King had beaten Bobby Riggs at tennis and dramatically changed the perception of female athletes. By the time I got out of college, I felt certain women would be in the NFL.

That summer, my mother took me to the Hastings Public Library to learn about being a girl. Just like taking tap and ballet lessons, going to the library for THE TALK was a rite of passage for Hastings girls of my generation.

Sitting with my fellow fourth graders, I watched the head librarian remove plastic cross sections of male and female torsos from a large cloth bag. She slid the penis of the male cross section into the vagina of the female cross section and explained how the man ejaculated, how his sperm swam to a waiting egg and how nine months later a baby was born. She showed pictures in a glossy book of the fetus growing month by month, a woman giving birth and breastfeeding.

Yuck!

After the reproduction lesson, we took a break. The librarian handed out Dixie cups of lukewarm lemonade and sugar cookies. The other girls and I tried to ignore the cross sections on the table. None of us knew what to say, so we consumed our snacks in silence.

"Now we are going to learn about menstruation," said the librarian, her lips pursed into a tight line. "Pay attention."

My stomach tightened into a knot as she explained that once a month, for forty years or so, I would start bleeding without any warning and have to wear a huge cotton pad called a "sanitary napkin" that attached to a belt worn around my waist. She demonstrated how to secure the belt and pad. "Most women menstruate four to six days per month."

I raised my hand. "Do boys bleed?"

"No, they don't."

"Why not?"

"That's the way God designed things," she said.

"That's not fair."

Other girls at the table nodded in agreement. Clearly, we were getting the short end of the stick; we had to carry babies in our stomachs, breastfeed AND wear sanitary napkins.

"What do boys do except ejaculate?" I asked.

The librarian glared at me, her expression as plastic as her anatomical cross sections. "I suggest you ask your parents."

Mothers streamed into the library, as if on cue, to collect their newly educated daughters. I followed mine out the door, my head hanging low, sick with this new reality.

How could I wear white football pants and play in the NFL if I could start bleeding at any time? What about the pad and the belt? It would definitely not work with the uniform pants. I would not be the next Larry Csonka.

When I got home I ran into my dad's study, relayed the horrible events that had unfolded at the library and challenged him. "You said I could be anything I wanted to be."

"Almost anything," he said.

"But..." I fell into his lap and cried.

"I'm sorry, honey," he said as he rubbed by shoulder. "That's just how it is."

Don't Go to Shreveport

Dallas, Texas – March 2005

Ryan's fundraising efforts stalled.

Even though three months remained on the contract, I didn't cancel it. I figured I'd let it run out while I explored other leads. Maybe he'd turn up something. As they liked to say in Texas, even a blind squirrel can find a nut now and again.

Late in March, while attending an investor forum being held at Southern Methodist University, I sat next to an entrepreneur named Larry. He founded a healthcare technology incubator around the same time Ruedger and I had started Lingualcare. We'd become friends, bonding over our shared struggles and helping each other with investor leads and introductions.

While commiserating over sticky blueberry muffins and weak coffee, Larry asked, "Have you thought about hosting an event for angel investors?"

I had not.

He went on to tell me that one of his portfolio companies had organized an investor dinner a few months ago at Maggiano's, a popular Italian restaurant with well-appointed private dining rooms. "They filled the whole financing round with guys from that event."

"I don't know who I would invite," I said. My only experience with big angels had been with the Kingsleys, and I certainly wasn't going to send them an invitation.

Larry offered to share his angel email list and added, "Call your accounting firm and law firm. They have clients who invest in deals like this. They might even offer to co-sponsor the event and help pay for the dinner."

It was worth a shot. We'd tried crazier things.

After checking Ruedger's calendar, I reserved a private room at Maggiano's for early May. Both our law firm and our accounting firm agreed to be sponsors and forward the invitation to a few select clients. We quickly accumulated over thirty RSVPs.

Two weeks before the Maggiano's dinner, Scott burst into my office, as excited as I'd ever seen him. "I think I've got a big angel who can fund the whole thing," he said.

He had my attention.

"It's a guy in Louisiana named Harry Ruskin who owns a bunch of truck stops full of video poker machines." Scott shook his head and smiled so wide I could see his molars. "The video poker machines spin off sixteen million a year in cash. *It's a gold mine!*"

I nodded, wondering, but not asking, why a guy like that wanted to invest in a dental company.

"When Ruedger comes next week for the Maggiano's meeting, go to Shreveport, have dinner with Beau, his deal guy, and pitch Ruskin the next morning."

It sounded too good to be true, one guy who could write an enormous check and solve our funding problem. But maybe it wasn't.

Maybe Harry Ruskin was *the one.*

* * *

Ruedger and I departed Dallas full of hope and drove the 200 miles to Shreveport anticipating a great meeting. Our hope began to diminish when we couldn't find Ruskin's office.

Ruedger had the address and the map I'd printed from MapQuest. Twice we passed the spot where Ruskin's office should have been, but neither of us saw anything that resembled an office building. We made a U-turn and another pass. That's when I spotted a bunker-like metal building set far back from the street. It looked more like a machine shop than an investor's office. I pulled into the parking lot and saw the small sign mounted on the metal building: *RUSKIN INTERESTS.*

I expected to find secondhand office furniture and linoleum floors when we came through the front door, but the inside of Harry Ruskin's office didn't match the outside. Filled with silky Chinese carpets, elaborate tapestries and ornate French furnishings, it looked more like a New Orleans bordello than a corporate office.

Beau led us through a set of carved wood doors into a room with the largest conference table I'd ever seen. It had to seat forty people. Burl wood, inlaid with an elaborate border of mother of pearl and onyx, the table would have been the most awesome thing in the room if it weren't for the oil painting on the far wall.

Harry Ruskin, at least eight feet tall and encased in a gilded frame, loomed above us, his bright blue eyes, penetrating and intense, staring down. Were he an English lord, this would surely have hung in the portrait gallery of his ancestral home.

"That must be Mr. Ruskin," I said, suppressing a giggle.

Beau nodded. "Yeah, he just had that done. Isn't it great?"

Megalomaniacal maybe. Definitely not great.

Ruedger shot me a look as we followed Beau into his office. I avoided his eyes. I too had serious doubts about the man responsible for the bizarre décor, but we were here, and it would be rude to just walk out.

"I have good news," said Beau as he scrolled through his email. "Mr. Ruskin's evening plans have changed, so he can join us for dinner."

We spent an hour walking Beau through our pitch deck and answering his questions. He wanted to be prepared for the presentation to Ruskin the next day. Then Beau gave us a rundown of Ruskin's many businesses, including the truck stops full of video poker machines, casino operations on Indian reservations in New Mexico, real estate holdings across the Southwest, and a security company that made video surveillance equipment.

On the way out, I noticed cameras blinking in the hallways, the lobby and over the front door.

As we left the building, Ruedger said, "That painting freaked me out. I don't even want to meet this crazy guy. Let's go back to Dallas tonight."

"He might not be as weird as his portrait." My words conveyed a conviction I didn't feel.

We followed Beau to the restaurant, an upscale steak and seafood place with clubby décor and lighting that would make my grandmother look like Sophia Loren.

An hour after the appointed meeting time, Mr. Ruskin had yet to appear. Out of deference to his boss, Beau wouldn't even order appetizers, so we sipped our drinks, made small talk and tried not to check our watches too frequently.

A flurry from the staff announced Ruskin's arrival. He stopped to greet people at the bar, kissed a waitress on the cheek and then made his way over to our table.

The portrait hadn't done his blue eyes justice – otherworldly, like a Star Trek character with laser eyes. He stood over six feet, with short gray hair and a Hemingway tan, the kind that came from spending time on the water sans sunscreen and hat.

After we ordered our food, the grilling commenced.

Who were our customers? Why did they buy? Why did we make gold brackets? How strong was our intellectual property? Why should he consider investing in our company? He asked us to give examples of things we'd done in the past that were successful. Where did we go to school? What did our parents do?

The barrage of questions continued through dinner. I barely touched my food.

"Where are you staying?" said Ruskin, suddenly shifting the conversation.

"The Holiday Inn," I said.

"Why don't you spend the night at my house tonight?" he said, smiling and looking over at Ruedger for confirmation. "My wife and kids are out of town and I've got plenty of room."

Ruedger hesitated, like he might answer in the affirmative, so I jumped in. "Thanks, but we've already checked into the hotel."

We hadn't, but I wasn't going to admit it.

"Well, just go get your stuff and check out." He was smiling, but his voice had an edge, like he wished to add "you stupid idiot" to the end of his last sentence.

I absolutely did not want to spend the night at Harry Ruskin's house. I could only imagine how many video cameras he had scattered around the property. He probably patented some kind of steam-proof lens that allowed him to spy on his guests in the shower.

"We don't want to impose," I said.

"It's not an imposition," he said. "I insist."

Ruedger's face wore a blank expression; he appeared to have lost his command of the English language.

Fuck.

"Thank you, but I'm going to decline."

Ruskin's laser stare passed all the way through me. I expected to hear a sizzle and smell burnt flesh. He signaled the waiter and handed him a credit card before I could intervene. Usually the poor entrepreneur had to pick up the check, so this wasn't a good sign.

After we pulled out of the parking lot, leaving Ruskin and Beau at the valet stand, I asked Ruedger, "What was that about?"

"He wanted to get cozy with you."

"Don't say that!!!"

"It's not too late to drive back to Dallas," said Ruedger. "He's not going to give us any money tomorrow since you turned him down."

The Holiday Inn offered no rest. The air conditioner under the window sounded like a Sherman tank, but it barely drowned out the screeching teenagers congregated in the pool area. I tried to fall asleep without allowing the bedspread, made of a petroleum-derived fabric, to touch any part of my body. It was slightly moist from the humid air and had stuck to my legs when I sat down on it earlier.

Wishing I'd never taken microbiology, I obsessed about Harry Ruskin's intentions and what manner of tiny creatures might be breeding beneath the bedspread's pink and green floral print.

The next morning, Beau took us back to Ruskin's private office. On the way, he said, "Mr. Ruskin is bidding on several Monet paintings this morning. There's an auction at Sotheby's. He'll be on the phone with his rep during part of the presentation, but don't worry, he can multitask."

Ruskin sat at a conference table for six. He had an ear bud in one ear and his cell phone and catalog of in front of him. He nodded when we entered the room but did not rise to greet us.

Ruedger attached his computer to the projector.

With a nod from Beau, I started the pitch.

I did my best to sound upbeat and positive as I went through the slide deck, but I had a hard time maintaining my rhythm because Ruskin gave no indication that he was listening. He seemed fixated on his catalog and whoever was on the other end of the phone line.

Finally, as I neared the end of the presentation, he asked, "Did you attend graduate school, or did you get your MBA online?"

His words stopped me like a phaser set on stun.

I wanted to dissolve.

I sat down and stopped speaking. I feared that if I opened my mouth, I would either break down crying or unleash the frustration that swirled in my gut like a cyclone.

When Ruedger realized that I wasn't going to finish the presentation, he stood up and started talking, too fast. He flew through the financial slides, running his words together and sounding more German than usual.

After Ruedger finished, Ruskin said, "I need to go to Dallas today. I was going to take my plane, but if you all want to give me a ride we could talk some more."

Was he insane? He treated us like shit and was asking for a ride to Dallas? I would rather chew off my arm than play chauffer to Ruskin.

Sensing my fragile emotional state, Ruedger said, "We aren't going back to Dallas."

With a nod to Beau, I packed my briefcase and exited Ruskin's office without shaking any hands. Ruedger could manage the formal goodbyes.

On the way to the lobby I stepped into the ladies' room and locked myself in the last stall. I braced myself against the wall and leaned over the toilet so my tears dripped into the bowl instead of running down my cheeks and smearing my mascara. I would not let that asshole know that he'd gotten to me.

It took a few minutes to calm down. As I exited the stall, I lifted my head high. That's when I saw it, the red blinking light in the corner above the mirror.

A video camera.

* * *

"Do you want to talk about it?" said Ruedger.

We were at a Cracker Barrel restaurant somewhere on Interstate 20 west of Shreveport, sitting on the porch in large white rocking chairs. Ceiling fans spun the hot air around us, creating a quasi-breeze. The noise from the restaurant and traffic on the interstate made it too loud to be relaxing, but compared to Ruskin's office, it felt like nirvana.

"I got my hopes up," I said. "That's why it feels so terrible. I thought we landed a big angel with a big checkbook who could solve all of our problems."

A silver bullet in the shape of a man.

"Ruskin is an asshole," said Ruedger. "That's why it feels terrible."

"Do you think it's because I'm a woman?"

"Ruskin shot an arrow at you, and he missed," said Ruedger. "Don't pick it up and ram it into your heart."

Maybe I'd been walking the tightrope between hope and pretense for so long, I'd completely lost perspective.

I rocked back and forth, sipping my iced tea. What if the Maggiano's thing didn't work? We needed at least two million dollars to make any real progress at Lingualcare, three would be better, and I was fresh out of good ideas.

"We should not have come here," I said. "I should have known better. A guy like that is not going to shift from roadside casinos to medical devices, no matter what his deal runner says."

"No, it's good that we came," said Ruedger. "I just don't know why yet..."

* * *

On the drive back to Dallas, I'd figured out why it was good we'd gone to Shreveport. It constituted a personal bottom – me succumbing to the "silver bullet investor" fantasy and not questioning the character of a man who could get a gaming license in the state of Louisiana. No matter what happened at Maggiano's, or any other investor meeting going forward, it would be better than Shreveport.

Shaking off the layer of slime I'd picked up in Ruskin's office, I began preparing for the Maggiano's dinner. My friend Larry suggested that we define the deal terms and include them in the presentation. "Smaller investors don't want to figure out terms," he said. "The large ones will negotiate with you anyway. Regardless, you should state your expectations up front."

So, Ruedger and I created a slide titled "Deal Terms." It included price per share, the minimum investment amount per investor and that they would receive common stock, the only class of shares offered by our company.

That night at Maggiano's, when I walked to the podium to pitch, I felt a weird sense of calm, like a battle-hardened veteran who knew they'd seen the worst. I pitched between dinner and dessert to a room full of attentive people. Afterward, attendees stuck around to ask more questions and several requested follow-up meetings.

One potential investor stood out in the crowd. His name was Jake. He'd attended the meeting both as an individual investor and as the representative of a group called the Longhorn Partners.

He shook my hand. "I get it," he said. "It's great."

Jake told me that he had built and sold a dental company that made products for oral surgeons. He liked the market and believed the future was in patient-specific products like ours.

"Do you think you could present to my group in a couple of weeks?" he said. "We invest as individuals, so you pitch to everyone. If enough of us want to pursue an investment, then we will assign a point person to lead the due diligence. In this case, it would be me."

"How long do you think the entire process would take?" I asked.

"Maybe sixty days, ninety at most," he said. "Each person will decide if they want in and for how much. Most write checks between fifty and a hundred thousand. We set a closing date and each individual pays in."

If we could close on our own terms in the next ninety days, all would be fine. Given our bank balance and sales projections, we had enough cash for six months, maybe more if we decreased our advertising spend.

* * *

In mid-June, I went to Austin to meet the Longhorn Partners. As their group had members in Dallas, Austin and Houston, they rotated the monthly meeting from city to city.

Their meeting date coincided with Will's and my annual trip to the Schlitterbahn, a popular waterpark located in New Braunfels, halfway between Austin and San Antonio. We were staying with a college friend of mine who lived in San Antonio. She had three boys of her own, one of whom was Will's age, and he could hang out with them while I went to Austin.

Will was not happy when it was time for me to go.

When I walked to the front door wearing my best blue suit and red shoes, briefcase in hand, Will looked up at me, wide eyed, lips pressed together in dissatisfaction.

"Tell me exactly when you will come back," he said.

I knelt on the cold tile floor and gathered him in my arms. He didn't resist, a sure sign of his unease. "I don't know yet, I'll try to be here before dinner," I said as I smoothed down his hair and pressed my nose into his forehead.

At age seven he was exploring independence, but still felt uneasy in unfamiliar surroundings when he couldn't locate either parent in his peripheral vision.

"That's a long time. Can you come back for lunch?"

"I'll come back as soon as I can."

My friend would take good care of Will and keep him entertained all day. But I felt the pull of sadness as I turned out of her driveway and saw Will, most of his front teeth now missing, smiling at me through the glass front door, waving goodbye.

The expression on his face reminded me of an incident that happened when he was two and a half years old. I had come home from work to find him staring out the bay window that faced our street. He had both hands and his nose pressed flat against the glass. I'd almost scolded him for dirtying the window, but then realized he was watching a baby squirrel under our big oak tree.

"What do you think that squirrel doing?" I asked.

"Waiting for his mommy to come home from the office."

His words landed hard on my chest. I knelt down and hugged him until he squirmed away to find his favorite airplane.

As he loaded passengers into the plane, making a boarding call in his sing-song voice, I watched the little squirrel until he scrambled up the oak tree. Hopefully the mother squirrel was out gathering nuts in a nearby yard, not roadkill.

Roadkill was a common sight in Texas – squirrels, opossums, armadillos and start-ups.

I had seen dead companies on the side of the start-up highway, the long faces of CEOs who bravely explained that "it's okay, I learned a lot" as they sold off computers, office furniture and all the other items they'd bought with a bank account full of hope.

As I passed the Austin city limit, I said aloud. "Please don't let Lingualcare be start-up roadkill."

My phone rang and I saw my mother's name on the caller ID. She knew I had a meeting in Austin.

"I want to put out a request to my prayer team for your meeting today. What time will you be speaking?" said my mother.

"Around two o'clock," I said. "But doesn't your group normally pray for people who are sick or facing some kind of tragedy?"

"Yes, but today we're going to pray for you. We're going to pray that the right money finds you, money that doesn't come with anything negative attached."

"You don't have to do that."

"I want to help," she said. "And this is the only way I know how."

* * *

I arrived at Ruedger's hotel at ten o'clock and found him at a table in the corner of the lobby. Bent over his computer, brows scrunched, Ruedger looked tired. He'd arrived in the U.S. the day before and had to be jetlagged.

"Coffee?" he asked.

I shook my head. "Water."

He got up and went to the hotel bar, where the hiss of an espresso machine promised a shot of energy. I paged through the slides on his computer, checking for typos or mistakes that would give the Longhorn Partners a reason to say no.

Ruedger returned with coffee, a bottle of water and a blueberry muffin with crumbles on top. He pulled the foil tops off two small containers of half and half and slowly stirred the contents into his Americano. He broke a muffin in half and handed it to me.

I told him about the phone call from my mother as I picked blueberries out of the muffin and ate them. "A whole bunch of church ladies in Nebraska, Kansas and Iowa will be praying for us at two o'clock," I said. "So we've got that going for us."

"We need all the help we can get."

"Are you in the dog house?" I said, brushing muffin crumbs from my pants.

Ruedger had abandoned his family mid-vacation to fly to Austin. Germans took their vacations seriously, so I knew his departure couldn't have gone over well.

"I'd rather be here than worrying about it from five thousand miles away," he said.

Having Ruedger at the presentation increased our chances of success, much more so than taking Scott along. He had a powerful presence. When he spoke in that deep, German-accented voice about technology and intellectual property, people listened.

We strategized about the meeting, agreeing that I would take the lead and he would chime in on technology and manufacturing.

Despite our efforts to map out how we would handle meetings, once they started we always went off-script. Like a battle plan, our meeting plans rarely survived the first minute of engagement. We had to adjust and react to the dynamics in the room. Fortunately, we'd done it enough times that we no longer stepped all over each other.

"We only have fifteen minutes for the slides and five minutes for questions and answers, so be brief," I reminded him.

"Just give me an ugly look if I talk too long," said Ruedger, laughing.

Ruedger had a habit of covering his nervousness with detail, delving into far more minutiae than was required or appreciated in most situations. And he talked fast, rarely pausing long enough to allow me to reclaim the floor.

"Except for Glasauer, Jake is the only person we've talked to who understands dental and has made real money in it," I said. "If we can sell the other partners on the financial opportunity, I think Jake's domain expertise will push them over the edge."

Before we left for the meeting, I stepped into the lobby bathroom, washed my hands and wiped the remains of the blueberry from my teeth with a paper towel. I inspected my pin-striped suit – no lint or stray hair stuck on the fabric and no muffin crumbs. I wiped a scuff mark from one of my red high-heeled shoes, the ones that communicated confidence I didn't always feel.

"You can do it," I said to the girl in the mirror.

* * *

Fourteen partners, all men in their thirties and forties sat at tables configured into a U shape. I stood in the middle. Ruedger took a chair at the end, near enough to the projector to hook it to his computer and advance the slides for me.

Ruedger started the PowerPoint.

I began to speak.

Something magical happened.

I didn't know if it was the welcoming energy in the room, the fact that I had given the presentation so many times that I could recite it while riding a rollercoaster blindfolded, or the efforts of my mother's prayer circle, but that afternoon the right words flowed from me effortlessly as one slide dissolved into the next.

Throughout the presentation the partners asked questions, not in a hostile or challenging way, simply requesting clarifications and confirmations. They smiled when I answered, took notes, nodded and smiled more – buying signals, like the ones we'd gotten so long ago at StarTech.

Ruedger addressed all the questions about our technology and patents, his answers on point and uncharacteristically succinct.

Jake walked us out. "Good job, you guys," he said. "You don't know this group so you don't have a reference point, but let me tell you, that's the best reaction I've seen since I joined. They liked it."

Ruedger and I crossed the lobby in silence. A bright blast of sunshine and hot air greeted us as we stepped onto the sidewalk.

It felt like a hug.

Two days later, Jake called. "We want to move forward. There's at least a million dollars of interest in the room, probably more."

I called Ruedger to share the news.

He had news of his own.

"Glasauer said he will commit a million if we get at least a million from the Longhorn Partners before the end of August," he said. "He thinks it will be easier to close if they know their money is not the only money coming in."

I hung up the phone and paced back and forth in my office. We had nine weeks to complete due diligence and close, nine weeks to secure the company's future, our employee's future and my financial future.

Please don't let anything go wrong.

Please.

But that was too much to hope for.

We Are Broke

Dallas, Texas – July 2005

It happened on a Monday morning near the end of July.

I'd just dropped off Will at summer camp and was stuck in traffic on Preston Road, feeling anxious about the long list of due diligence documents I needed to send over to the Longhorn Partners that morning, when my phone rang. I saw Scott's name on the caller ID.

"I just got a call from Chase bank," he said. "You guys are bouncing checks."

What? "We should have a couple hundred thousand dollars in the account," I said as my anxiety morphed into panic.

"That's what I thought," said Scott. "I'm in my car, but I'll be at the office in a few minutes. I'm going to log on to the account and see what's going on."

"Call me as soon as you can."

Scott no longer worked directly for us. He had taken a job running the Dallas branch of a virtual CFO firm based in Austin that provided fractional CFOs, controllers and staff accountants to small companies like Lingualcare. Although he still acted as our CFO, Scott installed a part-time controller at Lingualcare to do the day-to-day accounting work. Now he just reviewed monthly financials and accompanied me to investor meetings.

My low fuel light lit up a mile from the office. Great. I pulled into an Exxon station.

As the tank filled, I sat in my car and mentally went through the month's expenses and the orders we'd received. I knew how many cases came in each day because I listened to the beeps from the UPS guy's scanner. I could hear them from my office. Every beep equaled two thousand dollars. I kept a tally on the paper calendar pad that covered half my desk.

We could not be out of money. This had to be a banking error. Maybe something happened with our credit card processing.

I started the car and pulled away from the pump.

THUNK.

"STOP, LADY! STOP!!!"

In the rearview mirror, I saw the gas station manager, waving his hands and running toward my car, and the gas pump nozzle sticking out of my fuel tank.

I slammed on the brakes and waited for a Die Hard scene to unfold – the explosion, the giant orange and black fireball engulfing the station and the car at the pump next to mine catapulting through the air from the force of it.

But nothing happened.

Apparently, I wasn't the first person who'd driven off while still attached to the pump. The hose had a decoupling mechanism that kicked in when yanked too hard. The gas station owner shook his head as he removed the handle from my tank.

I should have gotten out to check if he'd closed my gas cap, but I was too embarrassed. I pulled into traffic, shaking from the adrenaline rush.

Scott called again before I arrived at the office. "There hasn't been a deposit into the checking account for three weeks," he said, "and the merchant account had less than two thousand dollars in it."

"I need to talk to Ruedger," I said.

I pulled into a grocery store parking lot, put the car in park and got out to check my gas cap. It was on, thankfully. I didn't have time to deal with a check engine light and a trip to the dealership. Then I called Ruedger and told him what was going on.

"We can't be broke in the middle of due diligence, it will kill the deal," I said. "I don't know what's going on, but we need cash right now, today. Do you think Glasauer would give us an advance on the million he committed to the financing?"

"I'll call him."

"We need it by Wednesday. Payroll runs on Thursday."

After we hung up, I drove to Lingualcare, but I didn't get out of the car right away. I needed to calm down before walking in the door. The employees searched my face every morning for signs of impending doom, reading my expression like tea leaves. I did not want to telegraph my panic.

Closing my eyes, I thought about the night before, about running after Will as he practiced riding his bicycle on our street. It had been hot, and both of us were red-faced and sweaty by the time he'd decided to call it quits. We ate fudgesicles on the front stoop and Will, unable to lick his faster than it melted, ended up covered in a sticky mess.

The memory of his happy, chocolatey face brought a smile to mine.

I got out of the car.

After successfully negotiating the employee gauntlet, and filling a mug with coffee, I went to my office and dug through the top drawer of my desk, searching for my key to the accounting office. I knew I had one. How long had it been since I'd walked in that office on my own, without Scott or the controller there? Maybe never.

I finally located the key under a pile of old business cards, still sealed in the envelope the locksmith had given me over a year ago when we moved in.

I unlocked the door and turned on the light. A piles of orders spilled over the basket marked "Receivables." I picked them up and mentally tallied them – over two hundred and twenty thousand dollars.

How was this possible? The controller came in two full days a week. He had thirty years of experience. I closed the door of the accounting office and called Scott to tell him about the ugly mess.

"I tried to find your controller this morning," said Scott. "He's not answering his phone. I have no idea what the hell is going on."

"Do you know the amount of the checks the bank needs to clear today?"

"About fifteen thousand."

"Can you help me run credit cards?" I asked.

"I'm on my way," said Scott, hanging up before I could say goodbye.

Ruedger called. "Glasauer said he would wire two hundred and fifty thousand in the morning," he said. "He's faxing over a convertible loan agreement for you to sign."

"Does he think I'm an idiot, running the company out of money?"

"No," said Ruedger. "But you need to figure out a better system for cash management. How could you sign checks with no cash in the bank?"

I wanted to blame the incompetent controller, but then I read the business card staring at me from the shiny stainless steel cardholder perched on the edge of my desk. It said Lea A. Ellermeier, Chief Executive Officer.

I owned this one.

I owned every single one.

Scott arrived within the hour, another controller in tow. She took the key to the accounting office from me and said, "I'm going to fix this. Don't you worry."

Scott closed the door to my office and sat down.

I told him about the emergency loan from Glasauer. "The wire should arrive on Wednesday," I said. "We won't miss payroll."

Scott shook his head. "If I'd logged into your account at the beginning of the month, I would have caught this. You're not the only one who dropped the ball."

He left, promising to check the deposits at least once a week going forward. "This will never happen again," he said.

When I peeked in the door of the accounting office at 2:00, I saw a clean desk, an empty trash can, a neat stack of manila folders next to the computer and the new controller packing up her briefcase.

"I processed about half the cards, more than enough to cover the pending checks," she said. "I'll be back tomorrow to do the rest and prepare payroll."

I turned off the light and locked the door behind her.

I'd dodged a bullet.

This time.

* * *

I didn't like looking too closely at money.

I'd never balanced my personal checkbook, not in my twenty-five years of being an account holder. But I'd also never bounced a check because I always rounded up to the nearest dollar and maintained a cushion, so my inattention to the details hadn't hurt me.

But what did that say about me?

At a networking event the year before, I'd heard a tech CEO say that his job consisted mostly of cash management. At the time, I scoffed. Tech founders were supposed to be anti-establishment visionaries who built disruptive products, rallied their troops to perform seemingly impossible tasks, inspired early customers to join them on the bleeding edge and bought cans of Silly String for Friday afternoon team-building events in the parking lot.

They weren't bean counters.

Managing cash wasn't fun or cool or sexy.

But the morning's events had been a wake-up call. Cash management was critical. It wouldn't manage itself.

My arms-length approach of scanning the monthly financials, approving expenses on a one-off basis and loosely tracking sales by the number of daily orders fell far short of what Lingualcare needed.

I was the last person to leave the office that day. As I turned off the lights in the lobby, set the alarm and locked the front door, I promised myself that I would dig deep into the weekly numbers and hire a full-time controller as soon as we closed the financing round. I couldn't afford to outsource it or ignore it any longer.

* * *

In mid-August, two weeks before our scheduled closing, one of the Longhorn Partners from Houston asked me to speak with his neighbor, an orthodontist with a big practice near the Galleria. The investor required one last data point before committing his money and declaring the due diligence process complete.

Ever since the meeting with Dr. Martin and the Kingsleys, I cringed whenever an investor said, "Let me run it by my dentist." It was a death knell. Like Dr. Martin, no dentist wanted to be responsible for a patient losing money, so their assessments always came out lukewarm to negative. But I had no choice. The investors drove the due diligence process.

Fortunately, the Houston orthodontist was open-minded, thoughtful and asked good questions. He even took the time to call Dr. Sam and get more clinical details before rendering his verdict – cautiously positive.

After he gave his thumbs-up, we gathered firm commitments from several members of the group who had declared early interest.

Summer vacations threatened to push our closing into September, but I hated to let the momentum wane, so I kept pushing. Glasauer had given us a deadline of August 31st to close the million dollars in order to get his matching funds. He would probably be willing to extend the date, but I'd rather avoid that conversation.

By August 28th, we had eight hundred and fifty thousand committed, a hundred and fifty thousand short of securing the matching funds. Several of the interested partners were on vacation and not responding to email. Jake believed they would commit, but probably not until after Labor Day.

Ruedger called me in the late afternoon of the 28th. He caught me daydreaming, staring out my office window thinking about what to pick up for dinner on the way home. I'd been serving Will way too much pizza, spaghetti and macaroni and cheese over the past four weeks.

"Let's do two closings, lock down the eight hundred and fifty on the table and see if Glasauer will match it right now," he suggested. "Then we can close the rest at the end of September."

"That would mean renegotiating with Glasauer. We risk him changing the terms and that could put the whole financing at risk."

"I'm worried we won't get anything if we don't close what's on the table," said Ruedger.

I shared his nervousness but was not prepared to concede defeat.

"We have a few more days," I said. "Let's see what the tide brings in."

Before leaving that night, I sent an update email to all of the Longhorn Partners, hoping to give them a nudge without sounding too desperate or pushy. I recognized that my priorities were rarely front and center in other people's minds. Friendly reminders went a long way.

The next morning one of the Longhorn Partners called me. When I saw his name on the caller ID, my stomach did a little flip flop. He'd already committed a hundred thousand dollars. I hoped he wasn't calling to back out.

I hesitated, then picked up the receiver.

"Hey Lea," he said. "A buddy of mine was in my office last night when your email arrived. I told him about Lingualcare and he wants to invest. He and I are in several other deals together, so I can vouch for him. Is it too late?"

"Do you know how much he wants to put in?" I said.

"Two fifty."

I could have kissed him.

"Send me his contact information and I'll get the paperwork out today."

On the last day of August, we closed $2,100,000, including Glasauer's money.

After I received the final signature page, I went out into the hallway and said, "Grab the chicken."

The chicken in question was a fluffy, orange-yellow stuffed bird about the size of a cantaloupe with a bright red beak and googly eyes. When someone squeezed his right wing, he played the chicken dance song often heard at baseball games.

Kathy had rescued the chicken from the clearance bin at Walgreens, and since his arrival in May, he'd assumed the role of company mascot, playing his little song whenever we hit our sales number or someone closed a long-shot customer.

As my team gathered around the door of my office I put the chicken on the parquet floor and announced the successful close of our financing.

Beth squeezed his fuzzy wing.

The chicken's feet moved up and down in time with the music, making his body rock back and forth. The black discs in his googly eyes bounced as he played, three choruses, each faster and more furious than the one before. People joined in, flapping their arms in time with the chicken's and stomping on the floor.

At the end of September, we closed an additional $425,000. Finally, we had enough funding to do some real marketing, hire more salespeople and make the numbers we'd been showing in our PowerPoint presentations since starting the company.

We had a chance.

Dreams Scale

Dallas, Texas – October 2005

Kathy, Cary and I, through much trial and error, had developed a successful direct selling formula and sales grew steadily. We landed on a messaging strategy that worked, selling the concept of being a radical, stepping out of the norm and trying something new. Our marketing pieces were irreverent and a little snarky, appealing to our customers' inner rebel.

We ran monthly direct mail and trade journal ad campaigns to sell online and in-person courses. Our inside salespeople followed up the prospects these activities generated. Six different orthodontists taught courses for us across the U.S., and a group of contract trainers performed on-site training for doctors who couldn't attend a course. The implementation of a Customer Relationship Management (CRM) system gave us visibility into the effectiveness of our marketing programs and sales rep activity. Our revenue became predictable and the factors needed to scale were no longer a mystery.

Every day information requests from potential new customers came in via the website, and the UPS guy started bringing our deliveries in plastic crates instead of carrying the individual packages in his arms. Lingualcare was on pace to more than double revenue from the year before.

I'd hoped that Knightsbridge would have a bigger impact on sales. But their core customer base, mostly older, price-sensitive orthodontists, turned out to not be our customer base. They never met their monthly goals.

When I thought about our progress year over year, I felt proud. But when I compared it to our closest competitor, Align Technology, I felt ridiculously small. Our market presence was microscopic compared to theirs. Of course, they'd raised $400,000,000 in investment capital while we'd raised only $4,000,000. We would never be able to compete at their level without an enormous cash infusion.

Back in 2002 when Ruedger, Thomas and I had started Lingualcare, we had big dreams, dreams of supplanting Invisalign as the leader in invisible orthodontic treatment. But over the last three years, as I'd struggled to keep the company from dying, I'd scaled my dreams down to a more manageable size. I thought in millions of dollars, not hundreds of millions. I cared more about providing secure jobs and decent benefits than seeing my name in *Fortune* magazine.

I no longer felt like an imposter when I handed someone my card.

I was a CEO, running a real company with employees.

Even though I had sales staff to send to the regional orthodontic meetings, I always attended one or two. Working the floor and talking to the poor souls who had the misfortune of making eye contact allowed me to hear unfiltered feedback from prospects and connect with customers. It also gave me a chance to scope out our competition.

That October, I worked the Pacific Coast Society of Orthodontists meeting with Kathy. During the lunch rush on the first day, John called me. I didn't want to leave our busy booth, so I let it go to voice mail. But he called back immediately. Fearing that something might be wrong with Will, I stepped into the aisle and took the call.

"I've got a job opportunity in Dallas," he said. "Your headhunter friend called me about it. Have you spoken to him?"

"No," I said.

"It's the perfect job for me, president of a digital advertising company," he said. "You need to call him and put in a good word."

"John, you know I can't do that," I said.

"Yes, you absolutely can," he said. "He respects you. He will listen to you."

"The booth is busy. Let me call you back when things slow down."

"You don't sound excited."

In that moment, I didn't feel excited at all. I felt annoyed. John expected me to call and push my friend to recommend him for a job. Did he not realize that my friend, a well-respected executive recruiter with two decades of experience, got paid large sums of money to do extensive background checks and talk to many, many references? Did he not know that asking me to "put in a good word" was amateurish?

"I'll call you back." I hung up and returned to the booth.

The rest of the day I thought about John returning to Dallas, about seeing him every day. Will would be thrilled to have his dad back, and for that reason alone I should have been happy. But I didn't feel happy. I felt dread.

I didn't love John. I didn't hate him either. I felt indifference, leaning toward irritation.

For the last few years, the immediate task of keeping our family financially afloat and managing our work schedules had given us an excuse not to address the growing abyss between us. But if John lived in Dallas full-time, it would be front and center.

I wouldn't be able to avoid the confrontation.

And I didn't think our marriage would survive.

You're Never Too Small for a Big Attraction

Dallas, Texas – January 2006

A fashionable after-work crowd jammed the brightly lit hotel ballroom. When I walked in a little before six o'clock and handed my coat to an attendant at the door, I felt relieved that I'd worn a silk dress and suit jacket to work that day, not my usual slouchy slacks and a sweater.

A local magazine hosted this annual party for their customers and prospects, and the guest list included executives from the city's largest and fastest-growing companies. I'd been invited by a friend who sold advertising for them.

Most of the networking events I attended were chock full of haggard, unshaven tech people desperately trying to convince anyone who would listen that their start-up was doing great. It was refreshing to see bright, stubble-free faces and a buffet with more than limp carrot sticks, chicken wings and tubs of ranch dressing.

I dutifully pinned the "Hi, My Name Is Lea" nametag to my lapel and made my way over to the mountain of cheese cubes and fresh grapes. I'd skipped lunch, and nothing tasted better than free food. After perusing the impressive spread, I filled a plate with Greek olives and mini spinach quiches. I'd need the sustenance to survive two hours of small talk.

I dreaded networking events, mostly because I sucked at chit-chat.

I had a set of standard conversation starters: "What do you do?" "Tell me about your company," "Are you from Dallas?" etc.

I didn't retain most of their answers. I was too consumed by my own problems. And I wasn't one of those people who asked probing follow-up questions, tuning in for a way to monetize the interaction.

I surveyed the room, which smelled of aftershave and sterno – lots of men in dark suits, much higher-end than the tech start-up crowd. I spotted a few women wearing the uniform favored by lawyers, consultants and accounts, a dark suit and appropriately cheery blouse. In the sea of dark suits, one woman stood out. She wore a fuchsia fur poncho and glittery four-inch spiked heels.

This was no lawyer or partner at Accenture. She looked like a celebrity.

She was talking to my friend from the magazine, who motioned me over. "You need to meet Kelly from the Dallas Cowboys Cheerleaders. I told her about your braces."

Kelly flashed me a huge smile and said, "I'd love to know more about your company."

I wanted to know more about her poncho. Was it dyed mink? Or fox? I fought back the urge to touch it.

Leaning in close to overcome the din of the party, I gave her my elevator pitch.

"Would you ever consider becoming a DCC sponsor?" she said. "We get lots of girls who can dance and look great otherwise, but they don't have perfect smiles."

I'd never thought about celebrity endorsement as an option for Lingualcare. I nodded. "Sure."

"We have a reality show on Country Music Television," she said. "If you guys became a sponsor and put braces on some of the girls, we could work you into the show."

Being on television would bring us visibility, but I hesitated to get too excited. Kelly hadn't mentioned the price. I assumed the sponsorship would be too expensive for a company our size.

She must have noticed my hesitation, because she kept selling.

"Do you attend tradeshows?" she said.

"Yes, we have our biggest show of the year in April."

"What would you think about having a couple of the girls in your booth signing swimsuit calendars?"

That got my attention. In the five years I'd been going to the AAO annual meetings, no company had hosted a celebrity in their booth. Dallas Cowboys Cheerleaders would definitely make a splash.

"The great thing about the calendars is that they are oversized," she said. "You can't fit them in the bags they hand out at tradeshows, so people have to carry them outside the bag. Others see it and ask where they can get one. Your booth will be mobbed."

A mob scene in our AAO booth -we needed that. I took her card and promised to call her the following week.

The next day, I ran the idea past Ruedger.

"Cheerleaders? Isn't that kind of cheesy?" he said.

As a German, Ruedger could not appreciate the sacred place that cheerleaders occupied in American pop culture.

Growing up, most of the girls I knew dreamed of wearing a short, pleated skirt and matching sweater with a megaphone applique to school on Fridays. Guys pined for them, but only the best-looking and most athletic boys could ever date one.

NFL cheerleaders breathed rarified air. They were talented dancers and gymnasts, chosen not just for good looks, but for their athletic ability. The Dallas Cowboys Cheerleaders set the bar for professional cheerleaders. They represented the best of the best of the best.

"It won't be cheesy, I promise," I said. "We can't afford a big booth, but maybe we can grab people with a big attraction."

Ruedger conceded. "You're the marketing guru," he said. "You decide."

The sponsorship was expensive – the largest amount I'd spent on a single marketing campaign – and it was potentially risky. On the negative side, our customers might find the skimpy uniforms offensive. On the positive side, the affiliation would get attention and link our company to a known brand associated with beauty.

Before I could agree to the sponsorship, I needed to call Dr. Sam to see if he would treat four Dallas Cowboys Cheerleaders for free.

He didn't hesitate. "Heck yeah! Bring them in."

I walked down to the breakroom, where Beth and Cary were brewing the 3:00 pot of coffee everyone relied on to get through the waning hours of the day. I told them about the impending deal with the Dallas Cowboys Cheerleaders.

"Are you crazy?" said Beth. "That's exploitive, those little shorts and all the cleavage. It demeans women. It sends the wrong message."

"I agree," said Cary. "That's not the image we want."

I reached my hand into the giant plastic container of Costco animal crackers and bit the head off a zebra. I hadn't expected this kind of negativity from the team.

Kathy, whose desk sat across from the breakroom door, walked in and joined us. "What are you saying about the Dallas Cowboys Cheerleaders?" She reached for the animal crackers and took a handful.

"Lea is going to hire them as spokespeople," said Beth. "She wants to bring them to AAO to sign swimsuit calendars."

"Are you joking?" Kathy said.

Beth opened her eyes wide and shook her head back and forth. She passed me a Styrofoam cup of coffee and then poured one for herself.

"Dr. Sam will put braces on them," I said as I stirred a package of fake sugar into my cup. "They will give testimonials in the booth."

"Oh Lord." Kathy laughed. "Did he pee his pants when you told him?'

FINDING THE EXIT

"We need to raise the company's profile, fill the booth with prospects," I said. "If you can do that for the same amount of money, I'm all ears."

"Can you give us a couple of days to brainstorm?" said Kathy. "I think Beth and Cary and I can come up with something better."

"You have two days," I said.

They filed out of the breakroom, leaving me with the open jar of animal crackers and a sudden burst of doubt. What had seemed like a great idea less than an hour ago now seemed precarious. What if the women who attended the AAO had the same reaction as my employees? How would I explain it to our new investors?

The next afternoon, Kathy came into my office and told me that after a two-hour brainstorming lunch, they hadn't been able to think of anything to compete with my cheerleader idea. "What are you going to do if it backfires?" she said. "A lot of female staff members come to the AAO, they could be turned off by those girls."

I shrugged and said, "I think it's worth a try."

After Kathy left, I thought about risk. If I had been afraid of taking risks, I would never have done half the crazy things I'd done in my life. I would have never moved to Texas, or taken the job in Berkeley, or left Mordix to start Lingualcare. Risk scared me, but it never stopped me, it had become that friend who said, "Come on, I dare you."

I signed the deal.

Kelly selected the girls who needed braces and within a month they became Dr. Sam's patients. Once the cheerleaders got their braces, I didn't put much energy into worrying about how our customers would react.

Something more urgent was consuming my attention.

After nine and a half years, I wanted out of my marriage to John.

Time to Go

Dallas, Texas – March 2006

John had returned to Dallas in November, triumphant. He'd landed the job at the digital advertising company without me having to call my headhunter friend.

While he'd been in Chicago, I'd rearranged my life. Will and I established a weekday routine that worked. The disruption that accompanied John's weekend guest appearances left me feeling out of sorts. Spending time with him felt like a chore.

His moving back was worse than his leaving. John wanted a wife, a romantic partner who focused her energy on him, not an entrepreneur obsessed with financings, customer issues and manufacturing problems.

Our emotional bond wasn't strong enough to distract me from the business, only Will could do that. John's sole means of grabbing my attention was to provoke me. We bickered constantly, ratcheting up the tension in our house to the point where I no longer wanted to come home from work.

Whenever I had an idle moment in my day, I fantasized about divorce. I scoured real estate websites, imagining where I would live. I built spreadsheets to calculate the costs of living alone and the impact of a divorce. I talked to divorced friends about their experiences, how they managed the goodbye part, the kids, the division of stuff and the messy court battles.

After closing the Longhorn Partners financing, Ruedger and I had raised our meager salaries and I could afford a place of my own, barely. Foremost on my mind was finding a home where Will would feel safe and happy, some place with a yard, close to Will's school and my office, but far enough from the house I shared with John that we wouldn't trip over each other at the grocery store.

In early March, while looking at online ads for rental homes, I saw a two-bedroom house on a street next to a beautiful park. The location fit all of my criteria, and the rent was in my range. I decided to drive by on my lunch hour to check it out.

My excitement plummeted as soon as I pulled into the driveway. The house had broken shingles over the porch, a big dent in the aluminum screen door, and landscaping in desperate need of water. I walked up the steps and peered into a large picture window. Hardwood floors and a fireplace made the living room appealing, but the kitchen cabinets and appliances screamed 1975.

Maybe the affordable, idyllic hideaway that I'd conjured up didn't exist.

Before returning to the office, I walked around the park. Moms, nannies and toddlers filled the playground with shouts and laughter. I pictured Will swinging on the swings, climbing to the top of the slide and playing football in the large grassy field with his school friends, one of whom lived a few blocks away. I looked over in the direction of Will's friend's house on Park Lane and I noticed a sign in front of a lovely gray brick house with black shutters – *FOR LEASE.*

I called the phone number on the sign. No one answered, so I left a message.

My excitement rose as I drove slowly past the immaculate little house with the well-kept yard. It would likely be out of my price range, but what if it wasn't?

The next day, the owner called and offered to show me the house during my lunch hour.

It was perfect.

I immediately fell in love with the remodeled kitchen, stone floor and new stainless steel appliances, the master bathroom with jetted tub and a big closet, the large bedroom and bathroom for Will and a third bedroom I could use for an office, with a wall of windows overlooking a wood deck and large backyard. The price was a few hundred dollars a month higher than what I'd budgeted, but I knew I could make it work.

"I put up the sign two days ago and I've had over sixty phone calls," said the young woman who answered the door. Her parents, who lived in Chicago, owned the house as an income property. She and her husband had been staying in it while their house in Highland Park was being remodeled. They planned to move out mid-April.

The house felt right.

"I need to leave my husband," I said. "I have a seven-year-old son and I can't move out unless I have a good place for us to go. This house would be perfect. Please tell your mom I promise to treat it like my own."

That night her mother called and left a message on my voice mail at work. She said, "The house is yours if you pass the background check."

Three days later I signed the lease.

I had six weeks to figure out an exit plan.

* * *

The company needed a marketing manager and another customer service person, but I couldn't fit one more employee in the space adjacent to the clinic.

The business of selling to doctors had proven to be a winner, while the clinic had become a distraction disproportionate to the revenue it produced. Dr. Sam longed to have his Fridays back and we needed a bigger office.

Ruedger and I talked about it at length. Even though he still believed the clinic model could work, we agreed that we didn't have the financial bandwidth to run both lines of business.

"Ok," he conceded. "Kill the clinic."

I contacted a commercial real estate broker before Ruedger could change his mind. She showed me office space nearby that would give us plenty of room to grow.

Then I started working on finding an orthodontist to take on the clinic patients and someone to rent the space and equipment. One of our clinical advisors, an orthodontist with an office ten minutes south of us, agreed to take the clinic patients and complete their treatment for a fixed fee. After signing the contract with him, the pieces fell into place.

I'd heard through a friend that a chain of dental clinics wanted to open an office in our neighborhood, so I called them. They liked our location and quickly agreed to rent the clinic and equipment for a price that covered our cost.

We scheduled the Lingualcare move for April 15th, three days before I planned to move into my new house on Park Lane.

Because there were boxes strewn all over our offices, no one noticed all the boxes from Overstock.com and Amazon piled up against my wall and under Ruedger's desk. I'd been shopping online for weeks, acquiring all the items I'd need for the new house: linens, pots and pans, flatware, dishes and rugs.

After signing the lease, I'd met with a divorce lawyer and had her draw up papers. I could not envision a scenario where John and I would live together again, and I knew from past experiences that once I'd reached the point of indifference in a relationship, I'd never go back.

John would be in Europe the week my landlord's daughter planned to vacate the house. Moving while he was five thousand miles appealed to me – no big fight, no ugly scene, no drama. But to pull it off in one day would require help.

I worked up the nerve to call my mother two weeks before the planned move. "I have a big favor to ask," I said.

I told her about the problems with my marriage, my desire to live separately, the new house and my plan to move with Will in a few weeks. Would she come to Dallas to help me pack, move and take care of Will? Mostly I needed her to help manage the emotional fallout from John, which I knew would be enormous.

John and my mother shared a close friendship. They held similar worldviews and frequently emailed each other news articles and political commentaries. When she stayed at our home, she spent her time commiserating with John. They had more in common with each other than I had with either of them.

"Are you mad at me?" I said.

"No, honey, I am just sad. This will be difficult for Will and for you. I'll pray for you."

"Please don't say anything to John," I said. "I want to tell him in my own time."

She agreed. Thrice divorced, my mother knew how ugly people could get when they fought over kids and money.

After hanging up, I called Ruedger and told him about my plans to leave John right after the clinic move. "I wanted you to know because I might be distracted," I said. "Please don't say anything to anyone at the company. I haven't even told Beth."

"I'm so sorry," he said. "If I can help you, please ask."

As I hung up the phone, I recalled Darryl Hannah's famous line from *Steel Magnolias*, "I will not allow my personal tragedy to affect my ability to do good hair," and it made me laugh out loud for the first time in weeks.

We spent Friday and Saturday moving out of the clinic and into our new space on Alpha Road. Although the new office was only a few miles from the clinic physically, psychologically it felt like we'd relocated to a new planet.

No more trying to figure out how to recruit clinic patients.

No more Dr. Sam locked in the bathroom.

No more staff flaking out at the last minute.

I drove to work on Monday feeling a weird combination of excitement about working in the new office and dread about my upcoming move. My mother would be flying in that night. I had to pick her up at the airport, but before I did that, I had to tell Will what was going on.

Although I'd rehearsed the conversation in my mind for months, I still hadn't found the words to tell him that I was breaking apart his family.

That afternoon, I picked up Will from school and brought him to the new office. I kept a bucket of toy soldiers in my file cabinet. As soon as Will arrived, he dug them out and began setting up a battle formation in the hallway.

I studied his profile, lips set in concentration as he focused on his task. What would his sweet face look like tomorrow? I ached thinking about it.

Instead of going home for dinner, I took Will to California Pizza Kitchen, his favorite restaurant. I asked about school. I asked about his friends. I tried to sound cheerful and happy, when in fact I felt too sick and scared to taste my food.

We drove south from California Pizza Kitchen instead of east, toward home.

"Where are we going?" said Will.

"I need to run an errand." I had a rug in the trunk of the car that had been delivered to the office that day, so that part was true.

I pulled into the driveway of the new house.

"Whose house is this?"

I unlocked the side door, the one next to the driveway, then opened the trunk, picked up the rug and carried it inside.

"Mom, what are we doing here?" Will's voice quivered.

I went back outside. He was standing in the driveway, arms folded. As I approached him, he ran to the backyard.

"Why are we here? You're scaring me. Whose house is this?" he shouted.

I reached out and pulled him to me. His skin felt damp through his shirt. I buried my nose in the top of his head. His hair smelled citrusy and sweaty, not like a baby's hair, but not like a man's either.

"This is our new house," I said. "I'm leaving your dad. You and I are moving here tomorrow. In a few minutes, we are going to the airport to pick up your grandmother. She's going to help."

"Does Dad know?"

"No. I'm going to tell him tonight."

I hugged Will. He struggled and tried to pull away, but I didn't release my hold. I was afraid to let him go, afraid to look into his eyes and see what I'd done. "I'm so sorry," I said when I finally eased my grip.

"Can we go now?"

Will was silent in the back seat.

"Are you okay?" I said.

"It's going to take me a little while to get used to the idea," he whispered.

Later that night, as my mother put Will to bed, guiding him into sleep with one book after another, I wrote John an email.

A brave person would call.

A brave person would deliver the news in person.

I wasn't brave.

As further proof of that, when John called at two in the morning, I let my mother answer the phone. I was afraid to talk to him, afraid that he would attack my resolve with all his persuasive power and convince me not to go through with the move.

My mother spokes in a soft tone. "She's not ready to talk to you yet. Please respect that and give her some time."

I imagined the panic John felt. He was thousands of miles away and couldn't do anything to stop me from moving out of the home we'd shared for nine years.

The next morning, I woke up and checked my email. John's reply waited for me in my inbox. I stared at the screen, willing myself to click on it.

My mother came into the office. "Don't open it," she said. "I'll read it for you."

I went into the kitchen, started a pot of coffee and sagged against the kitchen counter. I didn't want to deal with John's anger, his hurt, or his pain; I could barely cope with Will's and my own.

My mother and I packed with startling efficiency, and the movers pulled out of the driveway by 1:00 p.m. I only took a third of the furniture, a few household items, my personal possessions and Will's things. Guilt made me leave most of our shared belongings behind.

Will spent his first evening at the new house playing in the park across the street. From the kitchen window, I watched him throw a football to another boy about his age who I didn't recognize. I ate baby carrots dipped in garlic hummus, the only food I'd had since breakfast, while my mother washed silverware, wiping away the water spots before putting each piece carefully in the drawer.

All day she'd worked steadily, taking on one task after another to help me make a home here, without saying anything even remotely judgmental. Despite our differences, despite her close relationship with John, she was there, supporting me with her actions and her silence, being the mother I needed.

Breaking Up Is Hard to Do

Orange County, California – April 2006

After breaking up with the clinic, and breaking up with John, I had to break up with Knightsbridge, at least partially.

They could not afford to invest in marketing and sales to find the new customers we needed. In addition to sales commissions, the contract promised them tens of thousands of shares if we hit certain revenue targets. But they didn't deserve the promised stock grants when Lingualcare was paying for the growth.

Somehow, we needed to preserve the manufacturing part of the contract and kill the marketing and sales piece without destroying our relationship.

I called Mr. Kryptonite and asked for his advice. I figured with all the companies in his portfolio he'd seen more than a few partnerships fall apart.

"There is no easy way to do it," he said. "Try not to assign blame or throw accusations around. Show them the gap in the numbers and ask if they'll agree to let you out."

"As the contract is written, I can't sever one part without negating the rest of it," I said.

"That gives you the advantage. They just invested tons of money in that manufacturing plant. They won't want to lose it."

After talking with our lawyer, Ruedger and I decided to propose an amendment to the existing contract, a supplement that allowed us to maintain the manufacturing part of the agreement while removing the marketing commitments and sales commission payments.

I dreaded the confrontation.

Their attempt to screw me during the merger talks still bothered me. It had been hard to stay silent, but I'd kept my promise to Ruedger. I never let on that I knew what they'd done.

Now I had to sit across the table and have a hard discussion.

Nothing personal, just business.

Ruedger and I wanted to keep things friendly. That's why, at the last minute, we added an olive branch to the contract amendment, a consolation prize. If they signed, we would give them a portion of the stock they could have earned by achieving their milestones. They wouldn't have to do anything to get the stock except sign the contract.

I met Ruedger in San Diego and we drove to Carlsbad. He'd been in Mexicali for the last two weeks helping optimize the manufacturing lines.

"Mexicali will be ready to produce the first cases in a few weeks," he said. "We can't blow up the relationship today."

* * *

Davis knew something was up. Instead of his usual smile, he wore a grimace when he met us in the lobby. He ushered us into the conference room and then left to find Bart.

Despite the heat, I opened the blinds. Sunlight filled the small room. I sat down at the table and looked at the blank whiteboard. How many times had I been in this room, enthusiastically drawing on the whiteboard, conjuring up marketing plans and sales strategies that never came to fruition?

Davis returned with Bart. They brought bottles of water. I opened mine and took a long swig. The simple act of doing something basic, drinking water, calmed me.

Davis started, "So why are we here? What's with all the mystery?"

"Congratulations," I said. "Ruedger told me how great the Mexicali plant looks."

"You didn't ask for this meeting to compliment us on Mexicali," said Bart.

"No. We're here to discuss the marketing agreement," I said. "We want to terminate your selling rights."

Bart shifted his eyes to Davis, then to Ruedger and back to me.

Ruedger pulled copies of the contract amendment out of his briefcase and passed one to each person at the table.

"We don't want to end our manufacturing relationship," he said, "just the sales and marketing. So, we've prepared an amendment to the current agreement."

"We've invested a lot of money in building your sales," said Davis.

"The numbers don't reflect that," I said. I didn't want this to digress into accusations. I needed to stay on message, to stick to the script I'd mentally written on the way there.

"Come on, Lea, you can't just pull the rug out from under us."

"We recognize your efforts and the marketing investments you made." I turned the contract to the page with the option grant clause and showed Davis. "We're willing to give you these shares outright, even though you didn't hit the milestones."

"What about the customers we brought you?" said Davis.

I turned to the last page of the contract where we listed all the Knightsbridge customers who became our customers. "We will continue to pay the full sales commissions on these customers for the next twelve months."

They read it, page by page. I resisted the urge to justify and defend our position. They didn't hit the numbers. What else was there to say?

No one talked. The tension made it hard to breathe.

We had cause to terminate and technically, we could terminate the entire contract, including the manufacturing, which would put them in a terrible position. It would put us in a terrible position too, so I didn't want to go there.

I waited for the question, "And if we don't agree to this, then what happens?"

But Davis asked a different question. "What if we continue to sell, non-exclusively, and hit the milestones? Could we get the original number of shares promised?"

The contract amendment that Ruedger and I proposed would give them forty percent of the stock they would have earned had they achieved the milestones. If I were them, I'd take stock and run, not gamble more money on a maybe.

"Yes," I said, "but then we need to remove the guaranteed shares from the amendment."

Concern passed over Bart's face. "I'm not sure we want to do that," he said. He knew we were offering a good financial deal and a way out of a bad situation that allowed each party to save face.

Davis insisted. "I guarantee you we can hit our milestones, and I want the opportunity to vest all the stock."

Bart threw Davis a skeptical look. "Are you sure?"

Davis said, "Absolutely."

Ruedger started his laptop and deleted the olive branch clause.

We printed the new contracts. I signed on behalf of Lingualcare. Bart signed for Knightsbridge.

We all shook hands.

I was in the car and had the AC blasting before Ruedger made it out of the building.

Ruedger adjusted the radio until he found a classic rock station as I raced north to the Santa Ana Airport. Our flight didn't leave for several hours, but I couldn't wait to put distance between me and Knightsbridge. Ruedger didn't say anything, just stared out the window and listened to music.

We arrived at the airport four hours early, so I pulled into the parking lot of the IHOP directly across the street.

"Can I buy you lunch?" Ruedger said.

We both ordered iced tea and pancakes.

When the waiter brought my iced tea, I took a sip and started laughing, and then I couldn't stop. I laughed from the center of my being. Ruedger laughed, too. We'd stop for a few seconds, then look at each other and start again.

It had been a horrible month. Laughing the tension out of my body was better than crying hysterically.

I sipped the tea, perhaps the best I'd ever tasted, and giggled.

It was over.

I hoped it was the last breakup for a while.

Viva Las Vegas

Las Vegas, Nevada – May 2006

Going into the 2006 AAO meeting, my whole staff, with the exception of the three men on our sales team, complained about having the Dallas Cowboys Cheerleaders in our booth. They also hated my choice of booth attire.

I wanted us to stand out, so I ordered bright orange polo shirts with our logo emblazoned in dark blue. The eye rolling and whispers started as soon as I handed out the shirts at the company meeting prior to the show.

"Here's the good news about your new orange shirts," I said. "No one will mistake you for a Dallas Cowboys Cheerleader or an OrthoCo rep."

On the first day of the show, our two cheerleaders arrived at the Las Vegas Convention Center with Kelly's assistant, who acted as chaperone and wrangler. She'd shipped the swimsuit calendars to the hotel a few days earlier so we had them ready to go. The girls pulled off their tracksuits to reveal the iconic uniforms, tiny, blue, cleavage-enhancing halter tops, white hot pants, a little white vest with fringe and those awesome white cowboy boots.

Both cheerleaders had our braces behind their teeth.

Our booth, long and narrow, was positioned at the end of a wide aisle, visible from the opposite side of the convention center. We intentionally placed the sales counter where the cheerleaders sat in the middle, visible from three sides.

"Would you like a free swimsuit calendar?"

"How about a photo?"

It didn't take long for word to spread. Within an hour a mob descended on the Lingualcare booth. An empty booth repels people, but a crowded booth sucks people in.

We took photos of customers and prospects with the cheerleaders, our logo strategically positioned over their heads, and printed them out right then and there.

While people stood in line to meet the cheerleaders, our reps talked to them, showing the plastic models with our brackets and handing out brochures. Kelly's assistant managed the girls' interactions, replenished the stack of calendars when it got low and kept the line moving.

Our two cheerleaders could not have been more professional. They autographed calendars with a Sharpie, answered questions and opened their mouths to show their braces.

This was huge.

One commonly held assumption about lingual braces was that they interfered with speech. Both girls told potential customers how much they liked the product and affirmed that they had no problem speaking.

They enthusiastically posed for photos and smiled, smiled, smiled, hour after hour.

I was surprised by the number of female attendees who lined up for calendars and photos. Women easily outnumbered men in the line three to one. After eavesdropping on their conversations, I understood. Some recognized the girls from the Country Music Television show, others wanted to get a calendar autographed for a husband, boyfriend or son. I didn't hear any comments about sexual exploitation.

A few Mordix employees came over to spy. They stood far enough down the aisle to avoid a conversation, but close enough to observe the mob scene. It had been three years since Ruedger and I left, but they still treated us like enemies of the state.

Near the end of the day, Richard Riley, my nemesis from OrthoCo, showed up. We hadn't spoken since New Orleans, and as far I was concerned, if I never spoke to him again it would be just fine. I avoided his darting glances, but he waited on the edge of the crowd until I finished with a prospect and then cornered me.

"You guys are the talk of the show," he said. "I had to come over here and see what all the buzz was about."

He cast an envious gaze at the queue, and then inclined his head and winked at me. "How about a picture with the girls? You and me. Since you're the boss, you can cut the line."

Before I could explain why I would never, not in a hundred years, have my picture taken with an asshole like him, he darted to the front of the line and waved me over. I gritted my teeth while Richard put one arm around me and the other around a blonde cheerleader.

Say cheese.

Later that afternoon, Kathy pulled me aside. "They're so professional and sweet," she said. "I'm jealous, though. I wish I could fit into those little shorts."

We left the show with hundreds of leads.

No One Gets Rich Being Nice

Dallas, Texas – August 2006

At the end of August, we started sending a few orders per day to Mexicali so they could ramp up. Our plan was to slowly increase the number of orders going to Mexico while decreasing the orders going to Germany, until the transition was complete.

I didn't think we could switch from manufacturing in Germany to manufacturing in Mexicali with zero problems, but I didn't know how bad the problems would be, or how long it would take to sort them out.

The first issue we encountered was heat.

Our manufacturing process required a dental technician to cut the teeth from a plaster model one at a time and realign them in pink wax that resembled gum tissue. Because of patent issues with OrthoCo, we couldn't realign teeth with software; it had to be done by hand. Once completed, the wax setup was scanned into the computer and the process of designing customized brackets and wires began.

We included the wax setups in the packages sent to the orthodontists, along with the brackets and wires. Orthodontists showed the setups to their patients, so they could visualize what their teeth would look like at the end of treatment.

Soon after we began shipping products from Mexicali, orthodontists called to complain that the teeth weren't aligned properly in the setups. They emailed pictures to customer service. The teeth looked weird, not horrible, but off just enough to be noticeable.

Ruedger challenged the lab technicians in Mexicali. They swore the setups were designed to the specifications outlined in the work instructions. The dentist in charge of the lab assured us that he'd double-checked and approved every setup before scanning.

It took a week to figure out that the culprit wasn't poor workmanship, it was heat.

Our packages sat in the back of a UPS truck for hours waiting to cross the border from Mexicali to Calexico, California. The ambient temperature during the summer could reach 110 degrees, and it got much hotter in the truck.

We'd never had this problem with models from Germany, so it never occurred to us to check the melting temperature of the wax Hoffman used, the same wax we'd ordered for Mexicali because we wanted to replicate Hoffman's lab process to the letter.

The second problem was with the gold alloy used to make our brackets.

Hoffman used a brand of dental gold that could not be purchased in the United States. We bought the closest substitute available, an alloy with slightly less gold and slightly more silver. Testing showed that it met our biocompatibility and hardness requirements, but it appeared lighter and more silvery than Hoffman's gold.

Customers noticed the color difference immediately and complained.

"The brackets are silver, but you're charging me for gold," said one doctor.

"They are gold. I promise," I said. "I'll send you the material safety data sheet so you can see for yourself."

I instructed the customer service team to forward all the angry phone calls to me. One of the first calls I got was from an irate orthodontist in Kansas City. "I told the patient he had to pay a premium because the brackets are made of gold. How can I justify that now?" he yelled.

I reassured him. "It's hard for a patient to see color in the back of their mouth. Don't worry, it will be fine."

I hated to disappoint our customers and I didn't want them to think we were sacrificing quality to save money, but we had to transition to Mexico. We had to lower our cost of goods. Lingualcare would never be profitable as long as we bought products from Dr. Hoffman.

It took the better part of four months to work out the kinks and complete the transition. Many orthodontists grumbled, but only a few abandoned us.

* * *

Ruedger and I knew that the money we'd raised in 2005 might not get us to profitability, not unless we sacrificed our growth. That was always the dilemma, to focus on profit or growth. Profit bought us time and options. Growth bought us enterprise value.

When investors calculated the value of technology companies like ours, they based it on multiples of revenue, not on profitability. Ruedger and I both decided not to sacrifice growth for marginal profitability. Instead we would go back out and raise a bigger round, maybe eight to ten million dollars, enough to fuel real growth.

I contacted several Dallas investors who had turned us down three years ago to see if they wanted to take another look. One was the private investment arm of a famous oil family. My contact was no longer there, but his replacement agreed to see me.

Because I still hated going to investor meetings alone, I invited Scott to join me. We met outside Fountain Place, a distinctive, sixty-story glass I.M. Pei skyscraper. It was an iconic part of the downtown Dallas skyline, known for its angular design and the fountains that surround it. The oil family occupied several floors near the top.

"You ever met the oil guys?" asked Scott.

"No, but I've read about them."

"They didn't get here by being nice," he said as he pushed the elevator button. "All these oil patch guys are hard asses. Don't take it personally if they beat you up."

They couldn't be worse than Harry Ruskin.

The main lobby contained an amazing assortment of sparkling geodes and polished mineral samples, multicolored slices of the earth collected by men who drilled deep beneath its surface.

Our contact didn't belong to the oil family; he just worked for them. Short, athletic and in his early forties, he wore the wealthy version of office casual – wool pants, an expensive dress shirt with monogrammed cuffs, a Rolex and loafers polished to a high sheen.

"You and I have something in common," he said as we sat down in the conference room. "We both graduated from Hastings Senior High School."

Technically, I never graduated from high school, but I didn't bring that up.

He added, "I saw an article about you a few months ago in the Dallas Morning News."

The business section had done an article about me and had mentioned that I was from Hastings. I read the name on his card and then it clicked. "Your dad taught English at the high school," I said, envisioning the man in front of me thirty pounds heavier and wearing a ratty brown cardigan.

"You got it," he said. "I was five years ahead of you, so we didn't overlap, but I thought it was an interesting coincidence."

I did, too. It was weird that two Nebraska kids from a town of less than twenty thousand people wound up here, on the fortieth floor of an I.M. Pei skyscraper in Dallas, amongst the treasures of an infamous oil family. I wondered if the hometown connection would bring me any goodwill. Maybe it meant that he'd be less of an asshole.

Wrong.

He liked our story, but when I told him our pre-money valuation, he laughed out loud and shook his head.

"Your company doesn't merit an eight-figure valuation. You're looking at seven figures, and not high seven figures."

Scott jumped in. "Forget about the valuation for a minute. Do you like the company?"

"I like the concept, but it's still early stage, and that will be reflected in any term sheet we give you."

He agreed to discuss our deal with his colleagues at their Monday morning meeting and get back to me.

Outside, Scott and I sat on a bench next to the fountain. Water splashed all around us. Since the weather had cooled down, more people were eating lunch outside.

"I hate VCs," I said.

"They're all like that," said Scott. "It's never going to be like it was before 2001. They all lost too much money. Now they want to stack the terms in their favor, make you pay for their past sins. What about going back to the Longhorn guys or the Germans?"

"They don't have enough money," I said. "We need someone with deep pockets to lead the round."

I dreaded the prospect of more meetings like the one I'd just left. But I suspected every VCs we talked to would have the same attitude.

I wished there were another way.

I'd Prefer a Bridge Loan

Dallas, Texas – October 2006

On October 17th, I was in my office drinking coffee, picking at a banana nut muffin that I shouldn't have been eating and skimming the Wall Street Journal, when Ruedger called.

"I forwarded an email this morning. Did you read it?"

"No, I haven't worked my way through the pile yet," I said, scrolling through Outlook, looking for Ruedger's name. I saw it and double clicked.

3M Acquires Developer of 3-D Imaging Technology for Digital Dentistry, Brontes Technologies Inc.

I read the first line of the press release. It was dated yesterday, October 16th, 2006. 3M today acquired Brontes Technologies Inc., a Lexington, Mass.-based developer of proprietary 3-D imaging technology for $95M in cash.

"Do you know these guys?" I said. I put the phone on mute and took a big bite of the muffin, chewing while Ruedger talked.

"Never heard of them," said Ruedger, "but I did some research. They make a 3-D scanner like the one Mordix has, but the Brontes scanner is not commercially available. The company doesn't have any revenue."

I took the phone off mute. "How did they get ninety-five million dollars for a company with no revenue?"

We agreed to do some digging and see what we could find out about Brontes. This was the latest in a flurry of dental acquisitions by large companies over the past two years, but it was the first one I'd seen that wasn't a mature business.

Maybe there was hope for us.

I went to the Brontes website. Smart kids with Ivy League pedigrees developed the scanning technology at MIT. They had all the right ingredients – name brand investors, lots of patents, wunderkinds and East Coast cache.

Okay, maybe there wasn't hope for us.

A few hours later, I phoned Bart to discuss the latest batch of manufacturing problems. Before hanging up, I said, "Did you see that press release about 3M acquiring Brontes Technologies?"

"Yeah, I did. But I've never heard of them."

"No one has," I said. "How did they ever get ninety-five million dollars for that company?"

"Do you know the name of the banker who did the deal?"

"No," I said, "but I have a friend who knows people at one of the venture firms that financed the company."

"See what you can find out," said Bart.

I sent Mr. Kryptonite a note. He had an extensive network in Boston. The next day he called with a name, Miles Newgate. He worked for Jefferies in Waltham.

"You going to call him?"

"I'm not sure yet," I said. "Maybe."

He provided the phone number and email address. "Let me know what you find out," he said before hanging up.

According to my most recent calculations, without an infusion of cash, a big spike in revenue or dramatic cost cuts, Lingualcare would be out of money by the end of June 2007.

I'd started calling investors back in September. Scott and I had a few meetings like the unpleasant one with the oil family guy, but nothing that would turn into money soon. We needed a more substantial pipeline.

But I was tired.

I was tired of looking for money.

And I was tired of fighting with John.

He didn't want a divorce, so he refused to respond to the offers my attorney put on the table, and he would not go to co-parenting counseling. Instead he sent me rambling emails about why God didn't want us to break up and how our problems were actually my problems because he was perfectly happy.

I was struggling to help Will cope with the separation. Since we'd moved into the new house, he'd been drawing guns on the whiteboard next to the kitchen door, explaining to me that the size of the gun correlated to the amount of anger he felt each day. Some days he drew tanks, other days he drew rocket launchers and machine guns. I felt thankful the day he drew a small handgun.

Despite feeling overwhelmed by my personal life, I had to show up for Lingualcare and make something happen. There was no running from that responsibility.

* * *

At the end of November, I flew to Germany for a meeting with Mr. Glasauer to discuss our next financing. Ruedger and I stopped at St. Michael's to light candles before going to Glasauer's office.

Our footsteps broke the silence of the almost-empty church. The late afternoon sun cast shadows across the nave as I made my way over to the wrought iron rack of unlit candles. I put ten Euros in the tin box and started lighting.

For Will.

For Ruedger.

For more sales.

For the next right investor.

For John to let me go in peace.

For me.

Snow blew in our faces as we exited the church. Big, heavy flakes covered the cobblestones, making them slippery. Ever the optimist, I'd worn boots with heels. Ruedger offered me his arm as we negotiated the church steps and the cobblestone plaza.

"Did you light a candle for sales?" he said.

"Always. You?"

"Yes, and for Glasauer. We need his money."

"Does he have any?" I said.

"We're about to find out."

Ronnie and Glasauer greeted us warmly.

"Coffee?" said Glasauer.

The receptionist returned with cappuccinos and a large plate of Christmas cookies.

"When do you run out of money?" said Ronnie.

"Not until June."

"Seven months isn't much time. Do you have a plan?" asked Glasauer.

"We wanted to talk to you about a bridge loan," said Ruedger, "just in case it gets tight."

Bridge loans were a common instrument to use between financings. The company usually offered a discount on the price of the next financing round – fifteen or twenty percent – as an incentive to participate in the bridge.

"You need to find money somewhere else," Glasauer said.

I reached for a frosted gingerbread star, my all-time favorite German Christmas cookie.

"If we find money elsewhere, will you participate pro rata?" I asked, trying to determine if he didn't have any money or if he was just playing hard to get.

He smiled at me, knowingly. He had my number. "We can discuss it when you bring me a term sheet," he said.

I took three more cookies from the plate as Glasauer made a list of European firms he'd worked with recently. He offered to arrange meetings for us in January, but suggested we increase our efforts in the U.S., looking for money in California and on the East Coast.

"Since you have no commercial operation in Germany, it will be hard to get a European firm to invest," he said.

On the way out the door, Glasauer handed me a wrapped gift. "I wish you a happy Christmas, Lea."

I left with it tucked under my arm.

Ruedger left empty-handed.

I unwrapped the package on the way back to the Golden Adler. It contained a book with daily inspirational quotes called *Today Is My Best Day: Joy, Serenity, Fantasy & Success through positive Thinking, Planning and Action*. The mascot on the cover was a cartoon character, a cross between Big Bird from Sesame Street and a palm tree.

I'd have preferred a bridge loan.

On my last night in Germany, I paged through my dog-eared notebook, looking for Miles Newgate's phone number.

I'd been obsessing about Lingualcare's options and the implications of each. I didn't like the idea of raising a large financing with a venture capital partner that would take control of the company, and I'd given up on finding the perfect super angel. Maybe we could wrangle money out of a European VC, but that option felt even more like a long shot.

I kept circling back to the same questions. What if we sold Lingualcare now? Was it possible? Were we too early? We only had rights to sell our products in North and South America. Would that prevent a multinational company from looking at us?

I dialed Newgate's number.

Since it was Saturday afternoon in Boston, I wasn't surprised when no one answered the phone. I left a message on his voice mail, referenced the Brontes transaction and mentioned Mr. Kryptonite's contact at Charles River Ventures, hoping it would be enough to merit a call back. Maybe it was a waste of time, but if I didn't ask I'd never find out.

When All Else Fails, Listen to Tony Robbins

Dallas, Texas – January 2007

Hoping to get my bridge loan in Dallas, I called Jake to see if I could get on the Longhorn Partners' agenda for the January meeting.

"If you're going to ask for money, you need a reason," he said. "Bring us good news."

I didn't have any good news, and if I didn't make progress on fundraising I would have only bad news.

That night at home, while Will slept, I sat at the kitchen table and stared out at the park across the street, contemplating my next move. If I didn't get Lingualcare financed, I had enough money to survive for one month without a paycheck. After that I'd be pitching a tent in the park.

Will's blue and gold Notre Dame football jersey lay next to the sink, rumpled and dirty. I needed to wash it and hang it to dry so he could wear it the next morning. Since receiving it as a gift from his dad in October, it was the only shirt he would wear to school.

I understood. Will felt like his life was out of his control. He couldn't control his dad or me, but he could control what he wore to school, so he'd chosen Brady Quinn's jersey, number eight.

I filled the kitchen sink with water and added a dollop of dish soap. Little bits of the number had started to flake off, so I took extra care as I washed and rinsed it.

The next morning, Will drew a knife on the kitchen whiteboard, a big one with serrated edges, a Rambo knife. Was the knife an improvement over a gun?

I resisted the urge to wipe the board clean. He had the right to his feelings. I wouldn't erase them and I wouldn't minimize them.

* * *

"Did you ever read that Tony Robbins book I gave you?" my lunch companion asked.

We'd just finished our taco platters and had ordered a basket of sopapillas with cinnamon-honey dipping sauce. Normally I didn't eat a heavy lunch, but when I felt overwhelmed, Mexican food was my drug of choice.

"Tony has helped me a ton," she said. "My sales numbers are *way* up."

My friend worked in commercial real estate. Ever on the hunt for an edge, she read tons of business advice books and passed along the highlights, Cliff Notes personified.

I'd spent the last thirty minutes complaining about John dragging his feet on the divorce and Will drawing rocket launchers. I hadn't even gotten to the company running out of money when she brought up her favorite self-help guru.

"What is the upshot?" I said. "I promise to read the book later."

"When you go home tonight, sit down and think about two things you could do immediately that would change the trajectory of your life. Then take a step to make them happen." She smiled at me. "It's easy."

That night, after Will went to bed, I sat at the kitchen table and stared at a blank sheet of notebook paper and thought about what I needed: the company to stay alive, and to make some money so I could unwind my life with John.

I wrote:

1) Get on the Longhorn Partners February meeting agenda

2) Call Miles Newgate again

Even though it was late, I called Miles Newgate's office number and left the same message I'd left in December. Then I dialed the Longhorn Partners' deal manager and left him a message asking for a slot on their February agenda. Afterward, I opened my computer and wrote each of them an email. Although both actions felt small in comparison with the problems I faced, I went to bed feeling lighter.

Miles Newgate called me the next morning.

"I got your message in December," he said, "but the connection was bad and I couldn't make out your last name or your phone number. I'm glad you called me back."

I told him about Lingualcare, the financing situation and my desire to explore a sale of the company. I referenced the Brontes transaction.

"We got a premium price for Brontes because we ran an auction and had multiple parties bidding on the company," he said. "We set deadlines so bidders had to move at our pace."

Before I could ask the question that had been circling my brain, he said, "Our fee to enter an engagement is a hundred thousand dollars."

Yikes.

That would cut my runway by two months.

I called Ruedger to tell him about Newgate and his six-figure engagement fee.

"We don't have that kind of money," he said. "There is no point in even talking to him."

"I'm going to get a bridge loan from the Longhorn Partners," I said.

"Jake said you needed to bring good news," Ruedger reminded me.

"He did, but I'm not accepting that answer," I said. "I'm going to ask them myself."

That afternoon I heard from the Longhorn Partners' deal manager. He would give me fifteen minutes in front of the group at their February meeting.

* * *

The Longhorn Partners met at the Petroleum Club, a private sanctuary for oil and gas executives located on the 39th floor of the

Chase Tower in downtown Dallas. It was hard not to be dazzled by the opulent décor. I particularly liked the gold-plated bathroom fixtures and the crystal chandelier hanging in the foyer that was bigger than my car.

Their deal manager had squeezed me in during the lunch break, so I had to talk over the clink of silver on china plates. I hated presenting while people ate, but I made the best of it, going through my update quickly so I'd have time for questions before they kicked me out.

"I know our sales numbers are below the projections we gave you in 2005," I said, acknowledging Jake's concern that no one would want to invest since we lacked good news. "But we've dropped our cost of goods by fifty percent, and I believe we can hit future projections if we raise another five to eight million dollars. I'm not asking you for that money right now. Today we need a bridge loan, half a million dollars to buy us more time while we search for the right financing partner. We're offering a twenty-five percent discount on the price of the next round."

I didn't mention anything about Miles Newgate. Before we could make any decisions about a sale, we needed to secure the bridge loan. I did not want the money tied to progress on a sale.

"I'll put in another fifty thousand on those terms," said one of the youngest members of the group.

"I'm in," said another.

"Me, too."

Several of the partners nodded in agreement.

The deal manager asked me, "Do you have the paperwork ready to go?"

"Send a list of names and amounts. I'll have it to you by the end of the week," I said.

I called Ruedger as soon as I paid the eight-dollar parking fee and cleared the Chase underground garage. "They're in!" I said as soon as he answered.

"For how much?"

"I don't know yet. The deal manager is going to send me the commitments."

"What do you think?"

"Easily two hundred, maybe more. Can you get Glasauer to follow?"

"I'll call him once you have the total."

Two weeks later, we had four hundred thousand dollars in commitments from the Longhorn Partners. Glasauer put in another hundred.

At the end of March, we closed a half-million-dollar bridge loan.

We'd bought enough time to sell the company.

Since my first conversation with Miles Newgate, I'd spent many hours imagining what life would be like if we sold Lingualcare. What it would mean for our customers and the employees, and what it would mean for me?

I'd spent my career in technology, a world obsessed with building companies to the point where they could be taken public. In the go-go days of the Internet bubble, S-1 filings, lock out periods and the allocation of green shoe options dominated happy hour conversations. For my generation of tech entrepreneurs, no experience could compare with the magic of ringing the NASDAQ opening bell.

Now I had to explain to my inner idealist that a trade sale didn't equate to selling out my dreams. Although mergers and acquisitions weren't nearly as sexy or lucrative as ringing the bell, they still counted as a success.

It was still an exit.

* * *

After closing the bridge financing, I flew to Boston to meet Miles Newgate in person. Since I'd only planned to be in Boston for six hours, he'd rented a board room at the Logan Airport Hilton for our meeting.

About my height, with a trim build, lace-up shoes and an expensive tie, Miles had the confident, moneyed aura of a career Wall Street guy, the kind of guy who knew how to close a deal.

Before the meeting, I'd emailed him our pitch deck and a spreadsheet listing the many dental companies we had spoken to and contact information for executives at those companies. As far back as my Mordix days, I made it a point to introduce myself to executives of all the dental companies that had an orthodontic division. I'd stopped by their booths at the AAO and regional shows to say hello and update them on our progress.

Miles read through the list.

"I know M&A people at most of these companies," he told me. "They participated in the Brontes auction."

His recent experience with Brontes was a huge selling point, but the price was too high.

"Your fee is a problem," I said. "Is it negotiable?"

"What did you have in mind?"

"Sixty-five thousand." I'd come up with the number on the plane, something higher than fifty and lower than seventy-five.

He squinted as he considered the number, then nodded. "I can work with that."

Then he quoted me his minimum fee for the whole transaction, seven figures.

"We take a percentage," he explained. "If the selling price is over the minimum, then you pay us the percentage on top."

"I need to talk to my board," I said.

"For what it's worth, I think I can sell your company pretty fast. All those guys who lost out on Brontes are still in acquisition mode."

I called Mr. Kryptonite from the airport to ask his advice on convincing the board to approve Miles Newgate and his fee. Ruedger, Thomas and I would definitely vote for it. I needed Jake, Ronnie and Bart to vote for it too. I wouldn't sign the contract without unanimous approval.

"Bankers legitimize a process," he said. "I don't care what this guy charges, he's going to earn his money."

"What if the board wants me to sell the company without using a banker?"

"You can't run a company and a competitive process at the same time, and believe me, they want the competitive process. That's how they get the price up," he said. "Isn't there a former banker on your board?"

"Yes, Bart, the CEO of Knightsbridge," I said.

"Call him before the meeting and tell him what you need. He'll sell the board for you."

Bart required no convincing from me. Knightsbridge was a major shareholder; they'd make millions on the sale. He took the lead at the board meeting and convinced everyone to unanimously approve the engagement letter.

Miles scheduled the first round of meetings during the upcoming AAO meeting in Seattle. He rented a conference room at the Sheraton next to the convention center and confirmed appointments with six dental companies.

We'd prepared what bankers referred to as "the book." It was basically our pitch deck, financials and a letter outlining the process and key dates. The purpose of the AAO meetings was to introduce potential acquirers to the opportunity and entice them to take a next step.

Ruedger and I met with Miles the night before to prepare.

Over dinner at the Sheraton, he told us, "Don't get lost in the weeds. Tell them what they need to know to take a next step, answer their questions, but remember, it's a process. You'll have plenty of opportunities to fill in the details."

Our first meeting was with OrthoCo. Three of their executives attended, including my old friend Richard, who had recently been named CEO. He shook my hand at the beginning of the meeting, but then ignored me, choosing to direct his questions to Ruedger and Miles instead. I didn't care. He could be a jerk if he was willing to write a big check.

Two smaller dental companies came to see us that morning, but neither was a good fit. They both had business models like that of Knightsbridge, selling low-cost products and competing almost entirely on price.

After lunch, we met with the orthodontic division of XRDent. A large company with operations across the globe, XRDent made products for every specialty in dentistry and most of their growth came from acquisition. I'd never met the general manager of XRDent's orthodontic division, as he'd recently been transferred from another business unit. He brought along their head of sales and two technical guys who had a lively discussion with Ruedger about our patents.

The XRDent meeting ran twenty minutes longer than scheduled, and as they filed out of the conference room, the 3M guys arrived.

They eyed each other as they passed in the hallway and I thought I saw the gleam of competitive spirit in their eyes.

3M Unitek, 3M's orthodontic division, also had a new general manager, a Harvard/McKinsey guy who'd just been promoted out of the M&A group. He brought along Unitek's director of marketing and a technology guy fresh from their corporate office in St. Paul. Like the meeting with XRDent, the 3M meeting ran long because Ruedger and their technical guy jumped into a patent discussion.

When they finally left, Miles congratulated us. "I think the three companies you want in this process are all on the hook," he said.

Before the end of the week, OrthoCo, XRDent and 3M requested follow-up meetings in Dallas.

Technically, we were running a confidential process, but in a company of sixteen people secrets were hard to keep. After the AAO, and before any of the executives from the three orthodontic companies showed up in Dallas, I called an all-hands meeting in the conference room.

Because there weren't enough chairs, people leaned against the back wall. The room fell silent when I entered. No one smiled.

"Don't worry, we're not closing the doors," I said.

That produced a few chuckles.

"A few weeks ago, Ruedger and I hired an investment banker to find a buyer for the company," I said. "I won't be able to give you many details until we get closer to the end of the process. I am telling you this now because I don't want you to freak out when you see the parade of visitors during the next couple of months."

"If you sell to a company that's not in Dallas, are we going to have to move?" said one of the sales guys.

"Ideally, a buyer will keep the company as-is because you are our biggest assets and they would want to retain you," I said.

"Just tell me you're not going to sell to those assholes at OrthoCo," said Kathy.

I smiled, not wanting to tell her that we'd sell to whoever wrote the largest check, even if it was signed by those assholes at OrthoCo.

Smile When You Talk, You'll Sound Friendlier

Dallas, Texas – June 2007

In the deal memo, we asked for indications of interest and a price range to be submitted by the third week of June. Those who passed our minimum threshold would be allowed into an electronic due diligence room.

Before the internet became pervasive, companies set up a room in their building with binders where potential acquirers would camp out with an army of accountants and lawyers and comb through everything needed to make a buying decision. The electronic version made the process more manageable and less disruptive. We uploaded contracts, board minutes, formation documents, patent file wrappers, manufacturing specifications, customer complaints, financials and any other document we deemed relevant.

Miles warned us that each party would make additional document requests, visits to Dallas, visits to Mexicali and reference calls with our clinical advisors and customers. Ruedger and I would be inundated once the real due diligence began.

While preparing the electronic data room, Ruedger uncovered a problem. Lingualcare and EUROTOP currently shared intellectual property. After an acquisition, neither the acquirer nor Hoffman would want to continue the arrangement. We had to terminate the agreement and reassign the IP prior to any sale. We made a note to resolve the issue as we got closer to a sale.

Despite the warnings from Newgate, I was not prepared for the volume of work required to manage due diligence with three large corporations simultaneously. During July, I traveled non-stop between Dallas, California, New York and Mexico. Ruedger came for several weeks and together we managed plant tours in Mexicali, lunches in New York and detailed patent discussions in Dallas.

All three potential acquirers wanted to talk to our customers, specifically Dr. Sam, since he'd been with us the longest, and the Chicago doctor, because he bought more product than anyone else.

The Chicago doctor had no problem with taking calls. "Give them my cell number," he said. "They can call me anytime."

One particularly hectic afternoon I contacted Dr. Sam to ask if he would take a reference call from 3M. I called from the parking lot of the Texas Department of Motor Vehicles. I'd let my car registration lapse and needed to pick up new license plate stickers.

When I told him about the upcoming transaction, he said, "Well, that is good news. Will I be able to sell all of my stock?"

"Yes," I said.

"Wow, that will be big for you and Ruedger, won't it?"

"So it's fine if I give them your phone number?" I wanted to get him off the phone so I could go inside. The office closed in twenty minutes and I had no idea how long a line to expect.

"Well, not so fast. Before I agree to take any calls, I need to discuss something with you," he said. "Remember that new bracket I invented last year? I know I signed that agreement saying if I improved your design, then you'd own the improvement, but I don't think that's fair. I think you should pay me a royalty."

For a moment, I couldn't believe my ears.

Not only had he signed our Invention Assignment Agreement and received stock options in return, but the bracket he thought he'd invented had been invented by a Japanese orthodontist twenty years earlier. Ruedger had even sent Dr. Sam the Japanese patent drawings to prove it.

After all the bullshit I'd put up with at the clinic, and all the stock options we'd given him, he wanted to be paid for his reference. My teeth clenched with the realization that I had no choice. I would have to give in to his extortion.

I looked in my rearview mirror and smiled. I'd learned this trick from a telemarketer friend. If you smile when you talk, you sound friendly. It was the only thing I could do to offset my desire to say things I would later regret.

"I can't pay you a royalty because it would set a bad precedent for the other people who signed our Invention Assignment Agreement. But I can grant you additional stock options since you've done so much to help the company."

"How many?"

"Five thousand shares," I said, now smiling and lifting my eyebrows like a circus clown to maintain my happy tone.

"That's so sweet of you, Lea, thank you. Give my phone number to anyone you want."

* * *

"Mom, can we go home?" said Will. "I'm tired." He rubbed his eyes as he said it.

It was the last Wednesday night in July, and I was working late with our controller, preparing new financial projections for 3M. The remnants of Will's Chick-fil-A dinner sat on the corner of my desk. Even though my stomach was rumbling, I resisted the urge to eat the cold waffle fries.

The clock said nine-fifteen.

"Yes," I told him. "We can go home."

I picked up a half-eaten chicken nugget, dunked it in barbecue sauce and swallowed it before reaching to shut down my laptop. I noticed a reminder up on my Outlook calendar. Will had a dentist's appointment on Friday morning. Ruedger had scheduled a conference call at the same time. I would have to either reschedule the dental appointment or ask John to take Will.

I hated asking John for anything; it opened the door for him to berate me about my lack of organization and poor mothering skills.

As the computer powered down, I struggled to fill my lungs with air. Every breath stopped halfway. I sat down in my chair and focused on breathing deeply.

It took a few minutes.

What was wrong with me?

The following morning it happened again. I was driving to the office after dropping Will at summer camp when the phone rang. As Ruedger rattled off a list of things I needed to do before noon, I could not take a full breath.

"I might be having a heart attack," I said, interrupting him mid-sentence.

"Are you kidding?"

"No, I'm serious. I can't breathe. I have to call you back."

If my dad hadn't died at forty-eight, I might have been less concerned, but I had to take it seriously. I hung up and dialed my doctor's office.

"I need to come in right now. Something is wrong."

The nurse took me to a treatment room immediately and hooked up the EKG. My regular doctor wasn't in, but her father, the senior member of the practice, was. A steady man in his late sixties with thick white hair and rimless glasses, he listened to my heart and lungs and checked the EKG readout.

"You've got the heart of a sixteen-year-old," he said.

"I'm not having a heart attack?"

"No. What you're describing sounds like an anxiety attack. Are you under any stress?"

I couldn't hold back my tears. "Yes," I said between sobs.

He sent me home with prescriptions for Xanax and an albuterol inhaler, and a stern warning. "Take a nap. Stay off the phone. Don't go to your office today."

I promised.

After stopping at the pharmacy, I drove home.

The yard guys had parked their truck in my driveway, so I parked on the street. Leaning into the trunk, I grabbed my backpack and slung it over my shoulder. That's when I felt the weight shift and realized the top was unzipped. Powerless to change the laws of physics, I watched my laptop fly out in a perfect arc and hit the curb.

It contained my life – everything related to the transaction, to my divorce, all of it.

I held my breath and opened the top.

The screen formed a spider web of cracks. Pressing the power button yielded nothing.

It was dead.

When had I last run the back-up program, the one I was supposed to run each morning? It had been at least a month, okay, maybe two.

My lungs constricted with anxiety. I dug the inhaler out of my purse, leaned against the car and sucked in albuterol. Then I went inside, poured a glass of water and took a Xanax.

I didn't know what to do, so I did nothing.

Instead of calling Ruedger back, or tracking down our IT guy, I kicked off my high-heeled shoes and curled up on the sofa in my skirt and silk blouse, unconcerned about wrinkles and the subsequent dry-cleaning bill. I turned off my cell phone, pulled a knit throw over my shoulders and closed my eyes.

The doorbell woke me. I found Beth standing on the porch.

She followed me into the living room. "Ruedger called. He's worried. He said you thought you were having a heart attack." Her voice softened, almost to a whisper. "Are you okay?"

I told her about going to the doctor, the anxiety attack diagnosis and killing the laptop. "I don't know what to do," I said. "I can't figure it out."

In that moment, I felt like her lost little sister, the one passed out on the floor, surrounded by green lawn bags.

"Can you help me?"

She sat next to me on the sofa and hugged me. "Stay here," she said. "I'll take care of it." She left with my laptop tucked under her arm and a promise to call me if any due-diligence-related emergencies popped up.

I spent the day and night on the sofa, drifting in and out of Xanax-induced sleep, watching Star Wars DVDs, sipping Diet Coke and eating handfuls of the chocolate Teddy Grahams.

John had Will.

It was just me.

And Yoda.

The next day I got up early and went running, something I hadn't done in weeks. By the end of my run I felt calmer. I could breathe.

When I arrived at the office at 10:00, Beth was sitting at my desk with our IT guy.

"We ordered a new Dell laptop yesterday and had it shipped overnight," he said. "Your hard drive wasn't damaged. I'm transferring your data now." He gave me a stern look. "I set this to back up automatically, so be sure to put it in the docking station at least once a day."

"I promise," I said, and meant it.

It Never Hurts to Leave a Little Money on the Table

Dallas, Texas – August 2007

After weeks of due diligence, the date for final bids arrived. Not sure what that Friday would bring, I left my schedule open. I had nothing to do but pace up and down in the parking lot and make frequent trips to Starbucks for soy lattes.

Miles called at 10:00 to tell me he had received a bid from 3M. They bid below what we wanted, but in the right range.

One down, two to go.

The XRDent bid arrived at 4:30. It was higher than the 3M bid, but with different terms. 3M had offered all cash, our preference. XRDent offered cash and a lucrative earn-out.

Every entrepreneur I knew who accepted an earn-out either ended up bitterly disappointed or stuck in court fighting for their money. I wanted to avoid that option if possible.

The 5:00 deadline came and went without a bid from OrthoCo. I'd been on the phone with their M&A guy several times during the past two weeks. What was going on? I called him but got no answer. I called his boss. No answer. I called Miles. He hadn't heard anything.

Ruedger called me at 6:00, 1:00 in the morning in Germany.

"Why haven't you called me? What's going on?"

"OrthoCo didn't bid," I said.

"Did you call them?"

"Yes. No one is answering."

"They're going to try and screw us," said Ruedger.

"How can they screw us?" I said.

"They can wait until we announce the buyer, slap us with a patent lawsuit and kill our deal. Then they can try to buy us cheap."

"Don't get paranoid," I said. "We have two solid bids. Miles can work with those."

I forced myself to sound optimistic, but I wasn't. I didn't trust OrthoCo either. Why would they invest so much time in due diligence if they didn't intend to bid?

I called Miles on Monday

"We want all cash, so I'd like to sell the company to 3M, but their bid isn't high enough," I said. "Do you think you can get them to go higher?"

"Yes, since we have a higher bid in hand I think we can."

"I don't want an earn-out. It needs to be all cash," I added.

"I'll call them Thursday," he said. "We don't want to appear too anxious."

Ruedger arrived in Dallas on Wednesday afternoon and we flew to Los Angeles the next morning for a meeting with Knightsbridge.

We'd only been in the rental car a few minutes when my cell phone rang. It was Miles.

"I just talked to the head of M&A over at 3M Healthcare. I gave him our bottom line number. Harvard/McKinsey is probably going to call you to negotiate. Don't take his phone call. Let me handle it, okay?"

"Okay. I won't answer if he calls."

Just outside of Costa Mesa, California, my phone rang. Harvard/McKinsey's name flashed on the screen.

Ring.

I had hired Miles. I should let him do his job.

Ring.

But it was my company.

Ring.

It was my future.

I answered.

"Sorry it's loud here. I'm on a rafting trip in Washington state with my family," said Harvard/McKinsey.

I could hear the rush of water and what sounded like wind in the background.

"Corporate called me," he said. "I'd like to buy your company, but I can't get to your banker's number."

"I can't sell your number to my board," I countered.

"What number can you sell?" he asked.

I'd modeled so many different scenarios in my acquisition spreadsheet, I knew the numbers better than the multiplication tables I'd learned in fourth grade.

I also knew that the amount we were talking about was miniscule in the world of 3M. But I suspected this was not about money, it was about Harvard/McKinsey's ego. I'd dealt with guys like him before. He wanted to show his boss that he was a better negotiator than his counterparts in the M&A department. If I wanted to close a deal, I'd have to leave some money on the table.

I proposed a number four percent lower than the number Miles gave the corporate people, a number that would still make my stock worth several million dollars.

"Done," he said.

"The deal is only good today," I said. "The corporate guys need to fax me a Letter of Intent right now."

"Where should they send it?"

We were almost to the Bristol Street exit in Costa Mesa, an area I knew well. "Have them fax it to the business center at the Costa Mesa Hilton in Orange County."

Ruedger grinned as I hung up the phone.

"Did you just sell our company?"

"I think so."

We valeted the rental car, rushed through the lobby and retrieved the fax. I signed it and paid the business center guy five dollars to fax it back to the M&A department. I waited a few minutes and then called the corporate guy to confirm that he had received the countersigned document.

Ruedger and I huddled in the lobby and read the letter over and over, laughing and asking each other, "Can you believe it? Can this be true?"

Back in the car I called Miles and confessed that I'd taken Harvard/McKinsey's call and signed the Letter of Intent. He didn't give me a hard time, just asked me to fax him a copy when I arrived at my hotel in San Diego.

"So, what's next?" I asked Miles.

"We'll give them thirty days to complete any remaining due diligence," he said. "Then we'll announce the acquisition and close thirty days later."

"So, end of October?"

"End of October."

The employees knew that 3M had won the auction. They all owned Lingualcare stock and would make money on the sale. I cautioned them not to spend their money until it arrived in their bank accounts.

"It's not closed until it's closed," became my mantra.

September flew by.

One by one, we checked off the remaining open items on the due diligence list and worked through the specifics of the merger agreement, a fifty-seven-page document detailing every aspect of the transaction.

We negotiated a deal with Dr. Hoffman where each party assigned the shared IP to the territories each of us owned. I'd expected more resistance from him, but in the end, he saw the acquisition as positive. We had validated the product and its value. If Hoffman wanted to, he could follow a similar process and get a premium price for EUROTOP.

The last Friday in September, Ruedger and I went to Schwaebisch Hall to work with Mr. Glasauer on the mechanics of paying the German shareholders once the transaction closed. Their shares resided in brokerage accounts, so we couldn't just wire money like we could with U.S. shareholders.

After a full day of meetings, Ruedger, Glasauer, Ronnie and I went to the Golden Adler for a celebration dinner. Somehow it felt appropriate to celebrate with pork medallions and spätzle, the dish I'd eaten on my first visit to Schwaebisch Hall, on that cold March afternoon less than five years ago when we worked out the terms of our first financing.

Glasauer raised his glass. "I would toast Mr. Rubbert, but I don't think the credit for this success belongs to him. I think it belongs to you, Lea."

I disagreed, but I didn't protest too loudly. Ruedger was the yang to my yin. Neither of us could have managed it alone. We were a team.

* * *

On Monday, 3M planned to announce the acquisition via Business Wire and the whole world would know our secret.

While Ruedger navigated the autobahn, taking us from Glasauer's office back to the Frankfurt airport, I got out my laptop and built an email distribution list. I'd saved every email from every investor who had turned us down during the last five years and every naysayer doctor who had told me the product was not viable. I cut and pasted their names and email addresses into that distribution list, one by one. Then I added all my former Mordix colleagues and their board of directors. By the time I finished, I had 182 names.

When I landed in Dallas on Sunday night, I called John to tell him about the announcement that would go out the next day. He had no idea that I'd spent the summer working on this acquisition, only that I'd been busy and distracted.

"Congratulations," he said. "That's quite an accomplishment."

I must have caught him off guard because John hadn't said anything positive to me since I'd moved out a year and a half earlier. Maybe, with the promise of money on the table, he would finalize the divorce. Maybe we could move on.

"3M announced today it has entered into a definitive agreement to acquire Lingualcare Inc., a Dallas-based orthodontic technology and services company…"

I sent the press release to my distribution list and watched as good wishes and congratulatory emails rolled into my mailbox. Several of my Mordix colleagues responded, but I received nothing from Roscoe.

That night, to celebrate, I ordered Chinese takeout.

Will and I ate at the kitchen table. I listened intently as he recounted his day – the English test, forgotten math homework and scoring two touchdowns during morning recess football. I gave him my full attention, something I'd neglected to do during the last weeks as transaction details dominated my thoughts.

Near the end of our meal, I noticed the whiteboard next to the back door was blank.

"There's no gun on the whiteboard," I said.

"The marker doesn't work anymore," he said, digging into his lo mein noodles.

"Should I buy a new marker?"

"Not right now," he said.

Not right now.

I rose from the table to fill my water glass. I didn't want Will to see me fighting back tears. Friends had assured me that time and love would scab over the wounds left by the separation, but until that moment I didn't believe them. I felt like I'd destroyed Will's life, and I feared his anger and sadness would never diminish.

Maybe, just maybe, we'd both be okay.

I returned to the table to finish my Mongolian beef, resisting the urge to hug him.

Afterward

St. Paul, Minnesota – November 2008

A few days after the closing, Ruedger and I traveled to St. Paul to meet our new colleagues in the dental division. After a full day of meetings, they hosted a celebration dinner at a nearby brew pub for the people who had worked on our transaction.

Draft beer flowed freely and the waiter brought platter after platter of fried cheese sticks, buffalo wings, onion ring towers and mounds of Minnesota-style nachos, salty tortilla chips covered in orange cheese, hamburger and shredded iceberg lettuce.

Ruedger and I sat next to the IP attorney for the orthodontic division, a man who had worked closely with us throughout the closing process. I thanked him and confessed, "From the minute we made the announcement until we actually closed, I was afraid OrthoCo would send you guys a threatening letter and derail the transaction."

"Oh, they sent us a letter," he said, "right after the press release went out."

Ruedger put down his beer. "What did it say?"

"What you would expect," the attorney said. "They claimed your system infringed several of the Roberts patents and threatened to sue us if we purchased Lingualcare."

"Why didn't you tell me?" I said, glad that he hadn't, because no amount of Xanax would have gotten me through the month of October if I had known.

"They didn't have a case. There was no reason to worry you," said the lawyer.

The mystery of OrthoCo not making a bid had finally been solved. Ruedger called it. Rather than win the auction fair and square, they decided to scare off other buyers with threats of litigation. Without competitive bids, they could have acquired Lingualcare for half the price.

After toasts were made, beer glasses emptied and only a few naked tortilla chips littered the platters, people started putting on their coats to head home to their families.

Ruedger and I remained seated at our end of the table, finishing our drinks while our new boss paid the check. I was in no hurry to leave the warmth of the celebration and face the frigid Minnesota night.

I thought about the many hours we had spent hunched over dinner tables like this one, plotting, planning and trying to help each other not freak out about the next obstacle in our path. It seemed weird not to have a big problem to solve, no scary deadline to keep me awake half the night and no nightmares about OrthoCo dropping an atomic bomb on our fragile company.

What would I do with all that spare emotional energy?

As part of the sale, Ruedger and I had committed to stay with 3M to manage the integration process, but neither of us were suited for jobs that required I.D. badges and travel authorization forms. At some point, we'd leave.

Then what?

Ruedger had become my trusty sidekick.

I could not imagine a life without him in it.

When we stood up to leave, Ruedger took my coat from the back of my chair and held it for me. As I pulled it on, he leaned over and whispered.

"I've got an idea."

THE END

Acknowledgements

Completing this book required not a village, but a metropolis. I'd like to thank my writing tribe for their support, willingness to read early work, and for sharing their talents and insights to make this book all it could be: Joyce Maynard, Anjanette Fennell, Stuart Horwitz, Robert Bausch, Ann Hood, B.K. Loren, Andrea Askowitz, Hope Edelman, Eric Goodman, Adrea Peters, Amy Waterman, Aviva Rubin, Laura Mellow, Chris Greenslate, Melissa Warren Vincel, Mindy Davis, Hannah Kozak, Emily Kelting, Leigh Haber, Linda Hanher, Kris Schrader, Lorianne Gengo, Judy Johnson, Sylvia Symons, Rebecca Tuttle Schultze, Karen Gidley Mulvaney, Lindsey Muscato, Sudesh Kannan, Brandon Johnson, Dave Chandler, Kathy Mardis, Sunny Nunan, Sharon Walthew, Tom Hoitsma, Kim Bunting, Elizabeth Buckley Balmer, Suzanne Slonim and Pam Gerber. Special thanks to Amy Oscar and Christine Clemmer for showing me the light within, my editor Therese Arkenberg for her expertise and Gary Kaplow for his artistry.

Special thanks to my husband Ruedger Rubbert for always seeing past my flaws. Without you, this would have been a very different story.

Made in the USA
Coppell, TX
19 September 2021

62613369R00184